The Darkness Shall Be the Light:

T.S. Eliot's Journey to Faith

John O'Brien OFM

Other books by the author

Catch the Wind
Return to Gethsemane
My one Friend is Darkness
Rachel's Tears and Mary's Song
Love Rescue Me
Cry Me a River
Therese and the Little Way of Love and Healing
Clare of Assisi: A living Flame of Love
Waiting for God: From Trauma to Healing
With Thee Tender is the Night
Loneliness Knows My Name
Silent Music of Love: Teach Us to Pray
A Love Supreme
At Eternity's Gate: Artists of the Infinite

To Liam McCarthy, Eugene Bennett,
Eamonn O'Driscoll OFM
and Linda O'Halloran

*"Survive the dark
and you will
become
the light"*

(Roger Lee)

Contents

Introduction

Andrei Tarkovsky (+1986) was a Russian filmmaker, writer and film theorist. His films explored spiritual and metaphysical themes and are noted for their slow pacing and long takes, dreamlike visual imagery and preoccupation with nature and memory. He constantly found himself in conflict with the then ruling Communist Party. In 1966 Tarkovsky produced a film called 'Andrei Rublev' based loosely on the 15th century icon painter. Next to nothing is known about Rublev, so the film has little historical data. The Russia depicted in the film is brutish and gray. It is populated by louts, jesters and paranoid bureaucrats – made like the Russia of Tarkovsky's time. The film is like an anti-icon, not filled with the redeemed light of Christ, but with the darkness of a fallen world. This is the world Rublev wanders through. He mutters throughout the film – "only by prayer can the soul transcend the flesh". This world eludes him. It seems that Tarkovsky's bleak vision leaves no room for grace. All is blank.

Then, suddenly, things change. The stark black and white imagery bursts into bright colours. The camera shows us a montage of Rublev's most famous icons. The colour comes as a revelation. Beauty has usurped ugliness and hope overcomes despair. The icons are filmed first in gigantic close-up, as swirls and streaks. One thinks of modern painters such as Mondrian and Pollock. Then the camera pulls back and recognisable objects appear. We see the face of Christ. But then the soundtrack changes. The music breaks the silence and stillness of these holy images. Tarkovsky seems to suggest that the icons will never entirely escape the dark, sin-soaked world. Yet Tarkovsky seems to suggest that the icons offer us a vision of supremal beauty and transcendent truth, a glimpse of God's good kingdom.

The paintings produced by Rublev came from the deep darkness of the world he found. Picasso said that the purpose of art "is washing the dust of daily life off our souls". Rublev's works point out to us that the world we find is not the end. Hope overcomes despair. Art does not reproduce what we see. It makes us see (Klee). We see beyond to come to know

God's hand in our lives. Rublev's icons challenge our views of what we consider reality to be. As the harsh world of Russia produced Rublev's icons and Tarkovsky's film reflection so it is with our own world. The world can seem to us to be harsh, cold and bleak with little love. That is the experience of many. Yet if we can look beyond like Rublev we can see that God's hand is at work even here. The secret is to let God in and allow him to reshape and renew us as a new creation. Rublev's art and Tarkovsky's art in turn are the highest form of hope. They inspire us to hope and open in us a hope for the Divine. This is the journey we are on in this work.

Henri Nouwen (+1996) was a priest, writer and psychologist. All his life he was plagued by anxiety. He was beset with loneliness and insecurity. Yet from his suffering he produced many beautiful works that have helped millions. He, too, was influenced by Rublev. He had a copy of Rublev's icon of the Trinity which gave him solace.[1] He said Rublev wrote the icon to help those who lived in turbulent times to keep their hearts centered on God's love. This helps us understand Tarkovsky's view of Rublev. As we gaze on the icon in prayer, we come to experience a gentle invitation to participate in the intimate conversation of love that is taking place at the table and we are invited to enter in. During a difficult period in Nouwen's life, when verbal prayer had become almost impossible and during which time he felt emotional and mental fatigue which made him the easy victim of despair and fear, he spent time in gentle silence before the icon and that was the beginning of his healing. His gaze became prayer (p. 32 Behold the Lord). This gentle, silent prayer made his inner restlessness melt away and he felt himself lifted up into the circle of love, a circle that cannot be broken. In these meditations, based around T. S. Eliot's work, is an invitation to enter the "circle of love" and find peace. This is not meant just for believers. It is open to all. I have met so many who seek meaning and a reason to believe. These meditations are dedicated to them, also.

[1] see Henri Nouwen, Behold the Beauty of the Lord: Praying with Icons (Indiana: 2007).

Chapter One

The Waste Land: No Country for Old Men

What is it to be human? This is a question we face today. Yet what comes to mind are, often, examples of what it means not to be human. When we make mistakes and are unkind we say "I'm only human". Yet the truth is that when we do something unworthy we are not human. Maurice Zundel (+1975) when he was asked "Are you human?", answered "No, not yet". There are many obstacles to being human. Rabbi Abraham Heschel (+1972) said our age is an age that is losing what it means to be human. We have forgotten how to pray, how to think, how to cry, how to resist the lure of so many persuaders in our midst. We have "exchanged holiness for convenience, loyalty for success, love for power, wisdom for information, tradition for fashion".[1]

We legislate against murder, yet we wage war with ferocity and wipe out peoples. History is scarred with wars and more wars, with so many dead and so many tears. Our Western society looks upon people and nature in terms of usefulness. Our greed is destroying the planet. People are not cared for and many live lives of desperation and profound loneliness. We search for meaning but bad experiences tell us we have no value and our efforts have no meaning.

How do we break out of the "lie" that we have no value, that our efforts do not matter. We have to begin where we are. Our reality is often best captured by writers, artists and poets. Catharsis (a Greek word meaning "purification" or "cleansing" or "clarification") refers to the purification and purgation of emotions that results in renewal or restoration. Aristotle (+322BC) in his "Politics" speaks of how we relate to tragedy as a catharsis, a cleansing. We see our own lives acted out on the stage and we discover we are not alone. We can come to accept ourselves as we are.

[1] Abraham Heschel, Man's Quest for God: Studies in Prayer and Symbolism (New York: 1954), p. 150.

T.S. Eliot:

One of the people who helped me confront my "dark night" is the poet T.S. Eliot (+1965). He was a poet, essayist, publisher, playwright and a literary and social critic. Born in St. Louis, Missouri, to a prominent Boston family, he moved to England in 1914 at the age of 25 and would settle, work and marry there.

Eliot studied at Merton College, Oxford. He was introduced to American expatriate poet Ezra Pound (+1972). He was to have a profound influence on Eliot and encouraged the young Eliot on his quest. He helped publish "The Love Song of J. Alfred Prufrock" which was seen as a masterpiece of the Modernist movement. This was a reaction to the perceived excesses of Victorian poetry, with its emphasis on traditional formalism and ornate diction. The Modernists saw themselves as looking back to the best practices of poets in earlier periods and other cultures. Their models included Greek, Chinese and Japanese poets, the troubadours, Dante and the English Metaphysical poets. The Modernist era was also a time of experimentation in music. In 1913 Stravinsky's "The Rite of Spring" was first performed. The music was different from that which had gone before and initially was not well received. It was also at this time that jazz was becoming popular with its experimental rhythm. Eliot, in his turn, experimented with poetry.

In 1915 Eliot married Vivienne Haigh-Wood, a Cambridge governess (+1947). The marriage was an unhappy one with Vivienne having a number of health problems. She was also mentally afflicted and both she and Eliot grew increasingly apart. The period following the war was a difficult time for Eliot. His marriage had failed. Both he and Vivienne were suffering from nervous disorders. Eliot was told to rest by his doctor and he was given a leave of absence to do so by the bank for which he worked. The reason for his leave was cited as a "nervous breakdown". During his period of leave Eliot composed "The Waste Land". Eliot's state of mind – a state of emotional spiritual crisis – finds expression in his poem. His personal mood is transmuted into an epic poem. The Waste Land reads like a recapitulation of a life, all the scenes connected with that one life, the characters melding into each other as in a dream. Many voices speak and this helps show the brokenness of the poet. In being personal, Eliot reflected the brokenness of his age after the slaughter of World War I. He expressed the feelings of many of us who have experienced loneliness, alienation and so many voices speaking at us in disharmony. In the 1969 film "Midnight Cowboy", Harry Nilsson composed the song "Everybody's Talkin'"

> "Everybody's talking at me
> I don't hear a word they're saying
> Only the echoes of my mind.
> People stopping, staring,
> I can't see their faces
> Only the shadows of their eyes."

This helps us listen to the voices of the "Waste Land".

The Waste Land:

This was not the original title chosen by Eliot. He had initially wanted to call it "He Do the Police in Different Voices". This is a quotation from Dickens where a boy reads the news reports and reads them in different voices. He wanted to emphasise the multiplicity of voices that are heard in "The Waste Land". Throughout the 'Waste Land' different voices, languages interrupt each other. All is confused and broken. There is a multiplicity of changes in voices, scenery and time. We are a generation of detached voices, all speaking over each other. There is a searching for intimacy, communication and love that is not there anymore.

The work's epigraph is in four different languages – Latin, English, Greek and Italian. Already we see the different voices that are going to permeate the poem:

> "Nam Sybillam quidem Cumis ego ipse oculis meis vidi
> in ampulla pendere, et cum pueri illi dicerent: Στβμλλ
> τί Θέλεις; respondebat illa: άπσΘνειν Θελω."

For Ezra Pound
il miglior fabbro
(Epigraph)

This describes an encounter with the Cumean Sibyl, a famous prophet who was granted eternal life but forgot to request perennial youth. The Sibyl suffered the painful degradations of eternal old age. The translation says: "Once I saw with my own eyes the Cumean Sibyl hanging in a jar". She is asked in Greek: "Sibyl, what do you want?" And she replies "I want to die". The prospect of death as something to be desired is found throughout the poem. In the Waste Land in which he lives there is no real purpose, no real truth. Everything is without meaning. Death seems to be the one way out of all the pain of the Waste Land. All the emptiness of our lives can be soothed only by death. He dedicates the poem to Ezra Pound "il miglior fabbro". This reference is from Dante and it translates as "the better craftsman". Pound worked as an editor for "The Waste Land" and Eliot was grateful for this.

Eliot had thought of using Joseph Conrad's work "The Heart of Darkness". In this work Kurtz is discovered to have gone savagely mad in the depths of the jungle. Kurtz's death is reported by Marlow, the narrator of the story:

> "Did he live his life again in every detail of desire, temptation, and surrender during that supreme moment of complete knowledge? He cried in a whisper at some image, at some vision – he cried out twice, a cry that was not more than a breath – 'The horror! the horror!'"
>
> (The Heart of Darkness)

Pound was Eliot's guide in choosing the title "The Waste Land" and the work's epigraph. "The Waste Land" appeared in 1922, the same year as James Joyce's "Ulysses" and three years before F. Scott Fitzgerald's "The Great Gatsby" – his exploration of the jazz age, flappers and the attempt to escape the "horror".

Eliot describes the London of his day. It is a portrait of rush hour:

> "A crowd flowed over London Bridge, so many,
> I had not thought death had undone so many."

"We have left undone those things which we ought to have done; And we have done those things which we ought not to have done" goes the general confession in the order for Evening Prayer.

The poem returns to the thought of things undone, like the wind crossing "the brown land, unheard" in Part III, or the female voice later in the same section that laments: "Richmond and Kew / Undid me". Among the things the poem leaves undone so well is rhyme and Christopher Ricks has analysed beautifully the dead-rhyme here:

> "at once more richly a rhyme than any other could be, since it is the repetition of the very word itself, and yet more poverty-stricken than a rhyme could be, since it is not truly a rhyme at all, is not a creative co-operation of two things but instead has what is here the singleness of a consternation without parallel."

As though a parody of the water the loss of which the poem elsewhere regrets, it is the crowd that does the flowing here, and the prevailing fluent emptiness of purpose in the commuting traffic is nicely captured in Eliot's decision not to include a pronoun at all.

He uses the expression "unreal city" to refer to London. This is a phrase he borrowed from Charles Baudelaire. He composed a work called Les Fleurs du Mal (The Flowers of Evil). He looked at the changing nature of beauty in the rapidly industrialising Paris. He called Paris "unreal". Here Eliot applies the expression to London. This city is shrouded in fog, shrouding the living dead. We see a crowd on the bridge. Just before this Eliot had introduced a Madame Sosteris, "famous clairvoyante". She saw in her vision "crowds of people walking round in a ring". This is Dante's vision of Hell. The crowd in hell are those on the bridge. Eliot says: "I had not thought death had undone so many". We are in the Hell of the living dead. Eliot wished to express in poetic form the sadness he felt in the music of Beethoven to which he was listening at that time.

(i) The Burial of the Dead

This is the first section of "The Waste Land". The poem opens with a voice out of nowhere, purportedly the expression of some sort of collective experience. It shows a contrary attitude to Spring. Chaucer in his "Canterbury Tales" talks about "When April with his sweet showers has pierced to the root the drought of March". "The Burial of the Dead" is that which the Book of Common Prayer calls the funeral service, in the course of which the congregation is called to remember the "sure and certain hope of the Resurrection to eternal life". In this poem the returning Spring is not seen as a blessing but as a curse.

> "April is the cruelest month, breeding
> Lilacs out of the dead land, mixing
> Memory and desire, stirring
> Dull roots with spring rain.
> Winter kept us warm, covering
> Earth in forgetful snow, feeding
> A little life with dried tubers."
>
> (Burial of the Dead)

In "The Waste Land" Eliot hints at five elements, earth, air, fire, water and spirit. These correspond to the divisions of the "Waste Land". The "Burial of the Dead" presents us with the first element "earth". We remember the words of the burial rite "dust into dust". We return to dust when we die. The Book of Common Prayer cites chapter 11 of the Gospel of John. There we see our hope: that once we are buried there is hope for a resurrection and eternal life. Jesus says: "I am the Resurrection and the Life. The one who believes in me will live, even though they die" (Jn 11:25). The perspective of "The Waste Land" is different. It asks the question: "What if there is no resurrection, no rebirth?". We are just dust consigned to the grave.

The poem begins with "April is the cruelest month...". April refers to Spring, and re-awakening. It speaks of a renewal of nature. Winter is seen as a time of darkness and death, hibernation. April should not be the cruelest month. Yet this is not what Eliot says: "April breeds lilacs out of dead land"; it mixes "memory and desire, stirring dull roots with spring rain". The Spring rains do come but in the waste-land all the earth is dead. There are no roots. There is no prospect of re-birth. There is an absence of God, an absence of meaning, an absence of purpose. Modern life doesn't present us with any prospect of resurrection. There is no hope. People are dust. The rain stirs dull roots. There is nothing there. "Memory and desire" are mixed. There is a memory of a better time. There is a longing, a nostalgia for better times. There was a time when we had faith and hope. We desire something better to come but in the "Waste Land" this hope does not exist. The rain however falls on dull roots and this desire disappoints us. The rain provides all that is necessary for new life but in the Waste Land in which we live this is useless. In our disappointment, we see April only as the cruelest month. We live with these desires for a better life, a life of faith and hope. These desires are never realised in the "Waste Land". We are doomed to disappointment. In using the image of lilacs coming from the dead soil Eliot alludes to the Walt Whitman poem, "When Lilacs Last in the Dooryard Bloom'd".

> "When lilacs last in the dooryard bloom'd,
> and the great star early droop'd in the western sky in the night,
> I mourn'd, and yet shall mourn with ever-returning spring.
>
> Ever-returning spring, trinity sure to me you bring,
> Lilac blooming perennial and drooping star in the west,
> And thought of him I love."

Whitman's poem is a passionate elegy on the death of U.S. President Abraham Lincoln, assassinated in the spring of 1865 when the lilacs were blooming. In the poem's semiotic innovation, lilacs – traditionally a symbol of the renewal of the earth in spring – are now connected with mourning and anguish and death. In "The Waste Land" Eliot takes the semiotic innovation Whitman supplies but then uses it, in the manner of a literary Rosetta stone, as a means to understand the poem's complex allusions to the modern culture of death.[2] Semiotics, in language studies, refers to that which is signified by the words. Here the "lilacs" signify grief and loss. Then comes the paradox of "winter kept us warm, covering Earth in forgetful snow". Winter numbs us, causing us to forget. Spring strips away all the cold comfort we had. It was in Winter that we could paralyse or numb our negative feelings. Spring shows us how desolate the Waste Land is. He then speaks of Winter "feeding a little life with dried tubers" – another paradox. It feeds the dream of something occurring that does not nor cannot come to pass.

The first lines seem to be a reflection of what the Waste-Land is. It is desolate and hopeless. It reflects the world in which we live. Then, in the next few lines, a different voice comes in – something that happens a lot in the "Waste Land". There is a pile-up of broken images, sharing the brokenness of those in the Waste Land. Later the poet tells us "I will show you fear in a handful of dust". The "Book of Common Prayer" required handfuls of earth to be cast on the coffin while the priest intones, "Earth to earth, ashes to ashes, dust to dust" but in the Waste-Land there is no hope, just the end.

> "Summer surprised us, coming over the Starnbergersee
> With a shower of rain; we stopped in the colonnade,
> And went on in sunlight, into the Hofgarten,
> And drank coffee, and talked for an hour.
> Bin gar keine Russin, stamm' aus Litauen, echt deutsch.
> And when we were children, staying at the arch-duke's,
> My cousin's, he took me out on a sled,
> And I was frightened. He said, Marie,
> Marie, hold on tight. And down we went.
> In the mountains, there you feel free.
> I read, much of the night, and go south in the winter."

Here we have a line that takes us by surprise: "Summer surprised us, coming over the Starnbergersee". This comes from someone who stayed

---

[2] James E. Miller, The American Quest for a Supreme Fiction: Whitman's Legacy in the Personal Epic (Chicago: 1979), p. 101-125.

in Munich, in which the Hofgarten is a public park and the Starnbergersee, a nearby resort. The rain comes as a welcome intervention to the speaker of the opening lines. Then another voice breaks in, speaking in German: "I am not at all Russian, I am from Lithuania". Lithuania exemplified the ambiguities of political identity. It had declared independence from the Russian Empire in 1918. It resisted the attempts of the occupying Germans to retain it as a protectorate. It would soon find itself resisting the advances of Communist Russia. All is unstable. Nothing is permanent. There is really nothing to hold on to.

Then an aristocratic woman's voice breaks in. People in the Waste Land seem to exist in this self-enclosed obliviousness. The woman, in this case, can be identified. She was Countess Marie Von Wallersee-Larisch. The lines evoke the recollection of an intense, fearful pleasure associated with a dangerous freedom that life had subsequently denied her. She says, "I read, much of the night" – a confession that she now suffers from insomnia. All she has is her memories. Then there follows the statement about going south in the Winter. There is an aimlessness in Marie's movements.

In the closing lines of this part of the "Waste Land", the poet greets a friend. There is banter between them but then we hear –

> "That corpse you planted last year in your garden. Has it begun to sprout? Will it bloom this year?"

Corpses buried in the garden are like memories stored in the psyche. In the Madame Sosostris section of the poem, the poet has just reviewed in the cards of his fate all the buried corpses of his past that will not lie quietly buried. Principal among these corpses is a real corpse, buried: the lost sailor and friend who haunts the poet and appears to be the moving spirit haunting The Waste Land.

The musical presence in The Waste Land is undoubtedly Wagner. However Igor Stravinsky is influential too. Eliot attended performances of Diaghilev's ballets when the Ballets Russes visited London in 1921.

He spoke of the music of Stravinsky's Le Sacre du Printemps (The Rite of Spring) which, he said:

> "seem[s] to transform the rhythm of the steppes into the scream of the motor horn, the rattle of machinery, the grind of wheels, the beating of iron and steel, the roar of the underground railway, and the other barbaric cries of modern life; and to transform these despairing noises into music."

The Rite of Spring declines to obey most of the customary musical rules. It alternates all kinds of disharmony and sonic dissonance. Eliot does the same with the rhythms and voices of The Waste Land.

(ii) A Game of Chess

In the Game of Chess we see people in loveless relationships where there is no intimacy, no communication. The first section of The Waste Land speaks of no life after death. Here we see the world of the living Dead, consumed by loneliness and the desire for intimacy.

Simon and Garfunkel caught the pathos of failed communication between lovers in their song "The Dangling Conversation". The words begin:

> "It's a still life watercolour
> Of a now-late afternoon
> As the sun shines through the curtained lace
> And shadows wash the room
>
> And we sit and drink our coffee
> Couched in our indifference, like shells upon the shore
> You can hear the ocean roar
>
> In the dangling conversation
> And the superficial sighs
> The borders of our lives

And you read your Emily Dickinson
And I my Robert Frost
And we note our place with book markers
That measure what we've lost"

(The Dangling Conversation)

They use the image of a still life watercolour. They talk of Robert Frost and Emily Dickinson but not of their own personal feelings. They use words but they don't reach each others hearts. Their conversation measures what they've lost.

"Like a poem poorly written
We are verses out of rhythm
Couplets out of rhyme
In syncopated time

And the dangled conversation
And the superficial sighs
Are the borders of our lives

Yes, we speak of things that matter
With words that must be said
"Can analysis be worthwhile?"
"Is the theatre really dead?" "

(The Dangling Conversation)

These lines are like verses out of rhythm, couplets out of rhyme. They belong in The Waste Land – that is where they live. They try to speak of the things that "matter" and in doing so fail to speak of the things that really matter. They have become strangers to each other – they do not share any more, they are:

"Lost in the dangling conversation
And the superficial sighs
In the borders of our lives."

(The Dangling Conversation)

In this section of the epic, communication has broken down between husband and wife. All their communication is now a game of chess. Ezra Pound edited out the line: "The ivory men make company between us." The only way they communicate is through the chess figures. The title "A Game of Chess" takes its title from a work by the 17th century playwright Thomas Middleton. In Eliot's "A Game of Chess" we see fruitless, barren relationships where there is no intimacy, no love, no communication. The first woman is compared to Philomela, a character out of Ovid's "Metamorphoses" who is raped by her brother-in-law the King, who then cuts out her tongue to keep her quiet. She is unable to communicate her inner pain. No one hears. No one cares. The woman and her surroundings are aesthetically pleasing but at the same time are sterile and meaningless, as suggested by the song she sings.

This section begins:

> "The Chair she sat in, like a burnished throne,
> Glowed on the marble, where the glass
> Held up by standards wrought with fruited vines
> From which a golden Cupidon peeped out
> (Another hid his eyes behind his wing)
> Doubled the flames of sevenbranched candelabra
> Reflecting light upon the table as
> The glitter of her jewels rose to meet it,
> From satin cases poured in rich profusion;
> In vials of ivory and coloured glass
> Unstoppered, lurked her strange synthetic perfumes,
> Unguent, powdered, or liquid—troubled, confused
> And drowned the sense in odours; stirred by the air."

The first lines recall Shakespeare's "Anthony and Cleopatra". As Cleopatra's royal boat proceeds, the breezes and the water fall in love with her. This new Cleopatra occupies a claustrophobic place: "the room enclosed", full of pungent, artificial perfumes mixed with messy smoke from the fire. The atmosphere is not of lovesickness but of sickness and the need for fresh air. We hear of "her strange synthetic perfumes, unguent, powdered, or liquid-troubled confused". Another theme that

Eliot uses in "The Waste Land" is that of 'The Fisher King'. This is an Arthurian legend. When the King is wounded, the land and people are wounded. When the King is barren, the land is barren. There is no life. The King is the weakest in the 'Game of Chess' and when he falls the game is over.

We see the discussion between the lady and her husband. This discussion is a non-discussion. The lady asks "Why do you never speak. Speak." Her speech is insistent, pitiable, needy, exasperating. She is met with silence:

"Glowed into words, then would be savagely still.

"My nerves are bad tonight. Yes, bad. Stay with me.
"Speak to me. Why do you never speak. Speak.
    "What are you thinking of? What thinking? What?
"I never know what you are thinking. Think."

I think we are in rats' alley
Where the dead men lost their bones.

"What is that noise?"
        The wind under the door.
"What is that noise now? What is the wind doing?"
        Nothing again nothing.
"Do
You know nothing? Do you see nothing? Do you remember
"Nothing?"

I remember
Those are pearls that were his eyes.
"Are you alive, or not? Is there nothing in your head?"

But
O O O O that Shakespeherian Rag—
It's so elegant
So intelligent

"What shall I do now? What shall I do?"
"I shall rush out as I am, and walk the street
"With my hair down, so. What shall we do tomorrow?
"What shall we ever do?"

The hot water at ten.
And if it rains, a closed car at four.
And we shall play a game of chess,
Pressing lidless eyes and waiting for a knock upon the door."

All is "savagely still". A loss of communion and lack of intimacy can be a savage blow to a marriage. The woman speaks of her nerves being bad. There is no peace. She is aggressive and demands that her husband talk. It is an observer's look into what has crumbled. There is no prospect for understanding between the two. He says he thinks they are in rats' alley where the dead men lost their bones. The rats that live in the alleyways of London have only dead bones across which to scurry. The husband and wife are in the valley of the dead. There could be a reference here to the valley of the dry bones of Ezekiel 37.

She asks what is that noise. The answer is nothing. The fear of being nothing permeates the poem. Nothingness speaks of oblivion. There is nothing coming to save their marriage. She repeats the word "nothing" – "Do you know nothing. Do you see nothing. Do you remember nothing." He remembers those pearls that were his eyes. This is taken from "The Tempest" by Shakespeare. The drowned sailor goes to the bottom of the sea and is transformed. Shakespeare held out the hope of a re-birth. Eliot used this, also, in the first section of "The Waste Land". Yet the man in the Waste Land has this only as a memory. He is spiraling downward into oblivion. He is losing meaning, losing trust. It is a form of Dante's Inferno.

The wife asks "Are you alive or not? Is there nothing in your head?" He is as good as dead. He is one of the walking dead. Eliot was fascinated by the culture he lived in. It was a time known as the Jazz age. Shakespeare's work is now just a form of rag-time. High and low culture are collapsed onto themselves. The words of the Bard are now reduced to jazz and rag-time. They have no more depth than that for the people in the Waste Land. "What shall I do now? What shall I do?" are questions people face in the Waste Land where there is no meaning. "What shall we ever do?" This introduces the fear that if there is an eternity, the pain now will be everlasting. She answers with mundane things "the hot water at ten. And if it rains, a closed car at four." Then she says "we shall play a game of chess". This is all they shall ever do. They will, play, make strategies and remain forever lonely.

There is also an echo here of Shakespeare's King Lear. The word "nothing" rings through the play. Lear has asked his daughters to express their love. Cordelia is silent.

> "Lear: … what can you say to draw
> A third more opulent than your sisters? Speak.
>
> Cordelia: Nothing, my lord.
>
> Lear: Nothing!
>
> Cordelia: Nothing.
>
> Lear: Nothing will come of nothing: speak again."
>
> (King Lear)

Nothing can be done for our couple either. All they have is nothing: the nothingness that lies behind waiting for the hot water, looking forward to the taxi ordered for four and – in the meantime – play a game of chess.

The last section of "A Game of Chess" is one in a pub in London. The bartender's voice tells the people "It is time to go home". One of the ladies finds her body has been undermined by chemically induced miscarriages. She is told by her friend that she had better smarten herself up for her man or else risk losing him to another. Her friend tells her "You ought to be ashamed, I said, to look so antique". Lil is the lady's name. She has to bear children and look beautiful for her man. Again there is no intimacy, no love, no compassion. Lil is broken. Then a voice breaks in: "Hurry Up Please It's Time" – the voice of the bartender telling Lil and the people in the bar to go home. At the time Eliot was writing these stories in Margate, his wife was having an affair with the philosopher Bertrand Russell. This adds another layer of suffering to the words Eliot penned.

(iii) The Fire Sermon:

This section is named after a sermon given by the Buddha to warn his followers of the consuming power of human passion.

> "All things, O priests, are on fire ... The eye, O priests, is on fire; forms are on fire; eye-consciousness is on fire; impressions received by the eye are on fire; and whatever sensation, pleasant, unpleasant, or indifferent, originates in dependence on impressions received by the eye, that also is on fire."
>
> (Sermon of the Buddha)

Only by acquiring an obliviousness towards these desires is a person able to attain freedom from the tortuous feelings that characterise this bodily life. In quoting the Buddha, Eliot was following Wagner and Schopenhauer. Later in the poem he intertwines Buddhist and Christian conceptions of fire together. Eliot wrote bits of this poem while convalescing in Lake Leman (the French name for Lake Geneva). In this section Eliot says: "By the waters of Leman I sat down and wept...". This calls to mind the lament of the exiled Israelites ("By the waters of Babylon we sat and wept, when we remembered Zion [Ps 137]). In this section Eliot will see unfettered desire as leading to a corruption of love and ultimately abuse. No one hears the voice of the abused. No one cares. A deep loneliness reigns in The Waste Land. Sexual love is debased.

The section begins with a description of the Thames. Earlier he had spoken of the hordes crossing London Bridge, aimless and lost, the living dead. He begins:

> "The river's tent is broken: the last fingers of leaf
> Clutch and sink into the wet bank. The wind
> Crosses the brown land, unheard. The nymphs are departed.

Sweet Thames, run softly, till I end my song.
The river bears no empty bottles, sandwich papers,
Silk handkerchiefs, cardboard boxes, cigarette ends
Or other testimony of summer nights. The nymphs are
departed."

The trees that overlooked the Thames and gave shelter are now "broken". This is a term used throughout the Waste Land – all in which one trusted for security is "broken". He describes Autumn where "the last fingers of leaves clutch and sink into the wet bank". Everything is now exposed to the harshness and cruelty of Winter. We have moved from "April being the cruelest month…" to "the Summer surprised us…" to Autumn, here. This evokes the idea of the "Wheel of Time". We are caught in an unending cycle of pain. Everything spirals downward in an unending, monotonous tragedy. In the Waste Land, the "wind crosses the dry land…" This is not the land of Springtime but a parched, dry land. The wind is "unheard". There is no-one who hears its sound. He tells us "the nymphs are departed". This refers to ancient nature gods. These are no more. Nature has lost her magic. There is no communion of people. There is no gathering of people who would enjoy the seasons. In the Waste Land everyone has fled and everything is desolate. Any form of spiritual or natural comfort is gone. He then prays: "Sweet Thames, run softly, 'til I end my song". This desire for the Thames to run softly comes from an Edmund Spenser poem. He had written these words. Eliot's Thames, however, does not have the Elizabethan charm of Spenser's. Here the opening lines depict a squalid urban river, a scene of Autumnal decay.

Tiresias is one of the narrators of the Fire Sermon. He was an ancient Greek prophet who was punished by Hera. He wanted to die but could not. He was blind but even in his blindness he knew what was going on. Tiresias is a figure who crops up in the Waste Land. He is central to understanding the Epic poem of the 'Waste Land'. For Eliot the violation of the sublimity of sex has in all ages and cultures led to decay and degeneration and there is a necessity to purify the sinner's soul through suffering. His presence in the Waste Land is also symbolic. He connects the waste lands of Oedipus and the Fisher King, as well as the past and present. He is bi-sexual and blind. However with his experience of life he sees far more than those with sight. He can destroy our illusions, our joys, our hopes and fears. He shows us the boredom and emptiness of the "Waste Land" in which many live.

Eliot quotes "Parsifal" and the work of Wagner before he introduces Tiresias. The time of Tiresias is the "violet hour". The lonely lines of Sappho which address the evening star as the daily inspiration for homecoming are given a sad twist:

> "…the evening hour that strives
> Homeward, and brings the sailor home from sea,"

This refers to the time of evening when the typist returns home and is tired. Tiresias says:

> "The typist home at teatime, clears her breakfast, lights
> Her stove, and lays out food in tins."

"Still" refers to Philomela ("And still she cried, and still the world pursues"). Philomela was turned into a nightingale in a desperate attempt to free herself from the prison of brutality. She had lost trust in love and humanity. She was left with nothing but a bleeding wound (inside and out). She cried and the world pursued. "'Jug, Jug' she cried to dirty ears".

The house agent's clerk is adept at living in the world of non-connection: "His vanity requires no response / and makes a welcome of indifference". In Samuel Johnson's "Vanity of Human Wishes" hope may be doomed but love, patience and faith remain.

> "With these celestial Wisdom calms the Mind
> And makes the happiness she does not find".

There is nothing of such wisdom here. The typist and the clerk have a loveless encounter. The clerk is sexually abusive and leaves the typist hurt and alone.

"When lovely woman stoops to folly and
Paces about her room again, alone,
She smoothes her hair with automatic hand,
And puts a record on the gramophone."

We are told: "Her brain allows one half-formed thought to pass". This is far from the world of thought. Eliot manages to invoke a sad song from Goldsmith:

"When lovely woman stoops to folly,
And finds too late that men betray"

He rejects its sentimental moralism but retains the pathos. The typist is used, abused and lonely. She plays a record to distract her. She lives in a world where nobody listens or cares. She is like Philomela. She is deeply wounded and this inner pain is a living death. People who have suffered abuse know this place well. They are told to be silent. They often carry their pain with them causing them to limp through life as one already dead. This is 'The Waste Land'.

In Wagner's opera, Parsifal ends with the song of the children celebrating the end of Parsifal's Buddhist-like quest to overcome desire. Here in the Waste Land we hear another tune coming from a pub near the fish market. The scene is bewildering and confusing.

Wagner appears in the last section of the poem. Three water-nymphs appear in Das Rheingold, the opening opera in the Ring of the Nibelung cycle. The opera opens with their joyful shrieks of "Wallala weiala weia". They have been charged with looking after the precious Rhinegold. Only the one who has renounced love can steal the Rhinegold. The nymphs do not believe such a person exists. However they did not reckon on the evil Alberich who curses love readily and can take the gold. The rest of the story develops from this. Eliot points us towards the closing opera in the cycle – Götterdämmerung (The Twilight of the Gods) – at the beginning of the third Act in which the maidens reappear lamenting their loss and longing for a hero to restore their losses. Their cry now is "Weila leia Wallala leialola". Eliot enters Wagner's sound-world at the point of greatest loss...

"The river sweats
Oil and tar
The barges drift
With the turning tide
Red sails
Wide
To leeward, swing on the heavy spar.
The barges wash
Drifting logs
Down Greenwich reach
Past the Isle of Dogs.
       Weialala leia
       Wallala leialala
Elizabeth and Leicester
Beating oars
The stern was formed
A gilded shell
Red and gold
The brisk swell
Rippled both shores
Southwest wind
Carried down stream
The peal of bells
White towers
       Weialala leia
       Wallala leialala

"Trams and dusty trees.
Highbury bore me. Richmond and Kew
Undid me. By Richmond I raised my knees
Supine on the floor of a narrow canoe." "

The barges drift aimlessly down the Thames. The nymphs lament the loss of the Thames. "Weialala leia / Wallala leialala". Then Queen Elizabeth I and her doomed love affair is mentioned. The maidens or nymphs lament this. Elizabeth was the Virgin Queen. She did not marry perhaps because she did not want to be aligned with another country.

Then an unidentified female voice comes in. She speaks of "Trams and dusty trees". She is devastated by her encounters and is left shattered, broken and alone.

> " "I can connect
> Nothing with nothing.
> The broken fingernails of dirty hands.
> My people humble people who expect
> Nothing."
>   la la
>
> To Carthage then I came
> Burning burning burning burning
> O Lord Thou pluckest me out
> O Lord Thou pluckest
> burning"

One of the nymphs sings: "I can connect with nothing". All is broken and has fallen apart. We hear a final stab of the nymph's lyrical noise ("la la"). This is like an exhausted collapse into nothingness.

The final lines blend two voices. One is the Western voice of Augustine and the other the voice of the Buddha from the East. St. Augustine was made bishop of Carthage. He described Carthage as a "cauldron of unholy loves". Later in his "Confessions", Augustine addresses God who saved him from his sinfulness: "… thou pluckest me out, O Lord, thou pluckest me out". This harps back to the typist who sought music to pluck her out of her despondency and disappointment. She seeks something to help her in her despair. Eliot breaks up Augustine's prayer "Thou pluckest me out / Thou pluckest". The prayer is fragmented and unanswered. Augustine's words are hopeful but as they appear in "The Waste Land" they are contextless and appear meaningless, cut down. Eliot crosses the flames of sin and sexual addiction with the burning described by the Buddha in his sermon: "burning, burning, burning". There is a powerful sense here of the person falling to pieces. We sense "the apparent irrelevance and unrelatedness of things". The Fire Sermon ends with a floating unpunctuated participle: "burning".

(iv) Death by Water:

This is the shortest section of the poem. It describes a man, Phlebas the Phoenician who was drowned. Phlebas is a character Eliot created as far back as 1916/17. He wrote, in French, "Dans le Restaurant", a poem about an encounter between a customer and a waiter. The last lines of this poem constitute what we know as "Death by Water".

In the first part of the "Waste Land", "The Burial of the Dead", we see a Madame Sosostris. Eliot said that the absence of faith led to credulity of the wrong kind. G. K. Chesterton is believed to have said: "If you stop believing in God, you do not start believing in nothing but rather in everything, whether true or not". In Eliot's later work "The Four Quartets", in the poem entitled "The Dry Salvages" he describes those practitioners who prey on our credulity.

> "To report the behavior of the sea monster,
> Describe the horoscope, haruspicate or scry,
> Observe disease in signatures, evoke
> Biography from the wrinkles of the plan
> And tragedy of the fingers... all these are usual"

And he lists:

> "Pastimes and drugs, and features of the press:
> And always will be, some of them especially
> When there is distress of nations and perplexity
> Whether on the shores of Asia, or in the Edgware Road."

Like these peddlers and proponents of mystery we find Eliot's Madame Sosostris. She is a figure of spurious spiritual guidance. She approximately sees the future. She sees the drowned sailor (who appears in this section). She also foresaw the "Lady of the Rocks" (Part II of the poem), the one-eyed merchant (who appeared as Mr. Eugenides in Part III). Her inscrutability is strategic and financially advantageous.

This section reads:

"Phlebas the Phoenician, a fortnight dead,
Forgot the cry of gulls, and the deep sea swell
And the profit and loss.
   A current under sea
Picked his bones in whispers. As he rose and fell
He passed the stages of his age and youth
Entering the whirlpool.
   Gentile or Jew
O you who turn the wheel and look to windward,
Consider Phlebas, who was once handsome and tall as you."

The first card Madame Sosostris held was that of the Wheel. This describes the monotonous routine in which we are all trapped. The last card she produced was the fear of death. She tells us to fear "death by water" – this took place in "The Burial of the Dead". Now in this section what she predicted comes to pass.

We meet "Phlebas the Phoenician". The Phoenicians were a sea-faring people and traders in the Ancient world. They knew the seas. We can assume Phlebas was a skilled sailor but already he is dead. Death is irresistible and final throughout the poem. Even before physical death in the Waste Land we see the figures of people who are the living dead – in "The Burial of the Dead" Eliot spoke of those who "march asleep". For all intents and purposes they are already dead.

Phlebas had forgotten the "cry of gulls and the deep sea swell / and the profit and loss". Being a sailor these are things he would have known. But he has forgotten the things he was born to know. All became meaningless to him. He was no longer the person he was called to be. He lived in despair.

He had forgotten the sea and its nature. He had forgotten home and his very own identity. All that was precious to him had lost value. He had no purpose in life. He had forgotten his emotional purpose. He had let his feelings become numb. All he believed in, including his trade, "the profit and loss" had now been filled by "A current under sea". He could not control the sea. As a Phoenician he should have understood the sea. He had lost the ability to navigate and this leads to his physical death. Under the sea we hear of how his bones were picked in whispers. In the "Fire Sermon" we saw the rats scurrying over the bones of the dead, scuttling down the alleyways and the sound of the wind on the bones of the dead. Here nothing remains but the bones of Phlebas. "As he rose and fell" refers to the body of Phlebas in the sea. He is now only a floating body. Everything he accomplished is gone and now he floats above the sea. As he rose and fell he "passed the stages of his age and youth". Here we have the wheel image again. He is and always has been trapped by his circumstances. He enters the Whirlpool. He spirals downwards. This is like the layers of Hell in Dante's Inferno. This image was used in "The Burial of the Dead". Perhaps here there is an unexpected sense of light. As Dante goes downward into the deepest layer of Hell, he ultimately comes to a place where he can leave Hell (Inferno) and move away towards the light of love. There are some suchlike glimmers of hope in the "Waste Land". In the "Fire Sermon" there was the church of Magnus Martyr which came after the story of the typist. It gave a glimpse of another world, a fleeting glimpse – the church of Saint Magnus Martyr, a building with "inexplicable splendour of Ionian white and gold".

Eliot ends the section referring to all people – "Gentile or Jew". Paul in the Letter to the Ephesians spoke of the barriers between Gentile and Jew being broken down (see Ephesians 2:11-22). The wheel image comes back again – "O you who turn the wheel and look to windward". We are addressed here, we are the ones still turning the wheels of our lives. We are told to "Consider Phlebas". We are not to forget all the good that is around us and part of us. We are called to become the people we are meant to be. Phlebas was once "handsome and tall", but now he is no more. He had forgotten the things that were central in his life. His was a living death before Death by Drowning. His spiritual death led him to physical death.

(v) What the Thunder Said:

In Hebrew *'bat qol'* literally means daughter of a voice. It refers to thunder as the voice of God. In the Hindu sacred books, the Upanishads, the thunder speaks of thunder as being the voice of God. Eliot studied the Upanishads when he was at Harvard, as he had studied Buddhist texts. Eliot wrote this part of 'The Waste Land' when he was in Lausanne in Switzerland.

This section begins with the lines:

> "After the torchlight red on sweaty faces
> After the frosty silence in the gardens
> After the agony in stony places
> The shouting and the crying
> Prison and palace and reverberation
> Of thunder of spring over distant mountains
> He who was living is now dead
> We who were living are now dying
> With a little patience"

Eliot enters the spiritual underpinning of our reality as human beings. There are many Christian elements in this section. After the "torchlight red on sweaty faces" is a haunting image of hatred, like the mob that came to arrest Jesus in the Garden of Gethsemane. They arrive after the "frosty silence in the Garden". There Jesus prayed in agony but all was silent (see Mk 14:32-42). Then Eliot speaks of the "agony in stony places", the death Jesus would endure (see Mk 15:33-39, Lk 23:33-46, Mt 27:32-55). This harkens back to the book of Isaiah and the suffering servant (Is 52:13 – 53:12). He suffers through feeling alienated from his father. In the event of Jesus' arrest we hear "the shouting and the crying / Prison and palace and reverberation…" We hear of "thunder and spring over distant mountains". Is there still a possibility of the death and resurrection that he denied in the "Burial of the Dead"? We see the poem move through the seasons and now we are back in Spring – the wheel of monotonous time we have seen in the 'Waste Land'. Then our hope ends abruptly. Eliot says: "He who was living is now dead". Our hope for a resurrection doesn't seem to be real. The one in whom we had hoped is now dead. "We who were living are now dying"! Decay, loss and meaningless existence seem to be our lot. Eliot sees the glimmer of light coming in and here he wrestles with doubt and near-despair. But still there is a light. Death, as a real cessation of life, is no consolation – but even in this darkness Eliot is looking to another "who is now dead" but whose figure haunts Eliot.

The next part reads:

> "Here is no water but only rock
> Rock and no water and the sandy road
> The road winding above among the mountains
> Which are mountains of rock without water
> If there were water we should stop and drink
> Amongst the rock one cannot stop or think
> Sweat is dry and feet are in the sand
> If there were only water amongst the rock
> Dead mountain mouth of carious teeth that cannot spit
> Here one can neither stand nor lie nor sit
> There is not even silence in the mountains
> But dry sterile thunder without rain
> There is not even solitude in the mountains
> But red sullen faces sneer and snarl
> From doors of mudcracked houses"

The speaker continues: "Here is no water but only rock". The Waste Land is a dry, rocky, barren land. Jesus described himself as living water (see Jn 4:14 where he speaks to the Samaritan woman). In the Waste Land no-one knows this. There is no water, no healing, no salvation. The living water contrasts with the drowning water of the previous section. All we experience is harshness. When one reads of the "road winding above among the mountains", one thinks of a Moses figure receiving The Law from Yahweh (Exodus 20). Also, in Exodus 17 God brings water from the rock to quench the thirst of his people. This is a type of Christ but we have "mountains of rock without water". In the Waste Land our hope deceives. "If there were water", if there were healing "we should stop and drink". Should talk of a saviour figure exist, then we would find relief but there is none. "Among the rocks one cannot stop or think". This means we can find no relief. "Sweat is dry and feet are in the sand". There is no solid ground in which we can find our feet. In the Waste Land there is no rock that can produce water and we are left with nothing but despair. "Here one can neither stand nor lie nor sit". There is no relief, no rest, no hope in the Waste Land. The anguish and anxiety of the Waste Land overwhelms us.

We are told there isn't even silence in the mountains: "but dry sterile thunder without rain". There is no fertility, no growth, just the barren Waste Land. "There is not even solitude in the mountains". In the Burial of the Dead there was the image of the crowd on London Bridge shuffling aimlessly. Here we are alone on a crowded mountain. "Red sullen faces sneer and snarl". We have again the image of hostility and hatred. This is an oppressive, demonic image.

Eliot continues:

> "If there were water
> And no rock
> If there were rock
> And also water
> And water
> A spring
> A pool among the rock
> If there were the sound of water only
> Not the cicada
> And dry grass singing
> But sound of water over a rock
> Where the hermit-thrush sings in the pine trees
> Drip drop drip drop drop drop drop
> But there is no water
>
> Who is the third who walks always beside you?
> When I count, there are only you and I together
> But when I look ahead up the white road
> There is always another one walking beside you
> Gliding wrapt in a brown mantle, hooded
> I do not know whether a man or a woman
> –But who is that on the other side of you?"

If there were water, we would stop and drink but in the Waste Land where we are without hope. This piece reads like a prayer of petition for water. He seeks a "spring", "a pool among the rock…". He remembers events like the healing at the pool of Bethesda (Jn 5:1-16) and the healing at the pool of Siloam (Jn 9:6f). He prays even for the sound of water alone, that would be enough for us, "not the cicada / and dry grass singing". These are the sounds of emptiness. He longs to hear the hermit-thrush singing. This is in contrast to Philomela who was turned into a nightingale so that she could not speak of her rape. "But there is no water". The voice of petition is in vain.

Yet there is hope. In Luke 24:13-35 there is the story of Jesus walking with the disciples on the road to Emmaus. This happens after his resurrection. He has conquered death and his presence gives hope to the two disenchanted disciples. There are times in our lives when we sense we are not alone, when we sense a comforting presence. In the beginning of the poem we read: "He who was living is now dead". Here we have hope in the possibility of new life. Christ is the one who walks always beside us. In the other parts of the Waste Land there was no hope for such a possibility but here there is still hope. We do not recognise him initially. Here is the hope that the one for whom we longed is here beside us in the Waste Land. "When I count there are only you and I together" – this means when I use my senses I can only see two but deep in my spirit I recognise a mysterious other. The scientific mind tells me there are only two but I need a different form of intelligence to sense the other – we are left with the question "– But who is that on the other side of you?"

John McCarthy is a British journalist, writer and broadcaster. He was held hostage from 1986 to 1991. One day he was full of fear and anxiety:

> "One morning these fears became unbearable. I stood in my cell sinking into despair. I felt that I was literally sinking, being sucked down into a whirlpool. I was on my knees, gasping for air, drowning in hopelessness and helplessness. I thought that I was passing out. I could only think of one thing to say – "Help me please, oh God, help me!" The next

instant I was standing up, surrounded by a warm bright
light. I was dancing, full of joy. In the space of a minute,
despair had vanished, replaced by boundless optimism.
What had happened? I had never had any great faith,
despite a Church of England upbringing. But I felt that I had
to give thanks. But to what?"

(Some Other Rainbow, p. 98)

Later on in the poem we come to hear 'what the thunder said'. The scene
switches to the Ganges where the thunder rumbles. Eliot draws on the
traditional interpretation of "what the thunder says" as taken from the
Upanishads. The Thunder "gives", "sympathises" and "controls"
through its voice.

> "Ganga was sunken, and the limp leaves
> Waited for rain, while the black clouds
> Gathered far distant, over Himavant
> The jungle crouched, humped in silence.
> Then spoke the thunder
> DA
> Datta: what have we given?
> My friend, blood shaking my heart
> The awful daring of a moment's surrender
> Which an age of prudence can never retract
> By this, and this only, we have existed
> Which is not to be found in our obituaries
> Or in memories draped by the beneficent spider
> DA
> Dayadhvam: I have heard the key
> Turn in the door once and turn once only
> We think of the key, each in his prison
> Thinking of the key, each confirms a prison
> Only at nightfall, aethereal rumours
> Revive for a moment a broken Coriolanus
> DA
> Damyata: The boat responded
> Gaily, to the hand expert with sail and oar

The sea was calm, your heart would have responded
Gaily, when invited, beating obedient
To controlling hands

         I sat upon the shore
Fishing, with the arid plain behind me
Shall I at least set my lands in order?
London Bridge is falling down falling down falling down
Poi s'ascose nel foci che gli affina
Quando fiam uti chelidon–O swallow swallow
Le Prince d'Aquitaine à la tour abolie
These fragments I have shored against my ruins
Why then Ile fit you. Hieronymo's mad again.
Datta. Dayadhvam. Damyata.
         Shantih   shantih   shantih"

The thunder speaks for itself. The sacred river 'Ganga' is the sacred river of the Hindus. Everything waits for rain. "The jungle crouched, humped in silence". In Romans 8 Paul speaks of "the whole creation has been groaning in labour pains until now" (Rom 8:22). All of creation awaits healing. Now the thunder speaks. Everyone and everything longs for redemption. In the Waste Land all is broken. All the words the thunder speaks begin with the word 'Da' (give). The first phrase is Datta which means 'gives'. We hear "what shall we give?" Here the giving is a complete act of self-giving before the reality of another person. We are called to break out from the self-enclosure of personality. Eliot speaks of "the awful daring of a moment's surrender". Eliot spoke of this self surrender in a letter to Stephen Spender:

> "You don't really criticise any author to whom you have never surrendered yourself... Even just the bewildering minute counts; you have to give yourself up, and then recover yourself, and the third moment is having something to say, before you have wholly forgotten both surrender and recovery. Of course the self recovered is never the same as the self before it was given."

He is discussing literary criticism here but, as Frank Kermode says, he is describing at the same time something powerfully operative in all aspects of his mind, including his poetic genius – as it is described, for example, in the trailblazing early essay "Tradition and the Individual Talent".

The persons realise themselves through a process of submission to something greater than themselves. The process of self-surrender is bewildering and full of awe.

The next word the thunder speaks is Dayadhvam. This means "sympathise". The self has become a prison. We are people in isolation, "each mind keeping us as a solitary prisoner in its own dream of a world" (Eliot). The key is the key that has locked us "each in his own prison". He refers to the isolated, despairing figure of Coriolanus. We are isolated and alone. Each of us longs for a key. We are called to show compassion yet at the same time we are in too much pain.

The final command is Domyata (control). Here the emphasis is on giving up control. "The boat responded gaily to the hand expert". This remind us of Jesus calming the sea. The disciples were afraid but Jesus calmed them and the sea:

> "That day when evening came, he said to his disciples, "Let us go over to the other side." Leaving the crowd behind, they took him along, just as he was, in the boat. There were also other boats with him. A furious squall came up, and the waves broke over the boat, so that it was nearly swamped. Jesus was in the stern, sleeping on a cushion. The disciples woke him and said to him, "Teacher, don't you care if we drown?"
>
> He got up, rebuked the wind and said to the waves, "Quiet! Be still!" Then the wind died down and it was completely calm."

> (Mk 4:35-39)

Jesus is the key-holder. When we allow Jesus to guide us we find happiness – those who know God respond "gaily".

Then, at the very end, comes a shock. Once again we are thrust back into the Waste Land. The last lines are broken. There is no harmony, no rhyme, just disjointed voices out of time. Sometimes we hope but then we meet the voices of our fears and brokenness.

'What the Thunder Said' concludes with a collage of quotations from various sources: the nursery rhyme 'London Bridge is falling down' (suggesting the demise of London as the centre of a vast empire and trading power); Dante's Purgatorio ('Then dives him into the fire which refines him'); the Pervigilium Veneris, a Latin poem dating back nearly two thousand years, followed by a Tennyson poem ('O swallow swallow'); a sonnet by Gerard de Nerval ('the Prince of Aquitaine in the ruined tower'); Thomas Kyd's Elizabethan play The Spanish Tragedy (c. 1587); and finally, the word 'Shantih', which Eliot says is roughly equivalent to our phrase 'the peace which passeth understanding', repeated three times.

Jacques Lacan said that the naming of something in a repeated way can mean the lack of that thing. As Eliot repeats 'Shantih', this could mean the desire for the peace that passes all understanding but a peace he has not yet found.

No Country for Old Men

"No Country for Old Men" is a 2007 film written and directed by Joel and Ethan Coen (the Coen brothers), based on Cormac McCarthy's 2005 novel of the same name. The title of the film comes from a W. B. Yeats poem, "Sailing to Byzantium". Yeats was in his early sixties when he wrote this poem. The speaker is referring to the country he has left, saying it is "no country for old men". It is a country full of life and youth. There "all summer long" the world sings with sensual music "that makes the young neglect the old" whom Yeats describes as "monuments of unageing intellect".

"That is no country for old men. The young
In one another's arms, birds in the trees
– Those dying generations – at their song,
The salmon-falls, the mackerel-crowded seas,
Fish, flesh, or fowl, commend all summer long
Whatever is begotten, born, and dies.
Caught in that sensual music all neglect
Monuments of unageing intellect."

An aged man is "but a paltry thing". The poem presents the transience of life and the permanence of nature. The speaker wants to escape from the world where the wise are neglected. The poem expresses the difficulty of keeping one's soul alive in a fragile, failing body. The poet wants to leave behind the country he is in for a visionary journey to Byzantium. There he hopes to move past his mortality and become something like an immortal work of art. He hopes to find spiritual rebirth. In a 1931 BBC broadcast Yeats said:

"I am trying to write about the state of my soul, for it is right for an old man to make his soul, and some of my thoughts about that subject I have put into a poem called 'Sailing to Byzantium'. When Irishmen were illuminating the Book of Kells, and making the jewelled croziers in the National Museum, Byzantium was the centre of European civilisation and the source of its spiritual philosophy, so I symbolise the search for the spiritual life by a journey to that city."

The film "No Country for Old Men" thematically seems to be related to Ingmar Bergman's "The Seventh Seal" (1957). We meet a Knight here who comes home from the Crusades. He meets death but he hopes to cheat death by playing a game of chess. In 'No Country' Anton Chigurh (Javier Bardem) tosses a coin to see if the other will live or die. Chigurh wears black like the villain in old Westerns. Unlike Bergman's Death, Chigurh uses a cattle gun in place of a scythe. The hero in Bergman's film seeks moral certainty. He seeks God – but in Bergman's bleak vision God is silent. The Knight is left without hope. The Coen Brothers share this bleakness. It is a form of the "Waste Land". In Bergman's film the Knight fears the silence of God. He fears this means God isn't there and his life (lived mostly in Crusades) was, therefore, meaningless. The Knight wants God "to reach out his hand, show his face, speak to him". Likewise, uncertainty weighs on the aged sheriff Ed Tom Bell (played by Tommy Lee Jones) who longs for the promise of an earlier time. He remembers his family of the past who were sheriffs of the county.

The setting of 'No Country' recalls the old western, cowboy films with clear lines separating the good from the bad. In the end the good guy kills the bad guy and rides off into the sunset. 'No Country' breaks these conventions. The aged sheriff finds brutality and violence all around him. We expect a show-down in 'No Country' which never comes. Llewelyn Moss (Josh Brolin) is found dead and there is no shoot-out with Chigurh. At the end of the film we see Chigurh head off like the heroes of old. The 'bad guy' gets away. He takes the place occupied by the 'good guys' in the old films. Sheriff Bell confides to his deputy that he "always figured" God would come into his life sometime and help him make sense of the violent, chaotic world around him but this does not happen.

The wind is omnipresent in the film. Shots of three windmills appear at the beginning of the film. The film has no music, so the wind becomes the film's consistent score. Sheriff Bell is reminded that one of his forebears died a violent death. The violence and chaos has always been there. Sheriff Bell has a too romantic view of the past. In the Book of Ecclesiastes we read:

> "Vanity of vanities says the teacher,
> vanity of vanities! All is vanity"
>
> (Ecl 1:2)

"Vanity" translates the Hebrew word *'hebel'*. It could translate as 'all is meaningless'. Later on he says

> "What has been is what will be,
> and what has been done is what will be done;
> there is nothing new under the sun"
>
> (Ecl 1:9)

In 1:14 the author tells us: "I have seen all things that are done under the sun; all of them are vanity (meaningless), a chasing after the wind". The Hebrew word '*hebel*' which can be translated as vanity or meaningless originally meant a mere breath, nothing of substance. I think here of Donovan's "Catch the Wind" (1965). The world of Ecclesiastes is bleak as is the Coen vision of the world. The film ends with a slow, calm, monologue spoken by the sheriff. Eliot finished his poem "The Hollow Men" with the following lines:

"For Thine is the Kingdom

For Thine is
Life is
For Thine is the

This is the way the world ends
This is the way the world ends
This is the way the world ends
Not with a bang but with a whimper."

This seems to be the same for the end of the film. Sheriff Bell tells his wife about dreams he had. He is now retired. Bell is one of the men to whom the title refers. He finds this world has no place for him. He struggles to face the actual world of chaos and randomness and so he is lost. The Coens use the dreams to show Bell mourning the decent, lawful world he believed in but could not find. The world he dreamed of is an illusion – it is the '*hebel*' of Ecclesiastes. The story 'No Country' rejects justice when Chigurh escapes and just walks off.

In Sheriff Bell's dreams he tells his wife that his father featured in both his dreams. Bell is now the old man. The world Bell found was extremely dangerous and wild and he retires defeated because of this. The first dream was about money his father gave him and how he lost it. The entire film has been built around money and how the different groups search for the money Moss stole. All the characters who are concerned with the money end up dead or injured and/or morally empty. There is no saving grace.

Bell's losing the money evokes his loss of this world with its moral confusion and ambiguity – a world that seems to have no use for him anymore. Bell cannot see clearly.

Bell's second dream is about riding on horseback through the mountains with his father – getting as far away from civilisation as possible. Bell has always longed for a safer, more straightforward time but this does not exist. His father carried a light with him. It carries the hope of a great light up ahead. Bell hopes to return to the simple good his father represents. His dream is not a prophecy but a desire. He needs the certainty that, in the end, there will be warmth and life. He dreams of something he knows will never come true. The scene cuts to black – all there is is 'nothingness' (hebel). Bell's father rides ahead to prepare a place for Bell to follow. This is the end.

The bleakness of the vision of the "Waste Land" and "No Country for Old Men" speaks to that lonely place in which many people live. Those who have suffered trauma from war, violence and abuse know the negative world to which these works allude. We see the face of nothingness and despair. They express in words and film the negativity that can overcome us. Paradoxically, it is only when we face the darkness that we can allow the light come in. "How else but through a broken heart may Lord Christ enter in" (Oscar Wilde, The Ballad of Reading Gaol).

Is the Waste Land Completely Pessimistic

Mark Rothko was an artist who used colours and their interplay to express emotions. He was commissioned by John and Dominique de Menil to produce paintings for a chapel which became known as the Rothko chapel. Rothko used dark colours, which incorporated dark hues and texture effects. Rothko said it was like the light penetrating the darkness. The chapel is a meditation space where one can remain in silence and find hope. It is situated in Houston, Texas and was opened in 1971. Rothko, himself, had battled with depression and took his own life in 1970. He did not see the opening of the chapel.

I see something similar in Eliot's Waste Land. He confronts the darkness and emptiness of the Waste Land. The poem was born from his own pain yet it also reflects the pain of his age after the trauma of the first World War. It speaks to the loneliness and heartbreak of every age. Yet there are interactions of light just as those in the Rothko chapel. We spend most of our energy running away from pain. The Waste Land helps us look at our pain and loneliness and in doing so allow hope to enter. Jesus tells us: "Peace I leave with you: my peace I give you. I do not give to you as the world gives. Do not let your hearts be troubled and do not be afraid" (John 14:27). One day we hope to leave the Waste Land and know this peace.

"Shantih!   Shantih!   Shantih!"

Chapter 2

Ash Wednesday:

The Waste Land is a depressing place. Eliot's description speaks to many of our hearts. Yet fear keeps us there. Soren Kierkegaard (+1855) in his work 'Fear and Trembling' criticises attempts at easy religious consolation which cut too quickly to promises of a happy ending. Easy consolations leave out the distress, the anxiety, the paradox within faith. For Kierkegaard the cost of faith is always high. He points to Abraham and Isaac. He tells us to look at Jesus' mother Mary, as she is depicted in the Gospel of Luke. When she is told that she is to give birth, she is afraid. No-one else saw the angel. No-one could understand her (Fear and Trembling, p. 57). Mary and Abraham became great not by being exempt from distress, and torment, and paradox, but they became great through passing through these things. He warns us that fear is the great enemy in the spiritual life and courage is needed to overcome it. "Do not be afraid", Jesus constantly told his disciples. He saw how fear contracted their hearts, preventing them from loving or receiving love. Our hearts must be open and strong if we are to become fully human, and that is why Mary and Abraham are among the greatest spiritual examples. Kierkegaard calls this openheartedness "humble courage" and he understands how difficult it is to accomplish: "It is harder to receive love than to give it" (Fear and Trembling, p. 54). Deep down our anxieties and fears can convince us we are not worthy of love. Experiences in life can bring us to that place: the Waste Land – and fear can keep us there. To leave this place we must take Kierkegaard's 'leap of faith'. Paul Tillich described faith as having the courage to accept acceptance. It takes courage because we fear we will not receive love and end up disappointed as before. There is something of the Eternal in all of us but fear and hurt keep us isolated. Kierkegaard says:

> "Deep with every human being there still lives the anxiety
> over the possibility of being alone in the world, forgotten by

God, overlooked among the millions and millions in this enormous household."

(JP 140; Pap. VIII A 363, Journals and Papers)

George Bernanos says starkly:

> "There is in man a secret, incomprehensible hatred, not only of his fellowmen, but of himself. We can give this mysterious feeling whatever origin or explanation we want, but we must give it one. As far as we Christians are concerned, we believe that this hatred reflects another hatred, a thousand times more profound and lucid: the hatred of the ineffable spirit who was the most resplendent of all the luminaries of the abyss and who will never forgive us his cataclysmic fall. Outside the hypothesis of an original sin, that is, of an intrinsic contradiction within our nature, the notion of man does become quite clear, only it is no longer the notion of man. When this occurs, man has gone straight through the definition of man, like a handful of sand running between his fingers."
>
> (La liberté, pourquoi faire? (Paris: 1953), p. 252-253)

When we live in this Waste Land we find we do not love. "Hell is no longer being able to love" (Diary of a Country Priest, p. 181). Brokenness and self-hatred cut us off from others. We are isolated, just as the characters are in the 'Waste Land'. Self-loathing comes from a world in which there is little love and this lack of love is turned inwards. Deep down many do not love themselves and they run into distraction to escape being alone with their poor self-image. Teresa of Avila helps us face this fear. In the first mansion of "The Interior Castle" she points to our dignity in the eyes of God. She says:

> "The things of the soul must always be considered as plentiful, spacious, and large; to do so is not an exaggeration. The soul is capable of much more than we can imagine, and the sun that is in this royal chamber shines in all parts. it is very important for any soul that practices

prayer, whether little or much, not to hold itself back and stay in one corner."

(Interior Castle, 1:2:8)

Our experiences can cloud our self-image. We do not know our dignity in God's eyes. Here humility means our proper self-knowledge of who we are in the eyes of God. Teresa says: "Believe me, we shall practice much better through God's help than by being tied down to our own misery" (Interior Castle, 1:2:8) She tells us:

> "So I say, daughters, that we should set our eyes on Christ, our Good, and on His saints. There we shall learn true humility, the intellect will be enhanced, as I have said, and self-knowledge will not make one base and cowardly. Even though this is the first dwelling place, it is very rich and so precious."

(1:2:11)

We come to know ourselves as we come to know God and see ourselves in Him. When we look at Christ we hear God's Word to us in his Person and that word is Love. "The gate of entry to this Castle is prayer and reflection" (Interior Castle, 1:1:7). Our despair and loss can point to a felt sense of loss to the Divine.[1] We know things are not as they should be. As Soren pointed out: we have a spirit. Despair arises when we do not become the people we are meant to be.

> "Just as a physician might say that there very likely is not one single living human being who is completely healthy, so anyone who really knows mankind might say that there is not one single living human being who does not despair a little, who does not secretly harbour an unrest, an inner strife, a disharmony, an anxiety about an unknown something or something he does not even dare to try to know, an anxiety about some possibility in existence or an anxiety about himself, so that, just as a physician speaks of

---

[1] Harold Kushner, When Bad Things Happen to Good People (New York: 1981), p. 142f.

carrying an illness in the body, he walks around carrying a sickness of spirit that signals its presence at rare intervals in and through an anxiety he cannot explain."[2]

The opening pages of "The Sickness Unto Death" declare that human beings are not just bodies and minds, but spiritual beings, related to a higher power. We all face the task of becoming ourselves, constantly returning to the eternal source of our beings. When we feel despair it is born out of a longing to become truly ourselves but failing. It is when we relate to the higher power of God that we come to know ourselves as beloved of God and by his grace we become the person we are called to be. There is hope even if we think despair is the end.

Abraham Heschel also speaks of despair. He tells us about the Hebrew Bible and despair:

> "The Bible charts human beings wrestling with despair and with God. Through the words of the sacred text, God is present. The sacred text is ultimately not the human being's view of God, but of God's love and his need to love individual human beings. It shows us God's view and God's search for the human being from the perspective of the Bible. Who is humanity? A being in travail with God's dreams and designs, with God's dream of a world redeemed, of reconciliation of heaven and earth, of a humankind which is truly God's image, reflecting God's wisdom, justice and compassion."[3]

Rabbi Heschel speaks of the "blackout of God" in our age. He spoke of the lack of authenticity and the indifference that characterises much of religious experience. His work was a call to allow God enter our lives. Martin Buber tells the following story from the Hasidim. It is a story from Rabbi Menachem Mendl of Kotzk:

---

[2] Soren Kierkegaard, The Sickness Unto Death (Princeton: 1983) p. 26-27.

[3] Abraham Heschel, Who is Man (Stanford: 1965) p. 119.

"Where is the dwelling of God?" was the question with which the Rabbi of Kotzk surprised a number of learned men who happened to be visiting him. They laughed at him, saying, "What a thing to ask! Is not the whole world full of his glory!"
Then he answered his own question: "God dwells wherever man lets him in."[4]

Oscar Wilde said in his "Ballad of Reading Gaol"

"How else but through a broken heart
May Lord Christ enter in?"

Ash Wednesday:

After the time of the "Waste Land" T. S. Eliot said the pain he described there had abated. He no longer felt the pessimism he spoke of then. He longed, like many of his generation, to find peace and meaning after the First World War. He turned again to a life of faith. He visited St. Peter's in Rome and to the surprise of his brother he fell to his knees. He eventually joined the Anglican Church, the Anglo-Catholic part of it. During this time his wife, Vivienne, descended more and more into mental illness. Rabbi Heschel once said of his own search: "Dark is the world for me, for all its cities and stars. If not for the few signs of God's radiance, who could stand such agony, such darkness".[5]

Part I:

In "Ash Wednesday" Eliot entered a new phase in his life. He expresses how he battles with his new found faith. The rhythm and flow of the

---

[4] Martin Buber, Tales of the Hasidim, vol. 2 (New York: 1991) p. 277.

[5] This was taken from a conversation with Martin Luther King when they met at the sixty-eighth Convention of the Rabbinical Society in 1968. Ten days after this Convention Dr. King was murdered.

words in "Ash Wednesday" is more musical than that of "The Waste Land". Eliot always tried to express the inexpressible. A contemporary of Eliot's, Evelyn Underhill, was an expert on mysticism. She said of Eliot: "Were he a musician it is probable that the mystic could give his message to other musicians in terms of that art, far more accurately than language will allow him to do".[6]

Poetry can be seen as close to music. Duke Ellington once said: "Music is Prayer".[7] Duke Ellington also said: "You pray to God with music".[8] Poetry, music and prayer can affect us in ways that cannot be defined. I had heard of music being analogous to prayer, but I didn't fully understand until watching an interview with Rosanne Carter, the daughter of the late Johnny Cash, which formed part of Ken Burns' documentary 'Country Music'. One time her father asked her to join him on stage to perform one of his songs. She refused – some tension had built up between them over the years. Then she looked with love at her father and changed her mind. She sang "I Still Miss Someone". As she sang with her father she felt the animosity she bore him evaporate and she felt a loving communion with her father. The music healed her. As we pray, read poetry, listen to music, we can be led into that place of peace.

Ash Wednesday is the first day of the Lenten season. It is a time of repentance, turning again to God. This is the title Eliot gives to his poem.

Ash Wednesday: Part I: Because I do not hope to turn again

Eliot was influenced by a 17th century preacher Lancelot Andrewes and his 1619 sermon "On Repentance". In this sermon Andrewes speaks about the cost of conversion and the sensitive conscience. In his own

---

[6] Interview: "Talking Freely: T. S. Eliot and Tom Greenwell", Yorkshire Post (Leeds), 29 August 1961, p. 3.

[7] I discovered this in an article by Jon Pahl, Ph.D., "Music is Prayer: Reconsidering Secular Music", Journal of Lutheran Ethics, 2010.

[8] Janna Tull Steed, "Nothin' Without God: Duke Ellington's Prayerful Music", The Christian Century III (Oct. 12, 1994) p. 124.

1925 poem "The Hollow Men" Eliot hints at the struggle to convert. A potential convert, still hollow of belief, tries to make the Lord's Prayer ('For Thine is the Kingdom') his own prayer. On the right of the page are the eloquent responses of the given prayer; on the left, the potential convert struggles to utter the words, in vain:

"For Thine is"

The shadow of doubt and fear draws him back. He ventures once more, edging slightly further, only to fall, again, short of completion:

"For Thine is the"

The first line of this section "Because I do not hope to turn again" is related to the first line of a ballad by Guido Cavalcanti. Dante's poetry caught the attention of Cavalcanti when Dante was eighteen. They both believed in the seriousness of their art. They set themselves a goal – to understand and praise love itself. They saw poetry as a means to change the hearts of people in society and as a means to bring about change. They focused their attention on a lady whose beauty and spiritual qualities they interpreted as miraculous graces from Heaven. Beatrice would become this figure for Dante.

Cavalcanti was exiled in 1300 to Saranza – where he died soon after. In this place of exile, from which there was no hope of return, he wrote the ballad beginning:

"Perch' io non spero di tornar gia mai,
Ballatetta, in Toscana..."

which translates as "because I do not hope to turn again, Ballatetta, to Tuscany". The first poem of 'Ash Wednesday' consists of variations on this theme of inability to turn back. The poem begins:

"Because I do not hope to turn again
Because I do not hope
Because I do not hope to turn

Desiring this man's gift and that man's scope
I no longer strive to strive towards such things
(Why should the agèd eagle stretch its wings?)
Why should I mourn
The vanished power of the usual reign?"

When somebody seriously repents, he says farewell to his past. He is open to God and places himself in Him. Here he is resolute. He remembers Cavalcanti and the "apathy that comes after the emotions and the possibility of emotions are exhausted". Here it is a matter of the will. There is a desire in the poem in which love is attracted to the beloved. He begins with no hope to return to his old life. He wants to leave the Waste Land. A return to the past would be a return to torment. There is the "Desiring of this man's gift and that man's scope..." This was a world with no peace. A close parallel is found in the twenty-ninth sonnet of Shakespeare which begins:

"When in disgrace with fortune and men's eyes
I all alone be weep my outcast state..."

and which continues:

"Wishing me like to one more rich in hope,
Featured like him, like him with friends possessed,
Desiring this man's art, and that man's scope,
With what I most enjoy contented least;"

In this sonnet the speaker bemoans his status as an outcast and failure. He begins to feel better thinking about his beloved.

It is the thought of the beloved which transforms what would otherwise be despair and isolation. The sonnet becomes a picture of a sorrow which had hope and love in it. The sonnet finishes:

"Yet in these thoughts myself almost despising,
Haply I think on thee, and then my state,

> Like to the lark at break of day arising
> From sullen earth, sings hymns at heaven's gate"

The reader of Ash Wednesday is reminded that the contrition which is an essential element in true penitence is a sorrow proceeding from love, a sorrow which is not self-centered but upward looking. He is now detached: "Why should I mourn / The vanished power of the usual reign?". This can degenerate into cynicism or indifference, but he looks to the grace of God. The soul is exhausted by the struggle to submit to God. The aged eagle appears in Dante. The eagle flew up into the circle of fire, burnt off its feathers and fell blinded into a fountain of water from which its youth was renewed. New life issues from death.

There are also many biblical images of the eagle. One appears in Isaiah 40:31 –

> "...those who hope in the Lord
> will renew their strength.
> They will soar on wings like eagles;
> they will run and not grow weary,
> they will walk and not be faint."

In Deuteronomy 32:11 we read:

> "like an eagle that stirs up its nest
> and hovers over its young,
> that spreads its wings to catch them
> and carries them aloft."

This takes place in the desert when the Lord comes to help those who feel lost. This is an idea taken up by Thérèse of Lisieux. She is taken up by "the eagle" to God.

St. Teresa reminds us that "it is a shame... we don't understand ourselves or know who we are" (1 Interior Castle 1:2). We are afraid of entering into ourselves because we do not love ourselves. Instead we, as it were, stay on the outside and run away from silence and recollection.

Saint Teresa describes our state when we do not enter this space:

> "Not long ago a very learned man told me that souls who do not practice prayer are like people with paralysed or crippled bodies; even though they have hands and feet they cannot give orders to these hands and feet. Thus there are souls so ill and so accustomed to being involved in external matters that there is no remedy, nor does it seem they can enter within themselves. They are now so used to dealing always with the insects and vermin that are in the wall surrounding the castle that they have become almost like them. And though they have so rich a nature and the power to converse with none other than God, there is no remedy."
>
> (1 Interior Castle 1:6)

It is as if we choose the Waste Land because we are afraid to move away from it. Eliot has left the 'Waste Land' here and with nervous, faltering steps he climbs the stairway to God's heart.

The penitent hopes not to return to an older form of life. This allows him a certain detachment:

> "I no longer strive to strive towards such things...
> Why should I mourn
> The vanished power of the usual reign?"

However the penitent is always attracted to the way left behind. We are attached to ways of living and they continue even when we have the first zeal of conversion. When we become inordinately attached we become addicts. What we are addicted to shapes our vision. John of the Cross tells us:

> "It should be known that the Word, the Son of God, together with the Father and the Holy Spirit, is hidden by his essence and his presence in the innermost being of the soul. Individuals who want to find him should leave all things through affection and will, enter within themselves in

deepest recollection, and let all things be as though not. St. Augustine, addressing God in the Soliloquies, said: I did not find you without, Lord, because I wrongly sought you without, who were within.

God, then, is hidden in the soul, and there the good contemplative must seek him with love, exclaiming: 'Where have you hidden?'"

(Spiritual Canticle 1:6)

For John perfect detachment is attachment. Every fixation disables the will. It invites compulsion. Desire blocks out reason and common sense. The emotional constellation surrounding our fascination impairs and distorts our perception and judgement. The fixation of our will severely limits our freedom and choices. Yet, God abides within the innermost being of every creature, while continuing to transcend it entirely. God is the *ground* of our being. The person who would encounter God must pass through creation, not circumvent it. The new life we strive for is not negative. By the work of the Holy Spirit we hope to meet God and find the fullness of life in Him.

> "We are not speaking here of the mere absence of creatures, since that of itself would not strip the soul of them as long as it still coveted them. Instead, we are talking about the detachment of the will… for creatures. Only in that way are we left free and empty of our attachments for them, even if we continue to possess and to enjoy them."
>
> (1 Ascent of Mount Carmel, B:1-4)

Many people recovering from addiction speak of a conversion experience which helps them start a new life. This is exemplified by Bill Wilson, the founder of Alcoholics Anonymous. He described how he felt beaten by his addiction to drink, but one night he had an experience of God's love entering his life, and this enabled him to leave his addiction behind. There was still the pull of the old world but now he had a new orientation. Coming to know God and his love for us is what we become attached to and than we see all things in God. We can enjoy all things in Him. Vestiges of the past still intrude even if we think our memories are dead. They still seek a toe-hold on us.[9] The goal for us, in this time of change, is to draw on the strength of the Holy Spirit, the seal or guarantee of the new age's consummation and to wait with trust for the full transformation of our lives.

The poet hopes not "to turn again". The next part of the poem reads:

> "Because I do not hope to know
> The infirm glory of the positive hour
> Because I do not think
> Because I know I shall not know
> The one veritable transitory power
> Because I cannot drink
> There, where trees flower, and springs flow, for there is
> nothing again"

Regret for the past and for what might have been is valueless – "for there is nothing again". Repentance for the past is a good thing, but permanent remorse stunts growth. The poet rejoices "that things are as they are". The call to new life sustains him. He lives in hope. He knows, now, in himself that he does not wish to return – that he will not "know again" what he has known before or drink "there, where trees flower".

This elevating satisfaction is often shaken but not broken by the recurrence of pleasures the soul has renounced. We can find ourselves rebelling against the onset of new life. In Romans 7 Paul describes the state of the person: "To will is present with me; but how to perform that which is good I find not. I find then a law, that, when I would do good, evil is present with me. For I delight in the law of God after the inward man: But I see another law of my mind... O wretched man that I am! who shall deliver me from the body of this death? I thank God through Jesus Christ our Lord" (Rom 7: 18-25). Eliot says:

> "Because I cannot hope to turn again
> Consequently I rejoice, having to construct something
> Upon which to rejoice"

9 J. Paul Sampley, Waiting between the Times: Paul's Moral Reasoning (Minneapolis: 1991) p. 10, 13.

As the soul grows in love a measure of detachment and relief is achieved. There is a desire for deep relief and the peace of true faith. Eliot asks for this relief:

"Teach us to care and not to care
Teach us to sit still"

He plays on the word care (Latin: *cura*) with its meaning of "solicitude" and anxiety. He prays for sensitivity without anxiety, for an unselfish perspective. This is God's view and He is the end of the journey. He echoes Isaiah 30:7: "Their strength is to sit still".

The idea of stillness and silence is a challenge. Many are afraid of silence. We try to distract ourselves and when that doesn't work we seek a distraction from distraction, a phrase Eliot will use later.

Alison Woolley made a study of silence and how it empowers women.[10] She quotes Maria Harris: "If we would be wise women attending to silence which destroys, we need at the same time to be engaging the silence that creates and heals" (p. 254). The volunteers for Woolley's project to engage with silence were, in the main, those who responded to an invitation from the director of a centre which hosts silent retreats. Many of the women involved spoke of becoming aware of a loving, healing presence and this was a call to loving, faithful living. Woolley says there can be little doubt that there is a "Spirit-led turn towards transformational solitude, propelling women into the frontiers of spiritual awareness and imagination".

Sarah Coakley describes her use of silence when she worked in prisons.[11] She introduced the prisoners to silent meditation and this gave the prisoners peace and a better attitude towards life. They related to the exercise of silence. They discovered its healing power.

---

[10] Alison Woolley, Women Choosing Silence: Rationality and Transformation in Spiritual Practice (London: 2019).

[11] Sarah Coakley, God, Sexuality, and the Self (Cambridge: 2013).

These people show us a rediscovery in our time of what the mystics taught us. "God is love" (1 Jn 4:8,16). We are born to love and be loved. God is love and is the source of all love.

> "Philip said, "Lord, show us the Father and that will be enough for us."
> Jesus answered: "Don't you know me, Philip, even after I have been among you such a long time? Anyone who has seen me has seen the Father. How can you say, 'Show us the Father'? Don't you believe that I am in the Father, and that the Father is in me? The words I say to you I do not speak on my own authority. Rather, it is the Father, living in me, who is doing his work. Believe me when I say that I am in the Father and the Father is in me; or at least believe on the evidence of the works themselves. Very truly I tell you, whoever believes in me will do the works I have been doing, and they will do even greater things than these, because I am going to the Father. And I will do whatever you ask in my name, so that the Father may be glorified in the Son. You may ask me for anything in my name, and I will do it."
>
> (Jn 14:8-14)

Knowing Jesus is the same as knowing the Father. In verses 10-12 Jesus tells us that he dwells in the Father and the Father in Him. This empowers Jesus and those who believe in Him. The empowering presence of God is mediated by the Holy Spirit. The Spirit lives "with you and will be in you" (Jn 14:17). In silence we experience this Spirit and the presence of the Father and the Son whose presence he mediates. Jesus promises us this Holy Spirit:

> "If you love me, keep my commands. And I will ask the Father, and he will give you another advocate to help you and be with you forever— the Spirit of truth. The world cannot accept him, because it neither sees him nor knows him. But you know him, for he lives with you and will be in you. I will not leave you as orphans; I will come to you.

Before long, the world will not see me anymore, but you will see me. Because I live, you also will live. On that day you will realize that I am in my Father, and you are in me, and I am in you. Whoever has my commands and keeps them is the one who loves me. The one who loves me will be loved by my Father, and I too will love them and show myself to them."

Then Judas (not Judas Iscariot) said, "But, Lord, why do you intend to show yourself to us and not to the world?"

Jesus replied, "Anyone who loves me will obey my teaching. My Father will love them, and we will come to them and make our home with them. Anyone who does not love me will not obey my teaching. These words you hear are not my own; they belong to the Father who sent me."

(Jn 14:15-24)

The Advocate "the Holy Spirit" mediates the permanent presence of Jesus among us (Jn 14:15-17, etc.). Jesus promises us His return and indwelling in our being. In verse 23 Jesus promises that He and the Father "will come and make our dwelling with you". He lives with the Father in the heart of our being and their presence is mediated by the Holy Spirit. There is a play on words throughout the Gospel of John. One of the words is the Greek word "*menein*" which means remain or dwell. We see this in the first chapter:

"The next day John was there again with two of his disciples. When he saw Jesus passing by, he said, "Look, the Lamb of God!"

When the two disciples heard him say this, they followed Jesus. Turning around, Jesus saw them following and asked, "What do you want?"

They said, "Rabbi" (which means "Teacher"), "where are you staying?"

"Come," he replied, "and you will see.""

The word used here is "*menein*". Jesus here is with the Father – that is where He dwells and we are called to that one place of peace. This is accomplished in us by the work of the Holy Spirit. This puts words on the experience of silence we spoke of above.

Teresa of Avila tells us:

> "that we consider our soul to be like a castle made entirely out of a diamond or of very clear crystal, in which there are many rooms, just as in heaven there are many dwelling places. For in reflecting upon it carefully, Sisters, we realise that the soul of the just person is nothing else but a paradise where the Lord says He finds His delight. So then, what do you think that abode will be like where a King so powerful, so wise, so pure, so full of all good things takes His delight? I don't find anything comparable to the magnificent beauty of a should and its marvelous capacity. Indeed, our intellects, however keen, can hardly comprehend it, just as they cannot comprehend God; but He Himself says that He created us in His own image and likeness."

(1 Interior Castle 1:1)

It is by gentleness and silence that we can enter this sacred space and discover the God who lives in us and who delights in us. Love transforms us and leads us out of our loneliness and delivers us from the Waste Land. The most difficult thing for us is to accept we are loved and this inhibits us from entering in silence to be with The One who loves us. Teresa tells us: "Contemplative prayer is nothing else but a close sharing between friends: it means taking time to be alone with him who we know loves us" (Life 8:5). We become one with Jesus and the Father by the power of the Holy Spirit.

Part II:

The second part of Ash Wednesday begins with the line, "Lady, three white leopards sat under a juniper tree". The parts that go to make "Ash Wednesday" were originally published separately, but in 1930 Eliot combined them into one work. The leopards can be seen as a surreal image of death and destruction. The leopards feed on his flesh, destroying his sensual desires and leaving only his bones which have been purified by the "Lady" figure. She is associated with the Virgin Mary.

> "Lady, three white leopards sat under a juniper-tree
> In the cool of the day, having fed to sateity
> On my legs my heart my liver and that which had been contained
> In the hollow round of my skull. And God said
> Shall these bones live? shall these
> Bones live? And that which had been contained
> In the bones (which were already dry) said chirping:
> Because of the goodness of this Lady
> And because of her loveliness, and because
> She honours the Virgin in meditation,
> We shine with brightness."

True repentance means dying to old ways so that new life may emerge. Eliot's poem is modelled after Dante's Purgatoria. The whole work is the struggle between the world of time and the world of eternity, between the worlds of faith and evidence and between the world of self-sufficiency and repentance. It invokes a number of themes from Dante where he addresses repentance and cleansing before the figure of Beatrice. Eliot's lady is alternately Lady Poverty or renunciation, death, the Virgin Mary and a Beatrice-like figure. Dante speaks of encountering a beautiful lady, Matelda, picking flowers and singing. She shows Dante a garden with two streams which flow through it. The first is the Lethe which empties the mind of those who drink from it of all cancelled sin. The second is the Eunoe which for those who drink from it, enhances recollection of the good they have accomplished.. The Lethe water must be drunk before the Eunoe. This is Dante's description of his meeting with Matelda:

> "A lady all alone, who went along
> Singing and culling floweret after floweret,
> With which her pathway was all painted over.
> "Ah, beauteous lady, who in rays of love
> Dost warm thyself, if I may trust to looks,

Which the heart's witnesses are wont to be,
May the desire come unto thee to draw
Near to this river's bank," I said to her,
"So much that I might hear what thou art singing.
Thou makes me remember where and what
Proserpina that moment was when lost
Her mother her, and she herself the Spring." "

(Purgatoria, canto 28)

The lady in the second part is described as:

"...The Lady is withdrawn
In a white gown, to contemplation, in a white gown."

In the fourth part she appears as:

"Going in white and blue, in Mary's colour....
Who moved among the others as they walked,
Who then made strong the fountains and made fresh the springs
Made cool the dry rock and made firm the sand
.... wearing
White light folded, sheathing about her, folded....
The silent sister veiled in white and blue...."

In the sixth poem she is described as "blessed sister, holy mother". In Dante's pilgrimage he sought his beloved, Beatrice. She was described as: "going in white and blue, in Mary's colour...." Dante does not see her face because she is veiled. She is transformed and purified. She is now judge, intercessor, saviour and lover all in one. She becomes the mediator between the pilgrim soul and God. She represents to Dante the love of Jesus Christ.[12] "The lady" in her various guises is love incarnate. The lady is filled with the Holy Spirit. In the Paradiso Dante will meet Mary, the mother of Jesus. In this way Dante shows us how we are transformed by love.

---

[12] Charles Williams, The Figure of Beatrice: A Study in Dante (Cambridge: 2000), p. 8.

The scene Eliot describes here is "under a juniper tree / In the cool of the day". In the Bible we read of the prophet Elijah who became a hunted and despairing man. He had risked all for God before Ahab and his queen Jezebel, but now he finds himself alone, weak, and in danger and in despair. He lay under a juniper tree to rest and God came to him and eased his pain (1 Kings 19:3-9). "In the cool of the day" is a phrase that harkens back to the book of Genesis. In the cool of the day Adam and Eve heard the voice of God as he walked in the garden. It was then their consciences awoke and they became aware of their guilt and weakness (Gen 3:8-17).

All that was of the penitent has been devoured, dissolved and only the outside husks of bone remain – "the hollow round of my skull". The unarticulated bones lie blacking in the sun. How can there be any life for these bones – "shall these bones live". Eliot gets the vision of the blacked bones from the prophet Ezekiel. They represent the people in exile who have felt the pain of exile and the despair at the fading away of an older way of life. Ezekiel has a vision for those in despair. We read:

> "The hand of the Lord was on me, and he brought me out by the Spirit of the Lord and set me in the middle of a valley; it was full of bones. He led me back and forth among them, and I saw a great many bones on the floor of the valley, bones that were very dry. He asked me, "Son of man, can these bones live?"
> I said, "Sovereign Lord, you alone know."
> Then he said to me, "Prophesy to these bones and say to them, 'Dry bones, hear the word of the Lord! This is what the Sovereign Lord says to these bones: I will make breath enter you, and you will come to life. I will attach tendons to you and make flesh come upon you and cover you with skin; I will put breath in you, and you will come to life. Then you will know that I am the Lord.'"
> So I prophesied as I was commanded. And as I was prophesying, there was a noise, a rattling sound, and the bones came together, bone to bone. I looked, and tendons

and flesh appeared on them and skin covered them, but there was no breath in them.

Then he said to me, "Prophesy to the breath; prophesy, son of man, and say to it, 'This is what the Sovereign Lord says: Come, breath, from the four winds and breathe into these slain, that they may live.'" So I prophesied as he commanded me, and breath entered them; they came to life and stood up on their feet—a vast army.

Then he said to me: "Son of man, these bones are the people of Israel. They say, 'Our bones are dried up and our hope is gone; we are cut off.' Therefore prophesy and say to them: 'This is what the Sovereign Lord says: My people, I am going to open your graves and bring you up from them; I will bring you back to the land of Israel. Then you, my people, will know that I am the Lord, when I open your graves and bring you up from them. I will put my Spirit in you and you will live, and I will settle you in your own land. Then you will know that I the Lord have spoken, and I have done it, declares the Lord.'"

(Ez 37:1-14)

The book of Ezekiel associates sin and impurity with death. It associates holiness and purity with new life. The image of the new heart in chapter 36 moves from death (a heart of stone) to life (a heart of flesh). Here Ezekiel is given a vision of dead bodies which represent the nation. All that is left is dead dry bones, bleached white by the desert sun. God "re-creates" them, bringing firstly the tissues, then the bodies back to life. The final verse attributes this miracle of rebirth to God's power, showing how divine power (the Holy Spirit) can be a source of comfort and hope for the enslaved and powerless.

For Eliot the miracle of individual repentance and forgiveness is no less a miracle than that of the restoration of the chosen people. He hopes the Spirit will breathe new life into him as he did in Ezekiel's vision.

This miracle is made possible through the intercession of other souls. God's miracle of bringing the dead bones to life is accomplished through the heart of the prophet. Here, "the lady" is the mediator of God's grace.

> "Because of the goodness of this lady
> And because of her loveliness, and because
> She honours the Virgin in meditation,
> We shine with brightness"

Here "the lady" represents the love of Jesus. The penitent is met by forgiveness in confession and the penitent can begin a new life. He can be re-created by the Spirit. This is accomplished by the loving sacrifice of Jesus. The Christ-centred man participates in God's life by the Spirit. He is spiritual because his own spirit is surrendered to the Spirit of God.

Eliot says:

> "Prophesy to the wind, to the wind only for only
> The wind will listen. And the bones sang chirping"

Here Eliot remembers the promise of God through Ezekiel that God "shall put my Spirit in you, Dry people, and you shall live and I shall place you in your own land" (Ez 37:14). This is the hope that sustains Eliot.

> "Forgetting themselves and each other, united
> In the quiet of the desert"

This is a solid, firm assurance of victory after the dissolution and the seeming death. The 'song of the bones' harkens back to Dante. It is a song of thanksgiving:

> "For the garden
> Where all love ends"

At the end of his pilgrimage Dante finds that the Garden of Paradise is where earthly love and earthly passions find their fulfillment. The garden is in the desert: the rose (which is the Rose both of forgetfulness and memory – Lethe and Eunoe) becomes itself the garden. Dante "sees the company of the saints, rising tier upon tier, as a flower-clad hill is mirrored in a lake in the light below. This forms the centre of the heavenly Rose and its petals are the ranks of glorified saints".

> "In fashion of a white rose glorified
> Shone out on me that saintly chivalry
> When with his blood Christ won to be his bride"
>
> (Paradiso 31:1-3)

Where all love ends, love begins.

Part III:

In the third section the poet glimpses "The broad backed figure driest in blue and green" but is distracted by "stops and steps of the mind", memories of

> "….brown hair over the mouth blown,
> Lilac and brown hair"

The lures and call of the past are always present. One does not reach total Paradise in the here and now. Often when people begin their new life of repentance, they are assailed by temptation to go back to old ways. Some can begin to despair when they find old weaknesses and faults rearing their heads. They can despair when they find forgiveness and love difficult. These things can blind people to the fact they are loved by God.

When these doubts arise one sees "the deceitful face of hope and despair". This means that hope is no longer centered upon God and true contrition seems impossible.

> "At the first turning of the second stair
> I turned…."

The penitent continues his climb. Even now the penitent can be afflicted...

"At the second turning of the second stair
I left them twisting, turning below;
There were no more faces and the stair was dark,
Damp, jagged, like an old man's mouth drivelling, beyond
repair,
Or the toothed gullet of an aged shark."

It is as if the very centre of the personality had rotted away and become hollow. It is as if all his faculties and energies had collapsed like a broken stairway and were no longer there. Self-revulsion and self hate are always temptations, but in this state if one looks beyond oneself to the mercy and love of God, then one grows through one's temptations. When the will is tired and the strong worn, then the lures of the natural world and indulgence in it, appears anew as unbearably beautiful and its attractions as stronger than ever before. Old doubts reassert themselves. People, in this space, feel it is better to give up and go back to old ways.

"At the first turning of the third stair
Was a slotted window bellied like the fig's fruit
And beyond the hawthorn blossom and a pasture scene....

Blown hair is sweet, brown hair over the mouth blown,
Lilac and brown hair;
Distraction, music of the flute, stops and steps of the mind
over the third stair"

Here the penitent battles with his selfishness. He wants to put others first and give himself but he is pulled back by his selfishness. As through "a slotted window" he finds himself looking furtively at all the beauty which is perceived and enjoyed through the senses and which is always before his eyes. The halting rhythm of the lines suggest the distraction and wavering will, "the stops and steps of the mind". The sweetness of brown hair and all the things in which the soul may be indulged is embittered by an unspoken feeling of guilt. In some way the sin of the sinner infects all he sees. These, however, are temptations and he must bring to mind his God-directed renunciation and surrender. The penitent begins to find...

"....strength beyond hope and despair
Climbing the third stair."

He begins to discover strength in the unchanging love of God revealed in Jesus. He is empowered by the Holy Spirit when he comes to pray before God.

In Teresa of Avila's 'Interior Castle' the third dwelling place represents a victory for the soul. In Eliot's vision of the stairs the soul presses on in faith. The person begins to see all things in God. The soul finds a certain peace. Teresa tells us: Poisonous creatures rarely enter these dwelling places. If they enter they do no harm; rather they are the occasion of gain (3 IC 1:3). The poisonous creatures are the old ways of thinking; now the person is coming to know God and is entering into a relationship with him. The soul understands itself to be in a relationship with God. It begins to see it is loved and is on the way to healing, forgiveness and peace. The soul is invited to enter this loving relationship. The temptations of the past begin to recede. The soul begins to feel more joy and continues to progress towards greater fulfillment.

Part IV:

Beatrice in Dante's Commedia becomes the mediator between the pilgrim soul and God: "Going in white and blue, in Mary's colour". She moves through Dante's poem as intercessor and restorer of penitent souls. The lady in the fourth poem relates to the struggle against the temptation not to fix the will on the contemplation of the Word made flesh. Here the writer refers to the prologue of the Gospel of John.

> "In the beginning was the Word, and the Word was with God, and the Word was God. He was with God in the beginning. Through him all things were made; without him nothing was made that has been made. In him was life, and that life was the light of all mankind."

> (Jn 1:1-4)

"In the beginning" recalls Gen 1:1, "in the beginning God created the world". The 'Word' brings to mind Wisdom who was with God in the creation (Prov 8:30; Wisdom 7:25). In Hellenistic Greek the term for word is Logos – Logos is to the world what the soul is to the body. John uses the term logos. This 'logos' was with God and was God. Through the 'logos' all things came to be. Jesus was the 'logos made flesh' (Jn 1:14).

In Canto 28 of the Purgatorio the woman speaks to Dante of the garden he had entered. Then there follows a divine pageant. A brilliant light is seen approaching. We see a procession heralded by seven candlesticks, the seven spirits of God (the Holy Spirit is symbolised by the seven lights). Behind them in the midst of angels is a veiled lady clad in the robes of faith, hope and charity.

> "Who moved among the others as they walked,
> Who then made strong the fountains and made fresh the
> springs
>
> Made cool the dry rock and made firm the sand
> In blue of larkspur, blue of Mary's colour,
> Sovegna vos
>
> Here are the years that walk between, bearing
> Away the fiddles and the flutes, restoring
> One who moves in the time between sleep and waking,
> wearing
>
> White light folded, sheathed about her, folded."

Eliot says "the kind of pageantry which will be tedious to those, if there are any, who are unmoved by the splendour of the Revelation of Saint John. It belongs to the world of what I call the high dream and the modern world seems capable only of the low dream." (Selected Essays, P. 248). For Eliot we are in the realm of divine pageant, the high dream of which the modern world is incapable of appreciating. We have become accustomed to mediocrity. Eliot describes the 'lady' who intercedes with God for him.

"Who walked between the violet and the violet
Who walked between
The various ranks of varied green
Going in white and blue, in Mary's colour"

He prays to the woman to help him "redeem" time. This section of the poem is set on the border of Paradise. He prays for the healing of memories. There is a conflict between the old feelings and the new.

"Redeem the time, redeem the dream
The token of the word unheard, unspoken

Till the wind shake a thousand whispers from the yew

And after this our exile"

In Dante's poem the lady is silent

"So prayed I, and in that distance she
When she had looked, with longing smile, again
Turned to the Fount that flows eternally."

(Paradiso, 31:93ff)

Her glance towards the future, which symbolises the presence of God, is her prayer of intercession. Penitence and restoration have led Dante and now Eliot to Paradise. This is the Garden where God walks with man. Until they reach the joyful consummation people agonise and stay in exile.

"And after this our exile"

This comes from the prayer Salve Regina (Hail, Holy Queen). The prayer says: "And after this our exile show unto us the blessed fruit of they womb, Jesus".

The poet called to the woman 'Sovegna Nos' ('Remember Us'). The lady is both "blessed sister" of humanity and Holy Mother. She walked, earlier in the garden, concerned with trivial things and "then made strong the fountains and made fresh the springs". The poet could not drink of these in poem 1. The silent sister and mother becomes mindful of the poet's pain. The yew is a symbol of the eternal sorrow which embraces men and Christ. The poet prays to her to lead him from exile. Eliot doesn't close off this poem. It points to future hope. He has conquered both hope and despair. Now his faith has become stronger and he prays for regeneration which depends on the fruit of Mary's womb, Jesus.

Part V:

To understand Part V it helps to know about the double meaning of 'Word'. 'Word' can refer both to the Bible (as the word of God) and to Christ himself as God (with a capital, i.e. 'the Word'). So 'the Word' can be used to refer to Christ, who was both the Son of God and God himself in human form. This is what St. John means when he opens his Gospel: 'In the beginning was the Word, and the Word was with God, and the Word was God.' That is, 'the Word' is both the manifestation of God (Jesus, who was God come down in human form walking amongst us in the world) and the revelation of God (the Bible, the revealed truth of God).

In other words (as it were), the modern world no longer hears God, or heeds his 'word' (that is, Biblical scripture). Will the 'veiled sister' (often analysed as a version of the Virgin Mary) pray for those who 'oppose' God, who oppose 'the Word', those who walk in darkness? The repeated line 'O my people, what have I done unto thee', is Biblical, from Micah 6:3: God addresses these words to those who have forgotten him and fallen into idolatry, or worship of worldly things, instead of worshipping him.

We read in Micah:

> "Hear, you mountains, the Lord's accusation;
> listen, you everlasting foundations of the earth.
> For the Lord has a case against his people;
> he is lodging a charge against Israel.

"My people, what have I done to you?
How have I burdened you? Answer me.
I brought you up out of Egypt
and redeemed you from the land of slavery.
I sent Moses to lead you,
also Aaron and Miriam."

(Micah 6:1-4)

Having described the promise of Israel's restoration (4:1-4, 6-8; 5:1-15), Micah turns to look at Israel now. The poet depicts God using a sorrowful and bewildered tone to confront Israel. The double use of "My People" (6:3,5) conveys allusions to the Exodus. The poet makes clear that God does not deserve Israel's lack of love, stated so movingly through the double rhetorical question of the passage (6:3). This refrain is used in the Good Friday ceremony of the Veneration of the Cross. The Christian is led to meditate on the immense love of God shown in Jesus on the Cross and at the same time the horror of human evil which brought Him to the Cross.

The first part of poem 5 begins by telling us how the Word of God is unrecognised by the world. All existence is derived from the Word.

"If the lost word is lost, if the spent word is spent
If the unheard, unspoken
Word is unspoken, unheard;
Still is the unspoken word, the Word unheard,
The Word without a word, the Word within
The world and for the world;
And the light shone in darkness and
Against the Word the unstilled world still whirled
About the centre of the silent Word.

O my people, what have I done unto thee."

The world whirls "about the centre of the silent Word". Until redemption is accomplished we live in a fallen world in which there is much darkness. The Word made flesh is a light in the darkness (Jn 1:5).

We are being led by Eliot to think of ourselves in the Word. We are called to walk in the Light. Jesus said: "I have come into the world as a light, so that no one who believes in me should stay in darkness" (Jn 12:46). In the Letter of John we read: "Anyone who loves their brother and sister lives in the light, and there is nothing in them to make them stumble. But anyone who hates a brother or sister is in the darkness and walks around in the darkness. They do not know what they are doing because the darkness has blinded them" (1 Jn 2:10f).

Those who reject God's redemption and love face the consequences of frustration, fearfulness and emptiness.

> "For those who walk in darkness
> Both in the day time and in the night time
> The right time and the right place are not here
> No place of grace for those who avoid the face
> No time to rejoice for those who walk among noise and deny
> the voice"

We reject the word when we reject love. We bring hurt to those around us and when people need us our selfishness can blind us to their pain. We create the Waste Land.

The penitents, the souls, ask themselves this question

> "Where shall the word be found, where will the word
> Resound?"

The people must answer of themselves:

> "....not here, there is not enough silence"

We must go apart from our busy world and remain in silence before God and allow him to speak to our hearts. Then we can hear God's word and the Word made flesh.

Eliot shows the frustrations of those who do not give themselves to love...

"Will the veiled sister pray for
Those who walk in darkness, who chose thee and oppose
thee,
Those who are torn on the horn between season and season,
time and time, between
Hour and hour, word and word, power and power, those
who wait
In darkness?"

Eliot wonders does God care for such as these. The poet wonders whether there can be hope for him as he meditates on his own life and failures. He wonders will the "veiled sister pray for those who walk in darkness?" The answer lies in God's faithfulness. As we saw in the brief section from Micah, God always remains faithful and his offer of love is never withdrawn.

One time the singer Bruce Springsteen withdrew from his normal routine. He wanted to be alone. He had to discover whether he truly could live with himself. Could he live with the fact he had let others down? These were hard questions. His reflections gave birth to the album 'Nebraska' (1982). In the album Springsteen is emotionally closer to the characters he sings about and is less interested in judging them. In coming to know himself Springsteen could be kinder to others and ultimately to himself. He had come to a sense of self-acceptance.

When we have the courage to be still, then we can come to sense that we are loved and held by the love of God. The Spirit is at work in us.

When we deny the Word of love we become victims of our vacillating wills, not having the courage to be silent. Those who have suffered from addictions know this place only too well. Our full health lies in being embraced by God's love. John of the Cross says:

"In other sicknesses, following sound philosophy, contraries are cured by contraries, but love is incurable except by things in accord with love. The reason for this is that the love of God is the soul's health and the soul does not have full health until love is complete"

(Spiritual Canticle, 11:11)

Later on John tells us:

"...love of God is the soul's health and the soul does not have full health until love is complete. Sickness is nothing but the lack of health, and when the soul has not even a single degree of love she is dead. But when she possesses some degrees of love of God, no matter how few, she is then alive, yet very weak and infirm because of her little love. In the measure that love increases she will be healthier, and when love is perfect she will have full health."

(Spiritual Canticle, 12:11)

Eliot sees that in our heart there is rebellion, fear and we shy away from the love that would save us. He says:

"And are terrified and cannot surrender
And affirm before the world and deny between the rocks
In the last desert before the last blue rocks
The desert in the garden the garden in the desert
Of drouth, spitting from the mouth the withered apple-seed.
O my people."

We affirm God with our lips but in our hearts we rebel. We turn the Garden of Eden, all that is good, into a desert. Many of us are good at self-sabotage. We believe we are not good enough. Adam and Eve were conscious of shame and guilt before they were expelled from the Garden. However the love of God calls to us whenever we try to push him away. God calls us all the time: "My people". Francis Thompson (+1907) described God searching for us as "The Hound of Heaven". He had known failure and drug addiction, but he began to find peace when he surrendered to the Love that followed him. He said...

"I fled Him down the nights and down the days
I fled Him down the arches of the years
I fled Him down the labyrinthine ways
Of my own mind, and in the midst of tears
I hid from him, and under running laughter.
Up vistaed hopes I sped and shot precipitated
Adown titanic glooms of chasmèd fears,
From those strong feet that followed, followed after.
But with unhurrying chase and unperturbèd pace,
Deliberate speed, majestic instancy,
They beat, and a Voice beat,
More instant that the feet:
'All things betray thee, who betrays Me.'"
                    (Francis Thompson, The Hound of Heaven)

St. Paul says:

"What, then, shall we say in response to these things? If God is for us, who can be against us? He who did not spare his own Son, but gave him up for us all—how will he not also, along with him, graciously give us all things? Who will bring any charge against those whom God has chosen? It is God who justifies. Who then is the one who condemns? No one. Christ Jesus who died—more than that, who was raised to life—is at the right hand of God and is also interceding for us. Who shall separate us from the love of Christ? Shall trouble or hardship or persecution or famine or nakedness or danger or sword? As it is written:
    "For your sake we face death all day long;
    we are considered as sheep to be slaughtered."
No, in all these things we are more than conquerors through him who loved us. For I am convinced that neither death nor life, neither angels nor demons, neither the present nor the future, nor any powers, neither height nor depth, nor anything else in all creation, will be able to separate us from the love of God that is in Christ Jesus our Lord."
                    (Rom 8:31-39)

Part VI:

Here the poet comes to a form of realism. He recognises that in this life he is always on pilgrimage. We are being formed as new people but that doesn't mean we are already formed. The poet begins to accept himself.

> "Although I do not hope to turn again
> Although I do not hope
> Although I do not hope to turn"

Eliot began with the actual words of Cavalcanti – "Because I do not hope to turn again". Later in 'Ash Wednesday' these words become "Because I cannot hope to turn". The poet wavered. He regretted not being able to go back. The desire was still there. Here he has come to accept his weakness; he uses the word "although...". He can waver, as he says,
"

> Wavering between the profit and the loss
> In this brief transit where the dreams cross
> The dreamcrossed twilight between birth and dying
> (Bless me father) though I do not wish to wish these things
> From the wide window towards the granite shore
> The white sails still fly seaward, seaward flying
> Unbroken wings"

He brings his weakness before God. The expression "Bless me, Father" is used in Confession where he places his weakness to God through the ministry of the Confessor. He has been led by the Spirit to the place where he can confess and accept he is weak, but, now, he trusts in the loving mercy of God who welcomes him and is with him in his weakness. His strength to carry on is not his own. He is now free to be himself and not wear a mask. As he stands before God and knows he is loved, he is empowered to go on. Paul Tillich, in his work "The Courage to Be" said faith was "the Courage to Accept Acceptance". Really it is more often true that we do not accept ourselves; so it takes courage to accept that we are loved. In this is our healing. Eliot tells us...

".... in his will is our peace –
This is the sea whereto all things move"

This harks back to Dante. In his Paradiso he meets Piccarda Donati. Intitially Dante thinks she has an inferior place in Paradise, and where she could be more "friends" with God? The childlike simplicity of the pilgrim's language only adds to the potency of the question, a question that brings to the surface all our unspoken concern about unfairness continuing on into the realm of justice itself.

"But tell me: though you're happy here, do you
desire a higher place in order to
see more and to be still more close to Him?"

The pilgrim's question gives Piccarda the opportunity to explain that heaven is a place where one's desire is always satisfied, where desire cannot possibly exceed the measure of what one has and where it is always aligned with the will of the transcendent power. In other words, the souls of paradise are completely happy with the grace that is apportioned to them. Everything in paradise is paradise.

"And in His will there is our peace: that sea
to which all beings move – the beings He
creates or nature makes – such is His will."

Our happiness lies in fulfilling God's will, in being the person we are called to be, not in envying others or seeking higher places. This is life "In him we live and move and have our being" (Acts 17:28).

Now because of God's grace the poet can look at all creation and see its beauty in God. He is like Dante who left Purgatory. He meets the 'lady' who tells him:

"Ye are new-comers; and because I smile,"
Began she, "peradventure, in this place
Elect to human nature for is nest,
Some apprehension keeps you marvelling;

But the psalm 'Delectasti' giveth light
Which has the power to uncloud your intellect..."
(Purgatoria, canto 28, 76-81)

'Delecasti, ne, domino' is taken from Ps 92:4

"For you make me glad by your deeds, Lord;
I sing for joy at what your hands have done."

She ends her song with words from Ps 22:

"Singing like unto an enamoured lady
She, with the ending of her words, continued:
"Beati quorum tecta sunt peccata." "
(Purgatoria, canto 29; 1-3)

The Latin term means: "Blessed are those whose sin is forgiven". Only when we realise that we are loved, accepted and forgiven are we free to be ourselves. We find our peace in doing God's will and therein is our delight. Jesus teaches us this when he says: "My food is to do the will of my Father" (John 4:34).

The poet goes on:

"And the lost heart stiffens and rejoices
In the lost lilac and the lost sea voices"

The old delights are restored to him in new form. With God, John of the Cross tells us, we can rejoice in all things:

"Mine are the heavens and mine is the earth. Mine are the nations, the just are mine and mine the sinners. The angels are mine, and the Mother of God, and all things are mine; and God himself is mine and for me, because Christ is mine and all for me. What do you ask, then, and seek my soul? Yours is all of this, and all is for you. Do not engage your self in something less or pay heed to the crumbs that fall from your Father's table. Go forth and exult in your Glory!

Hide yourself in it and rejoice, and you will obtain the supplications of your heart."

(Excerpted from Sayings of Light and Love, 26-27
– St. John of the Cross)

It is in this Spirit that St. Francis wrote his "Canticle of the Creatures":

"Most High, all powerful, good Lord,
Yours are the praises, the glory, and the honour, and all blessing.

To You alone, Most High, do they belong,
and no human is worthy to mention Your name.

Praised be You, my Lord, with all Your creatures,
especially Sir Brother Sun,
Who is the day; and through whom You give us light.

And he is beautiful and radiant with great splendour;
and bears a likeness of You, Most High One.

Praised be You, my Lord, through Sister Moon and the stars,
in heaven you formed them clear and precious and beautiful.

Praised be You, my Lord, through Brother Wind,
and through the air, cloudy and serene, and every kind of weather
through which You give sustenance to Your creatures.

Praised be You, my Lord, through Sister Water,
which is very useful and humble and precious and chaste.

Praised be You, my Lord, through Brother Fire,
through whom you light the nigh,
and he is beautiful and playful and robust and strong.

Praised be You, my Lord, through our Sister Mother Earth,
who sustains us and governs us,
and who produces various fruits with coloured flowers and
herbs.
Praised be You, my Lord, through those who give pardon
for Your love,
and bear infirmity and tribulation.

Blessed are those who endure in peace
for by You, Most High, shall they be crowned.

Praised be You, my Lord, through our Sister Bodily Death,
from whom no living man can escape.

Woe to those who die in mortal sin.
Blessed are those whom death will find in Your most holy
will,
for the second death shall do them no harm.

Praise and bless my Lord and give Him thanks
and serve Him with great humility."

The fact of freedom and renewed vitality outweighs our anxiety and we find new strength. This does not mean that there are no obstacles ('rocks' as Eliot calls them). The penitent accepts his limitations because his trust and strength is in Another:

"This is the time of tension between dying and birth
The place of solitude where three dreams cross
Between blue rocks
But when the voices shaken from the yew-tree drift away
Let the other yew be shaken and reply."

The yew trees are the symbols of life and death. He is now content to wait on God, the patient one who is always faithful and loving, even when the poet drifts away. The Holy Spirit is the Spirit of Love and the source of all love. This love sustains the poet and is seen in the figure of the 'Lady' (whether it be a Beatrice, Matelda, or Our Lady). This love is his strength. One might say he doesn't draw Ash Wednesday to a conclusion. The formation of the new person is an ongoing process over the whole of one's life. We are sustained in this by the love of the Holy Spirit. 'Ash Wednesday' is a call to us to surrender to love and live our lives in love. It is a call to experience the acceptance of God's love and forgiveness. The poem ends:

"Blessèd sister, holy mother, spirit of the fountain, spirit
of the garden,
Suffer us not to mock ourselves with falsehood
Teach us to care and not to care
Teach us to sit still
Even among these rocks,
Our peace in His will
And even among these rocks
Sister, mother
And spirit of the river, spirit of the sea,
Suffer me not to be separated
And let my cry come unto Thee."

Chapter 3

Burnt Norton

Our quest for meaning is a quest for ultimate relationship and belonging, a quest in which our masks are set aside. We all have a common loneliness. Are we alone in this maze of the self, alone in this wilderness of time, alone in this silent universe, of which we are a part and yet in which we feel like strangers? Is there on-one to collect the tears, soothe the pain, understand the agony of the innocent, the poor, the sorrowing? Such questions terrify us and we run away from facing them. They are the questions of the Waste Land.

Carl Jung (+1961) was a Swiss psychiatrist and psychoanalyst who founded analytical psychology. Jung's work was influential in the fields of psychiatry, anthropology, literature, philosophy and religious studies. In his practice he found many people were afflicted with hopelessness and anxiety. In several chapters of his collected works he studied this and concluded that these problems were caused by, what he called, a spiritual problem. As more people fall victim to anxiety this feeds into society. This, on a mass scale, can lead to social unrest and see the rise of people like Hitler. He saw this in his lifetime with two world wars and the rise of totalitarian states. He hoped to inform people so that these events would not happen again. Jung believed that the emergence of this spiritual problem coincided with the declining influence that traditional religions, most prominently Christianity, have had on Western societies over the past several centuries.

Casting aside religion left people with problems. One of them was the fact that those who faced the questions of who they are and have they any value, have no sense of the Divine to give them meaning. He compares this situation to medieval man.

> "How totally different did the world appear to medieval man! For him the earth was eternally fixed and at rest in the

centre of the universe...Men were all children of God under the loving care of the Most High, who prepared them for eternal blessedness; and all knew exactly what they should do and how they should conduct themselves in order to rise from a corruptible world to an incorruptible and joyous existence. Such a life no longer seems real to us, even in our dreams."

(Carl Jung, The Spiritual Problem of Modern Man)

Jung believed, as well, that the rise of mass culture in society plunged people into this sea of loneliness. Modern society grew from the industrial revolution when large portions of the population left the countryside and lived in sprawling new cities. This gave birth to a mass society. This new form of existence...produced an individual who was unstable, insecure and suggestible (Carl Jung, The Fight with the Shadow). All round the individual is a large crowd and here the individual feels nullified. The industrial revolution also brought in a scientific mindset. In the 19th and even more so in the 20th century, social planners, politicians, and leaders of various industries, mesmerized by the fruits which scientific inquiry was producing in the fields of industry and medicine, came to believe that the methods of science could be used to remodel society. This led to the "Massification of Society". This meant an increase in uniformity and a drastic decrease in the importance of the individual. For in order to model and subsequently remake society based on scientific and rational principles, the uniqueness of the individual must be negated in favour of statistical averages, and the redesign of society enacted by a group of elites, or Technocrats, who view humans as nothing but abstractions, homogenous social units to be managed and manipulated. Jung predicted what we see so much of today. He says:

"Under the influence of scientific assumptions, not only the psyche but the individual man and, indeed, all individual events whatsoever suffer a leveling down and a process of blurring that distorts the picture of reality into a conceptual average. We ought not to underestimate the psychological effect of the statistical world-picture: it thrusts aside the individual in favour of anonymous units that pile up into mass formations...As a social unit he has lost his individuality and become a mere abstract number in the bureau of statistics. He can only play the role of an interchangeable unit of infinitesimal importance."

(Carl Jung, The Undiscovered Self)

The effects of losing religion and the massification of society have conspired to make many people see themselves as insignificant, impotent beings. Jung said that when the conscious attitude of the individual is deficient in a manner which is detrimental to psychological health, the self-regulating mechanism of the psyche will produce an unconscious compensation in the attempt to correct the faulty conscious attitude and bring the psyche back into relative balance. Those who suffer from this spiritual problem do not have internal strength to attain psychological health. They are imprisoned in their feelings of insignificance. This can give rise to an insatiable hunger for power.

"The individual's feeling of weakness, indeed of non-existence, [is] compensated by the eruption of hitherto unknown desires for power. It [is] the revolt of the powerless, the insatiable greed of the 'have-nots.'"

(Carl Jung, The Fight with the Shadow)

This lust for power can remain hidden in the unconscious. He wrote:

"If such a compensatory move of the unconscious is not integrated into consciousness in an individual, it leads to a neurosis or even to a psychosis."

(Carl Jung, The Fight with the Shadow)

People in this state are likely to gravitate towards collective ideologies, mass movements and institutions which they view as having the power they as individuals lack. One sees the rise of Alt-Right groups and ideologies in our time. He is on the road to state slavery. Jung wrote the following, chilling passage:

"Instead of the concrete individual, you have the names of organizations and, at the highest point, the abstract idea of the State as the principle of political reality. The moral responsibility of the individual is then inevitably replaced by the policy of the State. Instead of the moral and mental differentiation of the individual, you have public welfare and the raising of the living standard. The goal and meaning of individual life (which is the only real life) no longer lie in individual development but in the policy of the State, which is thrust upon the individual from outside...The individual is increasingly deprived of the moral decision as to how he should live his own life, and instead is ruled, fed, clothed, and educated as a social unit...and amused in accordance with the standards that give pleasure and satisfaction to the masses."

(Carl Jung, The Undiscovered Self)

Behind this facade lies a deep loneliness and anxiety which eats at the heart of human beings. In the face of growing state power many feel impotent, but Jung saw hope for a recovery in the rise of psychoanalysis. Here people faced up to their feelings and expressed them. Gradually they would become empowered and in this way help heal society. He did not exclude the role of religion. As people began to re-discover their inner world, they would again seek the Divine. He said:

"I am not altogether pessimistic about neurosis. In many cases we have to say, "Thank heaven he could make up his mind to be neurotic." Neurosis is really an attempt at self-cure...It is an attempt of the self-regulating psychic system to restore the balance, in no way different from the function of dreams – only rather more forceful and drastic."

(Carl Jung, The Tavistock Lectures)

Anxiety disorders are prevalent in our modern world, so much so that our age is called an age of anxiety. Jung saw our anxiety and neurosis as being signals to us that a change is needed in us. The pharmaceutical model helps alleviate symptoms. Jung, however, wanted to get to the source of our anxiety:

"We should not try to "get rid" of a neurosis, but rather to experience what it means, what it has to teach, what its purpose is."

(Carl Jung, Civilization in Transition)

The anxiety and neurosis is present to us at the moment, so we have to deal with it in the present.

"In constructing a theory which derives the neurosis from causes in the distant past, we are first and foremost following the tendency of our patient to lure us as far away as possible from the critical present...It is mainly in the present that the affective causes lie, and here alone are the possibilities of removing them."

(Carl Jung, Theory of Psychoanalysis)

Our suffering could have started in childhood. Our upbringing can influence us too. Our suffering, however, is in the present. Jung explained:

"It makes no difference that there were already conflicts in childhood, for the conflicts in childhood are different from the conflict of adults. Those who have suffered ever since childhood from a chronic neurosis do not suffer now from the same conflict they suffered from then."

(Carl Jung, Theory of Psychoanalysis)

Jung would quote Cleanthes (+230 BC) who was a Greek Stoic philosopher and successor to Zeno as the second head of the Stoic school in Athens: "The fates lead the willing, but drag the unwilling". The fates were the three goddesses of Greek mythology who weaved the fabric of our lives and shaped our destiny. Jung did not believe in the fates but he did believe we are each called, in a certain manner, to a life task. We are called to a biological life. We are also called to become the persons we are meant to be. We can deny this part of ourselves and self-sabotage. Jung says:

> "[we] have a mighty dislike of all intentional effort and are addicted to absolute laziness until circumstances prod [us] into action."
>
> (Carl Jung, The Theory of Psychoanalysis)

If we do not own our place in life then the call becomes like a chain around our necks (Cleanthes). Jung said that what matters is our attitude, our internal world. We often lack the courage to explore our own path in life. The neurotic, according to Jung, blames the obstacles in the path.

> "[The neurotic] draws back [from his life tasks] not because of any real impossibility but because of an artificial barrier invented by himself...From this moment on he suffers from an internal conflict. Now the realisation of his cowardice gets the upper hand, now defiance and pride. In either case his [energy] is engaged in a useless civil war, and the man becomes incapable of any new enterprise...His efficiency is reduced, he is not fully adapted, he has become – in a word – neurotic."
>
> (Carl Jung, The Theory of Psycholanalysis)

If we repress or deny this impulse of forming our own path, the energy does not disappear.

> "The energy stored up for the solution of the task flows back into the old riverbeds, the obsolete systems of the past, are filled up again."
>
> (Carl Jung, Freud and Psycholanalysis)

If we do not grow then we regress into infantile ways of adaption. As Bob Dylan said:

> "Pointed threats, they bluff with scorn
> Suicide remarks are torn
> From the fool's gold mouthpiece
> The hollow horn plays wasted words

Proves to warn that he not busy being born
Is busy dying"

                    (It's Alright, Ma [I'm Only Bleeding])

When we are in touch with what we are called to be we develop
depressions, compulsive thoughts and self-sabotage. They serve a
purpose in that they tell us we are descending down a dangerous life
path. Retreat from life leads to regression, and regression heightens
resistance to life (Jung, The Theory of Psychoanalysis). Each one of us
is unique and how we arrived at such a predicament is the unique story
of each of us.

Jung speaks of the hesitation of the neurotic:

> "The perpetual hesitation of the neurotic to launch out into
> life is readily explained by his desire to stand aside so as not
> to get involved in the dangerous struggle for existence. But
> anyone who refuses to experience life must stifle his desire
> to live – in other words, he must commit partial suicide."
>   (Carl Jung, Symbols of Transformation)

These are the people Elliot saw in the Waste-Land.

> "Unreal City,
> Under the brown fog of a winter dawn,
> A crowd flowed over London Bridge, so many,
> I had not thought death had undone so many."

So many people are examples of the living dead. They are those that
"death has undone". They live lives of desperation and no-one cares for
the other. The neurosis points out to us that we need to change the way
we look at ourselves and the world we live in.

> "The outbreak of the neurosis is not just a matter of chance.
> As a rule it is most critical. It is usually the moment when
> a new psychological adjustment, a new adaptation is
> demanded."
>   (Carl Jung, Freud and Psychoanalysis)

We need a new attitude, a "wholehearted dedication to life", which makes "the powerful urge to develop our own personality" (Jung). The psychic health of the individual demands we let go of past relationships and become the centre of a new system. Jung is not talking about trauma and its effects in the present. This needs processing and a separate form of analysis. We need a clear picture of who we are and where we are heading. Instead of fleeing from what we experience, our flaws and humanity, we need to come to accept ourselves. Neurosis gets worse if we ignore it. Many people fear what will happen to them if they take an honest look at themselves. When we come to self-acceptance, however, we do not have to expend so much energy in pretending to be what we are not. With a trusted person we can disclose ourselves. Jung spoke of the value of speaking to a therapist.

> "...one of the most important therapeutically effective factors is subjecting yourself to the objective judgment of others."
>
> (Carl Jung, The Theory of Psychoanalysis)

We often try to avoid the negative feelings and live as if they did not exist. However if we try to avoid the triggers that cause anxiety, our life becomes more and more restricted and anxiety and neurosis tighten their grip on us. The only way out is through. Jung reminds us:

> "Flight from life does not exempt us from the law of age and death. The neurotic who tries to wriggle out of the necessity of living wins nothing and only burdens himself with a constant foretaste of aging and dying, which must appear especially cruel on account of the total emptiness and meaninglessness of his life."
>
> (Carl Jung, Symbols of Transformation)

Neurosis prods us to find a path in life, an attitude to life that is more fulfilling. Neurosis can be a blessing instead of a curse. True healing begins when we "venture into the strange world with all its unforeseen possibilities" (Jung, Symbols of Transformation). Nobody can tell us the direction we should take. Jung saw the role of the therapist as enabling us to find our direction.

"What direction the patient's life should take in the future is not ours to judge. We must not imagine that we know better than his own nature, or we would prove ourselves educators of the worst kind… It is better to renounce any attempt to give direction, and simply to try to throw into relief everything that the analysis brings to light, so that the patient can see it clearly and be able to draw suitable conclusions. Anything he has not acquired himself he will not believe in the long run, and what he takes over from authority merely keeps him infantile. He should rather be put in the position to take his own life in hand."

(Carl Jung, Some Crucial Points in Psychoanalysis)

Jung did give some pointers. He warned against conformity. We don't have to subscribe to the inadequacies of life we find. The anxious person if he tries to conform too much will find he is trapped in his suffering.

"So it comes about that there are many neurotics whose inner decency prevents them from being at one with present-day morality and who cannot adapt themselves so long as the moral code has gaps in it which it is of the crying need of our age to fill."

(Carl Jung, Some Crucial Points in Psychoanalysis)

Many people who brought about change in society were those who followed their path and did not conform. I think of people like Martin Luther King, Jnr. I think of Van Gogh and Picasso in the world of art. I think of St. Francis and his self-surrender and life of poverty. I think of St. Clare who broke the norms of her society. In the world of science I think of Albert Einstein who broke with the perceived ideas of the past in understanding our world. The list goes on and can include many musicians, poets, writers and artists who beautify our world. Many people are ill because they have not yet found a new form for their finest aspirations. Instead of conforming the neurotics can be moved by an interior vision. Jung tells that those who have difficulty conforming:

"...are born and destined rather to be bearers of new cultural ideals. They are neurotic as long as they bow down before authority and refuse the freedom to which they are destined."

(Carl Jung)

In many other cases recovery can mean just facing up to the tasks life places before us. Now recovery can mean living our lives where we find ourselves.

"Previously, because of his illness, the patient stood partly or wholly outside life. Consequently he neglected many of his duties, either in regard to social achievement or in regards to his purely human tasks. He must get back to fulfilling these duties if he wants to become well again."
(Carl Jung, The Theory of Psychoanalysis)

A 17th century Carmelite called Br. Lawrence (born Nicholas Herman) wrote of "The Practice of the Presence of God". This extract helps us see what he meant.

"That he had always been governed by love, without selfish views; and that having resolved to make the love of GOD the end of all his actions, he had found reasons to be well satisfied with his method. That he was pleased when he could take up a straw from the ground for the love of GOD, seeking Him only, and nothing else, not even His gifts."
"That in order to form a habit of conversing with GOD continually, and referring all we do to Him; we must at first apply to Him with some diligence: but that after a little care we should find His love inwardly excite us to it without any difficulty."[1]

Br. Lawrence lived out what Jung advised. Every moment is lived in the presence of God and all we do can give glory to God. Every moment is

---

[1] Br. Lawrence, The Practice of the Presence of God, audiobook et Libri Vox, chapter 1.

an expression of our life with God. Jung had an inscription in Latin over the front door of his house in Zurich. The inscription reads in translation: "Bidden or not bidden, God is present". He said that this was to remind those entering that "awe of the Lord is the beginning of Wisdom" (Psalm 111.10).

Partners of God:

Abraham Joshua Heschel (+1972) whom we met earlier, was a Polish-born American Rabbi and one of the leading Jewish theologians and philosophers of the twentieth century. He left Poland a week before the Nazis invaded and he lost all his family in the Camps. He was sensitive, like Jung, to the spiritual needs of people today. His writing was a counterpoint to the nihilism he saw. He tried to teach a new generation their dignity in God and in this way he hoped to subvert any ideology that would give birth to groups like the Nazis. He wrote masterpieces in Yiddish, German and English.

Heschel said conformity to the crowd and mere repetition of the past obscure one's uniqueness and lead to drudgery and inner devastation. For Heschel there is no such thing as the average person. In real life the average person is non-existent. Average is a result of statistics. The only person who allows themselves to be "non-existent" are those who are "drowned in indifference and commonness". Such spiritual suicide is within the grasp of every person (Who is Man, p. 38f). The being of a person is never completely finished. Each person is constantly in a state of being born. We saw this in Eliot's Ash-Wednesday. Being human means "being on the way, striving, waiting, hoping" (Man is not Alone, p.207).

Essential to one's being human is the ability to stand alone. Solitude implies a period of rest and recovery from society's hysteria. Proximity to the crowd spells the death of creativity and uniqueness. I have to withdraw into stillness in order to become more human. Genuine solitude is in reality a search for genuine solidarity, for I am never alone, even in seclusion. For the human person "to be means to be with other human beings… existence is co-existence". Any analysis of being human which disregards social involvement and human interdependence misses the meaning of being human (Passion for Truth, p. 215).

Heschel says we always seek "ultimate being" and meaning. To be human is to pledge one's total existence to the truth that "the quest for significant being is the heart of existence" (Who is Man? p. 54-57). The quest for meaning, then, is to understand oneself, as well as the whole of humanity, in terms larger than the self. It is an attempt to grasp the ultimate relevance of human existence. The goal of each person is not the mere acceptance of being, but the relating of being to meaning, the searching for the way an image of being relates to meaning, the searching for the way or ways of coming into meaning. For to be human is to be involved. For to be human is to "to act and react, to wonder and respond". The quest for meaning is the quest for relationship to what is beyond being (Who is Man?, p. 66-68). He tells us that the Biblical writer begins, not with being, but with the manner of being, with being as a divine act, with being as creation (Who is Man? p. 69-72). We come face to face here with a deep loneliness inside. Do I really matter? Am I alone?

In sensing the searchers of all reality, we become aware of transcendent reality, of the absolute reality of the divine. In meditating on the prophets and others in the Bible we enter God's presence. In assenting that God exists, we bring the overpowering reality of God down to the level of conscious thought. Heschel said faith is "trust in Him, in whose presence stillness is a form of understanding" (The Prophets, p. 143). We begin with our question and as we review in stillness we sense the presence of another, the Divine. He tells us that while the worship of reason would be arrogance and betray a lack of intelligence, the rejection of reason is cowardice and would betray a lack of faith (Man is Not Alone, p. 159f).

Revelation tells us that God speaks. God's Spirit bursts forth from its hiddenness. It tells us that a person can endure the sheltering presence of God. The constant biblical reference to the cloud that surrounds each theophany to Moses is indicative of the basic truth that in all revelation there is concealment. God speaks but remains always mysterious. Divine revelation stands above the mystery. Revelation should be seen as the drama of God's search for his people. Again and again we falter and flee from his word, but God searches, all the time, for us. It is not the people's quest for God, but God's search for a people that bears the central theme of God's revelation.

In the Prophets we saw a God of care and concern. He is involved with his people, us. Our wounds are his. Heschel describes the suffering of God as "pathos". The prophets share in and convey this divine attentiveness to humanity. There is a hidden pathos that hovers over the history of humankind. It is this care of God that constitutes our greatness. Each person is called to be God's partner. God is in need of us (God in Search of Man, p. 156). Heschel says:

> "However, God is not indifferent to man's quest of Him. He is in need of man, in need of man's share in redemption. God who created the world is not at home in the world, in its dark alleys of misery, callousness and defiance."
>
> (God in Search of Man, p. 156f)

and later:

> "The words, "I am a stranger on earth" (Psalms 119:19), were interpreted to refer to God. God is a stranger in the world. The *Shechinah*, the presence of God, is in exile. Our task is to bring God back into the world, into our lives. To worship is to expand the presence of God in the world. To have faith in God is to reveal what is concealed."
>
> (God in Search of Man, p. 159)

Jewish life is rooted in Biblical faith and is a life shared with God. He partakes and feels all our senses. God is in need of us because he has freely chosen to make us partners in his enterprise, partners in his work of creation (Man is Not Alone, p. 241-243, p. 269). We share God's dream of a healed world where every tear will be wiped away. Our efforts are divine when we become aware of being partners with God. We can feel we are not needed, that our efforts are useless. We can fear we are unimportant to change things. We can be made feel worthless. Heschel points us to another reality. We learn we are infinitely valued by God and he has called us to be his partners in healing the world. All the prophetic writings point to a single revelation. There is a continuity, an all-embracing meaning that flows through every insight of the prophets. Every word they preach reflects the covenant of God with Israel, as well as the demands of the covenant. As a result, the affairs of human life are treated not as isolated incidents, but as parts of a great cosmic drama. God has a stake in human history. He has a stake in what takes place between humans. What characterises biblical faith is the profound concern of God for humanity. We are called to have faith in God's commitment to humanity and to play our part, the part given to each of us, in bringing God's love to humanity. We have a profound dignity no-one can take from us. We are not obliged to live in the Waste-Land.

Meeting Jesus (Heb 12:2):

Teresa of Avila described in her "Life" how she drifted for many years. She was neither one thing nor another. Then one day her faith was reawakened. She tells us:

> "Well, my soul now was tired; and, in spite of its desire, my wretched habits would not allow it rest. It happened to me that one day entering the oratory I saw a statue they had borrowed for a certain feast to be celebrated in the house. It represented the much wounded Christ and was very devotional so that beholding it I was utterly distressed in seeing Him that way, for it well represented what He suffered…"

> (Life 9:1)

She felt the love in her heart awakened by the love of God revealed in Jesus. She realised how much he suffered so as to call us to new life in him. Teresa strove to picture Christ who lives in us. She remembered the scenes where Jesus was all alone. She was determined to remain with him in love and to let that be the cornerstone in her life. This led her to bring God's love to those around her.

Fyodor Dostoyevsky (+1881) had a somewhat similar experience to Teresa. One day in Switzerland he saw Holbein's "Dead Christ", a disturbing painting. His wife describes the effect the painting had on him.

> "The painting had a crushing impact on Fyodor Mikhailovich. He stood there as if stunned. And I did not have the strength to look at it – it was so painful for me, particularly in my sickly condition – and I went into other rooms. When I came back after fifteen or twenty minutes, I found him still riveted to the same spot in front of the painting. His agitated face had a kind of dread in it, something I had noticed more than once during the first moments of an epileptic seizure.
>
> Quietly I took my husband by the arm, led him to another room and sat him down on a bench, expecting the attack from one minute to the next. Luckily this did not happen. He calmed down little by little and left the museum, but insisted on returning once again to view this painting which had struck him so powerfully."

This had a profound effect on Dostoyevsky. He realised, as if for the first time, how real Jesus' sufferings were and how real his compassion and love for us really is. This moment informed his writings from then on.

Teresa learnt to pray more profoundly after her experience. She would remain in solitude with the one she now knew loved her. In the book of her "Life" she writes about perseverance in staying in the presence of the one who loves us:

> "I trust then in the mercy of God, who never fails to repay anyone who has taken Him for a friend. For mental prayer

in my opinion is nothing else than an intimate sharing between friends; it means taking time frequently to be alone with Him who we know loves us. In order that love be true and the friendship endure, the wills of the friends must be in accord. The will of the Lord, it is already known, cannot be at fault; our will is vicious, sensual, and ungrateful."

(Life 8:5)

In coming to know Jesus and giving herself to him she came to know herself and her mission in life. She became more human and loving. In her relationship with the living God, by the power of the Holy Spirit, she became the person she was called to be. She became God's partner in his healing work.

In prayer Teresa heard the interior words: "Búscate en mi, búscame en ti" (Seek yourself in me, seek me in yourself). She put these words into one of her poems.

"Soul, you must seek
yourself in Me
And in yourself seek Me.

With such skill, soul,
Love could portray
you in Me
That a painter well gifted
Could never show
So finely that image.

For love you were
fashioned
Deep within me
Painted so beautiful, so fair;
If, my beloved, I
should lose you,
Soul, in yourself seek Me.

Well I know that you
will discover
Yourself portrayed
in my heart
So lifelike drawn
It will be a delight to behold
Yourself so well painted.

And should by chance
you do not know
Where to find Me,
Do not go here and there;
But if you wish to find Me,
In yourself seek Me.

Soul, since you are
My room,
My house and dwelling,
If at any time,
Through your
distracted ways
I find the door
tightly closed.

Teresa, by her genius, gives full expression here to many biblical themes. Poetry is an excellent way to convey the mystery of the scriptures. One of the themes she catches here is Paul's use of the term "in Christ". We see one example of Paul's use of "in Christ" in Romans. Romans 8:1 provides another variation of the phrase: "There is now no condemnation for those who are *in Christ Jesus*." The Complete Jewish Bible may provide a clarification in its translation: "Therefore, there is no longer any condemnation awaiting those who are *in union with* the Messiah Yeshua." (Yeshua is the commonly accepted Hebrew name translated into Greek and Latin as Iesus, or into English as Jesus).

Galations 2:20, while it may not use the phrase in all translations, may further explain the concept. "I have been crucified with Christ, and it is no longer I who live, but Christ lives in me. So the life I now live in the body, I live because of the faithfulness of the Son of God, who loved me and gave himself for me." To Paul his old life as Saul of Tarsus, persecutor of Christians, was gone. Saul was dead, crucified as Christ was. His new life through a full-bonded union with Christ was represented by his new name, Paul the apostle. His life was completely subsumed by the life of Christ. This is not a physical movement into a place or person, but a metaphysical or spiritual replacement.

To be "in Christ" for Paul is the same as possessing the Holy Spirit and being led by him. By the Holy Spirit Jesus is present to all times and places and lives in us. He reveals to us our mission in life. By his power we come to live in the presence of God. He pours out the love of God into our hearts (Rom 5:5).

Teresa now lives "in Christ" and her writings call us to that same peace. We will still have troubles but at the centre of our being is peace. She tells us wait in patience in that peace to face the trials of our world. We incarnate a new reality, now:

"Let nothing trouble you,
Let nothing scare you,
All is fleeting,
God alone is unchanging.

Patience
Everything obtains.
Who possesses God
Nothing wants.
God alone suffices."

(Poem on Patience)

In her poem on seeking Jesus she tells us "it will be a delight to behold yourself so well painted". This is Jesus speaking to Teresa. We are God's work of art – all of humanity is. All the people I quoted thus far in this chapter remind us of our dignity in God. Our tragedy is we often do not listen.

Towards The Four Quartets:

Eliot was a lonely person. In the 1930's his marriage to Vivienne ended and she was sectioned, living out the rest of her days in a mental hospital. Those who knew Eliot, like Virginia Woolf and the 'Bloomsbury Set', often felt he presented himself to them with a mask. He wanted to hide the vulnerable, lonely man that was inside. He wrote from this place of loneliness. If one listens to his reading of his poetry one hears the loneliness in his voice. Yet, in spite of this, he had a great sense of humour. He loved the Marx Brothers films and he corresponded with Groucho Marx. In 1939 he wrote some fun-poetry, "Old Possum's Book of Practical Cats". Andrew Lloyd Webber loved this work and the musical 'Cats' was born, one of the most successful shows in Broadway and the West End in London. Lloyd Webber phoned Trevor Nunn to collaborate with him. Nunn thought, "this is going to be difficult". Eliot explored major themes in his writing. Nunn had to laugh to himself when he heard it was about 'Cats'. 'Cats' was first performed in the West End in 1981. Indeed there is a theatricality in all of Eliot's works. Eliot loved modern music and this influence fed into his poetry. In 1922 in his monthly "London Letter", published in The Dial magazine, Eliot wrote about the music hall entertainer, Marie Lloyd, who died that year.

C.S. Lewis and Eliot disagreed on many things. Lewis was more of a traditionalist while Eliot was seen as a modernist. They disagreed about the poet John Milton. Lewis loved him while Eliot didn't. This was the occasion of a beautiful (if somewhat unusual) compliment from Lewis to Eliot. Lewis said that those who loved Milton were like those who lived within the wall of China. They were safe and secure. Outside the wall lived the Barbarians, except for a certain Mr. Eliot who fasted and prayed among them.

The Four Quartets has a more musical quality again. Eliot had listened to Beethoven's String Quartet, no. 15. He thought there was...

> "a heavenly or more than human gaiety about some of his later things which one imagines might come to oneself as

the fruit of reconciliation and relief after immense suffering. I should like to get something of that into verse before I die".

(Letter to Stephen Spender, 1931)

He had not yet begun his work on The Four Quartets, but the idea was there in germ. The title Four Quartets tells us of the poems musical inspiration. What matters is how the four pieces work together – four become one. The words have a rhythm and to appreciate Four Quartets one has to listen to it being read. The poem helps to redirect our values and our desires. As a young man in 1910 Eliot had a type of mystical experience. Lyndall Gordon describes this experience as follows:

> "Then in June there came the indescribable Silence in the midst of the clatter of graduation, the exhortations of practical men, the questions of parents, the frivolity of millinery and strawberries in the Yard. Suddenly able to shed the world, he experienced a fugitive sensation of peace that he would try all his life to recapture."[2]

In 1934 Eliot visited Burnt Norton with Emily Hale. The original Norton House burnt down in 1741. He had loved Emily when he was younger but a whirlwind romance with Vivienne Haigh-Wood led to their subsequent marriage, which resulted in much heartbreak for both. Eliot renewed his friendship with Emily Hale but he felt he could not marry her. He, at the time, wanted to remain celibate. In the rose garden of Burnt Norton he had a similar experience to what he had in New England. He felt love again in his heart, in a moment of silence.

The epigraph of Four Quartets comes from the philosopher Heraclitus (circa 501 BC). The poem begins with two epigraphs taken from the fragments of Heraclitus:

---

[2] Lyndall Gordon, The Imperfect Life of T. S. Eliot (London: 2012), P. 48f.

τοῦ λόγου δὲ ἐόντος ξυνοῦ ζώουσιν οἱ πολλοί
ὡς ἰδίαν ἔχοντες φρόνησιν
     — I. p. 77. Fr. 2.

ὁδὸς ἄνω κάτω μία καὶ ὡυτή
     — I. p. 89 Fr. 60.

The first may be translated, "Though wisdom is common, the many live as if they have wisdom of their own"; the second, "the way upward and the way downward is one and the same".

Heraclitus believed the world existed in accordance with 'Logos'. This can mean "word", "reason" or "account". The word "Logos" is found in the Gospel of John 1:1-4. Heraclitus was famous for his idea that the world is in flux or changing. It is illuminating to look at St. Augustine and how close he is to Heraclitus. We are called to understand "God the Word who is God, with thee God; Which word is spoken for all eternity, and in it all things spoken eternally" (Confessions, Book XI, ch.7). Augustine goes on to speak of those who do not understand the mystery:

> "They do not yet understand thee, O thou Wisdom of God, and Light of our minds, nor yet do they understand how those things are made by thee and in thee … Who shall be able to hold and fix it, that for a while it may be still, and may catch a glimpse of thy ever-fixed eternity, and compare it with the times that never stand, that so he may see how these things are not to be compared together? That he may understand … that all which is both past and future is created and doth flow out from that which is always present."
>
> (Confessions, Book XI, ch.11)

This is contained in the first sentence. The world is always changing, in flux or becoming. The second statement in the epigraph can be thought of as us getting in touch with the higher Logos (the way up) and living in accord with the divine will or Logos (the way down).

Burnt Norton:

This is the first of the poems that go to make up The Four Quartets. Eliot begins with a meditation on time. As we saw he was influenced by Augustine who wrote about time:

> "For what is time? Who can readily and briefly explain this? ...If no one asks me, I know; if I wish to explain it to one that asketh, I know not; yet I say boldly that I know, that if nothing passed away, time past were not; and if nothing were, time present were not....But the present, should it always be present, and never pass into time past, verily it should not be time, but eternity."
>
> (The Confessions of Saint Augustine, Book XI)[3]

Augustine and many others wrestled with the meaning of time. How to look at us as time-bound creatures is important to us. We need to give meaning to our experience, our time on earth.

Eliot begins the poem:

> "Time present and time past
> Are both perhaps present in time future,
> And time future contained in time past.
> If all time is eternally present
> All time is unredeemable.
> What might have been is an abstraction
> Remaining a perpetual possibility
> Only in a world of speculation.
> What might have been and what has been
> Point to one end, which is always present."

Eliot is influenced by Dante, here again. In Dante's Paradiso (Canto XVII, 16-18) he speaks of the point at which all things are present:

---

[3] The Confessions of Saint Augustine, translated by Edward B. Pusey (Rockville, MD: 2008), p. 166f.

> "So thou beholds the contingent things
> Ere in themselves they are, fixing thine eyes
> Upon the point in which all times are present"

The still point is where eternity meets time in the incarnation of the 'Word made flesh' (Jn 1:14). He gives meaning to our lives when we are "in him". Eliot said in his Chorus VII of "The Rock":

> "Then came, at a predetermined moment, a moment in time and of time,
> A moment not out of time, but in time, in what we call history: transecting, bisecting the world of time, a moment in time but not like a moment of time,
> A moment in time but time was made through that moment: for without the meaning there is no time, and that moment of time gave the meaning."

The incarnation of the spiritual occurs in a moment of time but does not resemble a moment of time. Thus the historic sense is translated into the spiritual sense. This moment refers to the Incarnation of the Word. The incarnation of the spiritual occurs in a moment of time. This leads ultimately to Jesus' passion and death. This is not thought of as a single historic event but as a perpetual act operative in time. Jesus' passion continues to the end of time (Pascal). His passion continues in his people:

> "He is in agony wherever there is a human being that struggles with sadness, fear, anxiety, in a situation where there is no way out, as he was that day. We can do nothing for the Jesus who was suffering then but we can do something for the Jesus who is in agony today. Every day we hear of tragedies that occur, sometimes in our own building, in the apartment across the hall, without anyone being aware of it.
> How many Mount of Olives, how many Gethsemanes in the heart of our cities!"

The Passion is intimately connected with the Eucharist. Here the life-giving events of Jesus' life, death and resurrection are made present. Jesus gives meaning to our time, our lives, when we give ourselves to him. In coming to know Jesus we find ourselves; we come to know ourselves. Pascal tells us: "there is a God-shaped vacuum in the heart of every man which cannot be filled by any created thing, but only by God the creator made known by Jesus Christ."

Friedrick Nietzsche (+1900) was a German philosopher, cultural critic, composer, poet, philologist. In his work "Ecce Homo", he saw himself as being the first real psychologist: "Before me there simply was no psychology". This is a grandiose boast but when you consider that Sigmund Freud, Carl Jung and Alfred Adler were influenced by Nietzsche there is some substance to his boast. He sought to find a way of becoming the person we are meant to be. He, too, looked at time. He said:

> "What, if some day or night a demon were to steal after you into your loneliest loneliness and say to you: "This life as you now live it and have lived it, you will have to live once more and innumerable times more; and there will be nothing new in it, but every pain and every joy and every thought and everything unutterably small or great in your life will have to return to you, all in the same succession and sequence – even this spider in the moonlight between the trees, and even this moment and I myself . The eternal hourglass of existence is turned upside down again and again, and you with it, speck of dust!" "
>
> (The Gay Science [New York: 1974] p. 273)

Nietzsche claimed a timeless moment inspired his ideas of eternal recurrence. He believed that time, infinitely repeated in the future and the past would allow him have eternity in the now. It would give meaning to the 'now' and living the moment.

This idea replicates Dante's idea of Hell. There the doomed eternally, obsessively, repeat the sin that earned them damnation.

"But when events draw near, or are, our minds
Are empty, and were none to bring us news
We should know nothing of your human state."

(Inferno 10.94-105)

The souls here know the past and the future but not the present. We can only repent and change, make choices, in the present. Hell began in time (Inferno 34:121-126). Hell begins in time and must be chosen. Choosing in life must cause a change, a time that differs from the time before.

Eliot in his play 'The Family Reunion' said:

"I can guess about the past and what you mean about the future;
But a present is missing, needed to connect them."[4]

Soren Kierkegaard sums up the significance of the moment. He said life "must be lived forward, but understood backwards".[5] Our past informs us. We are called to become the people God called us to be – this is our end, our telos. The Greek word 'telos' has the sense of a goal. Our choices, now, determine whether we will achieve this goal. We are called by God to be the ones he knows us to be.

In the 'Waste Land' Eliot spoke of a woman bearing flowers out of sunlight. He says:

"You gave me hyacinths first a year ago;
"They called me the hyacinth girl."
—Yet when we came back, late, from the Hyacinth garden,
Your arms full, and your hair wet, I could not
Speak, and my eyes failed, I was neither
Living nor dead, and I knew nothing,
Looking into the heart of light"

(Burial of the Dead)

[4] T. S. Eliot, The Family Reunion Part II, scene II, in Complete Poems and Plays (New York: 1980), p. 272.

[5] Soren Kierkegaard, Papers and Journals, A Selection (London: 1996), p. 161 (43IV A164).

He saw in the Hyacinth girl (the gift of maternal love) an image of despair. He cannot accept the offered flowers, he cannot speak and his eyes fail. He is like Dante, looking on Satan, he is neither alive nor dead (Inferno, 34:22-27).

When Eliot met Emily Hale she rekindled love again for the poet. By this time he had separated from Vivienne, even though they did not divorce. Vivienne was sectioned at this stage and would die a few years later.

Eliot experienced a moment of eternity when he was in the rose-garden with Emily. There were two pools in the garden:

> "And the pool was filled with water out of sunlight,
> And the lotos rose, quietly, quietly,
> The surface glittered out of heart of light,
> And they were behind us, reflected in the pool."

In the midst of the autumn heat and vibrant air the "unheard music" and the "unseen eyebeam" bring new life. This experience of the divine enables the poet to interact fruitfully with the world. In the rose-garden of Burnt Norton a gray-brown desolate empty pool becomes transfigured by a glittering light. The pool, littered with moss and leaves, is filled with the sun's light through which he sees "the lotos rose". The poet's being has been enlightened. We do not know exactly what Eliot's experience was. St. Paul in Romans tells us: "…God's love has been poured into our hearts through the Holy Spirit, who has been given to us" (Rom 5:5).

While Eliot was a student at Harvard he studied the 'lotos' symbol in relation to the Hindu true self (the atman) and the Buddhist absolute emptiness (shunyata). In each of these traditions heart-mind transforms through direct realisation of one's true identity, symbolised by the lotos.

In the Bhagavad Gita Arjuna sees Krishna's infinite form. He says: "Brahma, the Lord, throned on the lotus seat".[6] In the Buddhist tradition

---

[6] The Bhagavad Gita, XI: 1:5 in Hindu Scriptures (London: 1966), p. 295.

the pure 'lotos' of the true self rises out of the muddy water of experience.

The rose has come to occupy a central place in Christianity. We have the rosary. In Paradiso Dante, after seeing the only true heaven, is momentarily blinded by the light. Dante's "multifoliate rose" in Canto XXX radiates the "Heaven of pure light".

> "So great a light, how vast the amplitude
> Is of this Rose in its extremest leaves!
> My vision in the vastness and the height
> Lost not itself, but comprehended all
> The quantity and quality of that gladness.
> There near and far nor add nor take away."
>
> (Canto XXX)

Dante sees that a ray of light from God descends from God and is reflected back up into a flame-like arrangement of souls centered on God. In Canto XXXIII, the supreme light of God is so dazzling that Dante has to turn away:

> "I saw within its depths how it conceives
> All things in a single volume bound by Love,
> Of which the universe is the scattered leaves."

The Word and immanent reality are one. All things are formed in the Word of God and come to rest in him. Eliot and Dante experience the world of eternity in the world of time. In the poem of Eliot there are subtle and profound interactions between the two traditions – the "lotos" (emptiness or true self) and the "rose" (fullness of the divine) – which reverberate throughout the poem. Eliot and Dante felt a sense of belonging. They felt God had come close to them and they saw themselves living life and seeing life from that place. Eliot did not trust private revelations which is why he chose a major tradition of Christianity. He was attracted to Catholicism and he chose Anglo-Catholicism over Roman Catholicism. Eliot and Dante were affirmed as human beings by their experience. Eliot, in Burnt Norton, tells us how hard it is to communicate the essence of his experience. He says of words:

> "And all is always now. Words strain,
> Crack and sometimes break, under the burden,
> Under the tension, slip, slide, perish,
> Decay with imprecision, will not stay in place..."

Eliot cannot stay too long in this phase. He returns again to existence here, after his glimpse of eternity.

Eliot spoke of meditation. He met Virginia Woolf who asked him about his new-found faith and he told her of his meditation practices. He wrote of his practice:

> "I myself should not choose to read very much at a time. To read two or three passages ... to attend closely to every word, to ponder on the quotations read for a little while and try to fix them in my mind, so that they may continue to affect me while my attention is engrossed with the affairs of the day: that is enough for me in twenty-four hours, and enough, I imagine, even for those more practiced in meditation than I."[7]

Augustine had spoken of his search for God. He said:

> "Late have I love you, beauty so old and so new: late have I loved you. And see, you were within and I was in the external world and sought you there, and in my unlovely state I plunged into those lovely created things which you made. You were with me, and I was not with you. The lovely things kept me far from you, though if they did not have their existence in you, they had no existence at all. You called and cried out loud and shattered my deafness. You

[7] T. S. Eliot, "Preface" in Thoughts for Meditation: A Way to Recovery from Within, related by N. Gangulee (London: 1951), p. 11-14.

were radiant and resplendent, you put to flight my
blindness. You were fragrant, and I drew in my breath and
now pant after you. I tasted you, and I feel but hunger and
thirst for you. You touched me, and I am set on fire to attain
the peace which is yours."

(Confessions, Book 10, 26)

It was from within that Augustine found himself. Eliot and Augustine
sensed a hunger within. We seek a Paradise within. "For there is"
Augustine says "a dim glimmering of light yet unput-out in men"
(Confessions Book X, ch23). Eliot is trying throughout Burnt Norton to
fix our attention on the "cause and end of movement", that "one end that
is always present". He reflects on retrieving timeless moments in the
endless flux of temporal existence, which stay with us. The rose garden
is filled with echoes from the present situation and from inner recesses
of memory. A feeling of finding a new world, a new life enters the poem.

"Footfalls echo in the memory
Down the passage which we did not take
Towards the door we never opened
Into the rose-garden. My words echo
Thus, in your mind.
                    But to what purpose
Disturbing the dust on a bowl of rose-leaves
I do not know."

Later he hears the bird speak again. The role of the bird has antecedents
in Romanticism; as in Wordsworth's 'To the Cuckoo', Shelley's 'To a
Skylark' and Keats' 'Ode to a Nightingale' in which the bird with
individual variations functions as the voice of an invisible, potential
world. Keats, once said: " 'Our first world' may be the world of one's
earlier life, the Garden of Eden, or some unrealized personal past."[8] In
us there is an infinite longing for such a world. Eliot in the rose-garden
glimpsed it.

---

[8] John Keats, quoted in Herman Servotte and Ethel Grene, Annotations to T. S. Eliot's Four
Quartets (Bloomington, Indiana: 2010), p. 106.

> "Go, said the bird, for the leaves were full of children,
> Hidden excitedly, containing laughter.
> Go, go, go, said the bird: human kind
> Cannot bear very much reality."

The brief glimpse he had of Eternity does not last. "Human kind cannot bear very much reality". He has to return to the mundane, the mud of ordinary life. The bird that initially invited the visitors into the garden ("quick, said the bird, find them, find them") now asks them to leave their "first world".

> "Time past and time future
> What might have been and what has been
> Point to one end, which is always present."

Louis Mantz comments on Four Quartets. He says:

> "A meditative poem is a work that creates an interior drama of mind; this dramatic action is usually (though not always) created by some form of self-address, in which the mind grasps firmly a problem or situation deliberately evoked by the memory, brings it forward toward the full light of consciousness, and concludes with a moment of illumination, where the poet's self has, for a time, found an answer to its conflicts."[9]

The second movement of Burnt Norton begins with the 'lotos rose' now changed into an earth-bound metaphor: "Garlic and sapphires in the mud / Clot the bedded axle-tree". The axle-tree (axis of the world, symbolically equated with the Tree of Life), reconciles all things, becoming a fixed point at the centre of the turning world. Garlic and sapphire, artery and boar, heaven and earth are gathered together.

> "At the still point of the turning world. Neither flesh nor
> fleshless;

---

[9] Louis Mantz, The Meditative Poem: An Anthology of Seventeenth-Century Verse (New York: 1963), p. 330.

Neither from nor towards; at the still point, there the dance
is,
But neither arrest nor movement. And do not call it fixity,
Where past and future are gathered. Neither movement
from nor towards"

The still point is God and the world in motion is around him. This is an idea Eliot got from is reading of Thomas Aquinas, Bonaventure, the Pseudo-Dionysus.

Bonaventure in his 'Itinerarium Mentis in Deum'[10] sees all things united in God. Creation reflects God who is the source of all. He says: "The Magnitude of things … clearly manifests … the wisdom and goodness of the triune God (itin 1:14). God "is within all things but not enclosed; outside all things but not excluded, above all things but not aloof, below all things but not debased" (Itin 5:8). He speaks of God as one "whose centre is everywhere and whose circumference is nowhere" (5:8). Therefore the origin, magnitude, beauty and fullness of all created things are the very "footprints" and fingerprints (vestige) of God. He also said:

"Therefore, open your eyes, alert the ears of your spirit,
open your lips and apply your heart so that in all creatures
you may see, hear, praise, love and worship, glorify and
honour your God, lest the whole world rise against you."
(Itinerarium, 1:15)

This is our gateway to silence, where God can speak to our hearts. This is what Eliot is calling us to. In the stillness of the moment God can speak. In silence he comes to us.

Describing the climax of one of his own early experiences, for example, Augustine writes: 'In the flash of a trembling glance my mind came to Ultimate Reality, Absolute Being, – that which is.' Also worth noting is Augustine's famous description of an experience which he shared once

---

[10] Bonaventure, The Soul's Journey Into God, trans. E. Cousins (New York: 1978).

with Monica his mother. They were at Ostia and were leaning out of a certain window overlooking the garden. Already, we are told, they had begun a gradual 'inward ascent' by thinking and speaking, marveling at God's works and discussing with each other concerning that life 'by which all things come to be, both those that have been and those that are to be'. Augustine then continues:

> "And the life itself never comes to be, but is as it was and shall be ever more, because it is neither past nor future but present only, for it is eternal. And as we talked and yearned after it, we touched it – and hardly touched it – with the full beat of our heart. And we sighed and left there impawned the first fruits of the spirit, and we relapsed into articulate speech, where every word has beginning and ending. And how little, O Lord, it is like unto thy Word."

Here, as in the opening movement of Eliot's poem, the stated object of contemplation, namely that living and eternal Reality, the Word which is always present, is viewed in terms of its relationship to time past and time future. For the protagonist in 'Burnt Norton', however, even a momentary experience of such reality is unbearable. He is prone to be distracted and his inward intellectual ascent to Eternal Life, or to the Paradise within, appears much more hesitant and more subjectively self-conscious than that of Augustine and Monica. But even for Augustine the core of the experience is transitory and is realised only in part and only for an instant. 'We touched it', he writes, 'and hardly touched it (attigimus eam modice) with the full beat of our heart.'

St. Teresa of Avila said that "pure prayer" only lasted a few minutes and then one returned to ordinary life.

Eliot tells us:

> "The inner freedom from the practical desire,
> The release from action and suffering, release from the inner
> And the outer compulsion, yet surrounded

By a grace of sense, a white light still and moving,
Erhebung without motion, concentration
Without elimination, both a new world
And the old made explicit, understood
In the completion of its partial ecstasy,
The resolution of its partial horror."

These lines show the consequences of his experience in the rose garden – "only through time is time conquered". He "must be still and still moving" and he must become "surrounded by a grace of sense". He now has a more contemplative view of the world and he is now open to genuinely reciprocal relationships with the world in the midst of the 'logos' common to all. "Through [logos] him all things were made; no one thing came into being except through him." (Jn 1:3). He recognises that the "still point" does not release him from the limits of time-bound existence but it does govern the way he views the world and his interaction with it. It brings release from attachments to desire and action, compulsion and it brings Erbebung (exaltation to consciousness).

His contemplative experience led him to reflection and meditation. He sought the help of a living tradition to centre his reflections.

"The detail of the pattern is movement,
As in the figure of the ten stairs.
Desire itself is movement
Not in itself desirable;
Love is itself unmoving,
Only the cause and end of movement,
Timeless, and undesiring..."

Later in the poem Eliot tells us:

"The Word in the desert
Is most attacked by voices of temptation,
The crying shadow in the funeral dance,
The loud lament of the disconsolate chimera."

The Word made flesh is Jesus. In the Gospels of Matthew and Luke, Jesus is "driven into the desert" by the Spirit where he is tempted (Mtt 4:1-11; Lk 4:1-13, see also Mk 1:12-13). As Jesus experienced agony and temptations so we too in our age face temptations proper to our age. We face the desert of our age. The Word of God is love. We are held in God's love.

> "Desire itself is movement
> Not in itself desirable;
> Love is itself unmoving,
> Only the cause and end of movement,
> Timeless, and undesiring..."

He uses phrases borrowed from Aristotle here, but the one he refers to is still the God of Jesus Christ.

The method employed by Eliot is very similar to the mystical writer, Pseudo-Dionysius. He would make a statement (God is ...) then he would say (God is not ...), in this way leading us to see God is beyond our categories. Eliot says:

> "Neither from nor towards; at the still point, there the dance is,
> But neither arrest nor movement. And do not call it fixity,
> Where past and future are gathered. Neither movement from nor towards,
> Neither ascent nor decline."

Compare this with the following quote from Pseudo-Dionysius:

> "It is not immobile, nor in motion, or at rest,
> and has no power, and is not power or light,
> and does not live, and is not life;
> nor is it personal essence, or eternity, or time."[11]

---

[11] Dionysius the Areopagite: The Divine Names and Mystical Theology (London: 1920), p. 200.

God is ever mysterious. Our words "crack and sometimes break, under the burden" of putting words on God and our experience. He escapes our categories as does our experience. Karl Barth said it was impossible to talk of God and yet we must. We are all called to a life with God. Faith and contemplation are the fruits of being human. However, we draw back in fear. Kierkegaard said every human being has potential possibilities, yet to be realised. Between the possibility and actualisation there is anxiety. This can be crippling, but Kierkegaard points out it can also be life-affirming. The anxiety can signal to us a call to actualise our potential.[12] Fear can hold us back. We prefer to stay in a comfort zone, but this zone gets smaller and smaller and in the end provides no comfort. Jung compared this non-movement to a 'living death'. We live lives of quiet desperation (Thoreau). Eliot, in his poetry, fires our imagination and invites us into the 'rose garden'.

In the third movement of Burnt Norton we leave the atmosphere of the rose garden and we find ourselves in the darkness of the London Underground (The Tube). The people here are dominated by distracted and empty thoughts. The death-undone faces that flowed over London Bridge in The Waste Land are echoed here. The people are frightened, confused and almost dead. These masks for human faces recall the headpieces "filled with straw" in "The Hollow Man" where:

"…between the motion
And the act
Falls the shadow"

The unhealthy atmosphere also recalls the yellow putrid fog in "The Love Song of J Alfred Prufrock" that settles in the tedious streets, "the burnt-out ends of smoky days", the "dull head among windy spaces". One of Eliot's most memorable phrases – "Distracted from distraction by distraction" – catches the negativity of this "twittering world" where there is only "tumid apathy".

For Eliot the way of darkness of John of the Cross and proposes that the way up and down are, mystically, the same:

---

[12] Soren Kierkegaard, The Concept of Anxiety (Princeton: 1981).

"Descend lower, descend only
Into the world of perpetual solitude,
World not world, but that which is not world,
Internal darkness, deprivation
And destitution of all property,
Desiccation of the world of sense,
Evacuation of the world of fancy,
Inoperancy of the world of spirit"

According to Saint John of the Cross one's faith journey passes through a "Dark Night of the Soul", another term for the Cross, on its way to becoming true. The idea of "soul" used by John of the Cross is close to the Hebrew word 'Nephesh' used in the Hebrew Bible. Nephesh refers to the whole person in their bodily and spiritual unity. Eliot sees this as part of our journey.

He then describes the modern "desert". He says:

"Neither plenitude nor vacancy. Only a flicker
Over the strained time-ridden faces
Distracted from distraction by distraction
Filled with fancies and empty of meaning
Tumid apathy with no concentration
Men and bits of paper, whirled by the cold wind
That blows before and after time,
Wind in and out of unwholesome lungs
Time before and time after.
Eructation of unhealthy souls"

Here we are tempted. We can get "distracted from distraction by distraction" living in tumid apathy. Fear and anxiety can overcome us. We can feel unworthy and unfree to change or make a difference. Yet with his reference to John of the Cross God is present in this darkness, just like he was present in the rose-garden. In the Book of Genesis: "the Spirit of God was hovering over the water" (Gen 1:2). The waters of chaos are the loneliness of modern people.

He goes on to say:

> "Into the faded air, the torpid
> Driven on the wind that sweeps the gloomy hills of London,
> Hampstead and Clerkenwell, Campden and Putney,
> Highgate, Primrose and Ludgate."

Eliot's image of the descent into the London Underground reflects his journey into his innermost depths. Nietzsche said we do not become the people we are meant to be because we are afraid to enter our innermost depths. We run away from this – "distraction from distraction". Eliot entered the depths of his own being. This is symbolised by 'The Waste Land' of his earlier years. Here the depths of his being are symbolised by the faces in the Underground. Jung said only when we accept the parts of ourselves that we do not like can we be cured. This is the journey we are on.

The people in the Tube are like those of the Waste Land. There is another sense in which these others can share the journey of Eliot from The Waste Land to the peace of the rose garden. The words of the poem can involve many different interpretations which enrich each other. Jung said: "Bidden or not bidden, God is present". He is ever at work in our darkness.

The fourth movement of Burnt Norton is very compressed. It reads:

> "Time and the bell have buried the day,
> The black cloud carries the sun away.
> Will the sunflower turn to us, will the clematis
> Stray down, bend to us; tendril and spray
> Clutch and cling?
>
> Chill
> Fingers of yew be curled
> Down on us? After the kingfisher's wing
> Has answered light to light, and is silent, the light is still
> At the still point of the turning world."

The bell can signal a funeral bell but it can also signal a call to prayer, a call to break out of ordinary time. During the Mass a bell is rung when the bread and wine are consecrated. There are images here of new life and hope that a sunflower will greet the new dawn. One emerges from the darkness of the preceding section with a double sensation: the extinction of death and the delicate warmth of nature's light. Eliot associated the yew tree, often found in English churchyards, with both death and new life in resurrection. In response to the question "will the sunflower, will the clematis turn to us?" the Kingfisher answers "light to light". New light, new life breaks through the cloud.

In the fifth movement we find poetic and figurative moments have made a sanctuary for the soul, in the midst of a deep struggle with ourself. He reflects on the troubling question of how words can evoke redemptive possibilities drawn from experience. Recalling the rhetorical difficulties of his own verbal process, he says:

> "Words move, music moves
> Only in time; but that which is only living
> Can only die. Words, after speech, reach
> Into the silence."

Words can only give a glimpse into the peace that arises from silence. The poet can evoke realities that exist beyond words. The poet strives to "reach / The stillness, as a Chinese jar still / Moves perpetually in its stillness." This becomes a spiritual practice for the poet. This stillness is not just the absence of sound:

> "Not the stillness of the violin, while the note lasts,
> Not that only, but the co-existence,
> Or say that the end precedes the beginning,
> And the end and the beginning were always there
> Before the beginning and after the end.
> And all is always now."

In the stillness of the moment we allow God speak and we can talk to the one we know loves us. In the poem the spiritual pilgrim descends into inner stillness, into the quietude of the soul and returns to articulate, as best he can, the practices of purgation, devotion and faith.

> "The Word in the desert
> Is most attacked by voices of temptation,
> The crying shadow in the funeral dance,
> The loud lament of the disconsolate chimera."

He goes from the inability of words to the perfect expression of God, his Word. Ironically for the poet the threatening voices of temptation, doubt and mistrust that populate our world open the door for the spiritual quest. The Spirit of God's Word is always active.

He goes on:

> "The detail of the pattern is movement,
> As in the figure of the ten stairs.
> Desire itself is movement
> Not in itself desirable;
> Love is itself unmoving,
> Only the cause and end of movement,
> Timeless, and undesiring
> Except in the aspect of time
> Caught in the form of limitation
> Between un-being and being."

Here he recalls John of the Cross's "figure of the ten stairs" of the mystical ladder of love, representing spiritual ascent in our souls. We recall the saying of Jesus: "whoever humbles himself will be exalted" (e.g. Mtt 23:12). This means the way down is the way up. The soul comes to surrender itself to love. The soul loves God. God loves the soul. Theres is a union of love achieved by the Holy Spirit and in the union of the Holy Spirit.

The last lines of Burnt Norton reaffirm manifestations of the still point:

"Sudden in a shaft of sunlight
Even while the dust moves
There rises the hidden laughter
Of children in the foliage
Quick now, here, now, always—
Ridiculous the waste sad time
Stretching before and after."

The scene in the garden is evoked again. He refers to the time before and after illumination. In the "first world" of inner stillness time past and time present are held by a taste of Eden. They are recalled subsequently through meditation and brought back into life. We can use our experience to give us hope in the world as we find it. We see the world with new eyes.

Chapter 4

East Coker:

In 'Burnt Norton' we saw how Eliot began his recovery of self from within. John of the Cross was one of the people he used to make sense of his experience. Teresa of Avila was intimately associated with John. Teresa tells us about how the fire of love is enkindled in us and is for others:

> "This fire of love in you enkindles the souls of others, and with every other virtue you will be always awakening them…"
>
> (Teresa of Avila, Interior Castle, VII:4:14)

By the power of the Holy Spirit God brings the person into a profound relationship with Him. In this way, each person is unique and chosen. We come to be the people we are called to be.

> "God, being God, seeks to make us gods by participation, just as fire makes all things into fire."
>
> (John of the Cross, Sayings of Light and Love, 106)

God's love is the source of all love and sets our hearts on fire with love. The desire for love is infused in all of us and we find its fulfillment in God. Because of circumstances many do not follow this road. In reading Eliot the way of discovering love becomes new for a new generation. East Coker was written during the war and it helped people. Ultimately 'The Dry Salvages' and 'Little Gidding' were added and became 'The Four Quartets'.

Teresa and John lived in "harsh times" (Life 33:5). The Spanish Inquisition was in full flow and it cast a long shadow.[1] At this time those

---

[1] see Gillian T. W. Ahlgren, Entering Teresa of Avila's Interior Castle: A Reader's Companion (New York: 2005), 5-18.

who taught mental prayer were under suspicion. As time went on there was the Valdés Index of Prohibited Books. Teresa experienced many people who were opposed to her way of thinking. In 1575 the Valladolid tribunal of the Inquisition ordered a theological review of her 'Life' for orthodoxy. The censor, Domingo Bañez said that her work was not suitable for just anyone to read, but for learned men, "experienced and of Christian discretion".[2]

In this climate people like Teresa and John sensed the whisper of God calling them to a deeper relationship with him and deeper personal authenticity. Teresa lost her mother when she was twelve years old and after that she went to a school run by Augustinian nuns. Teresa's father was a prosperous merchant but he was not of "pure blood" (Teresa's paternal grandfather had converted to Christianity from Judaism and was prosecuted by the Inquisition). Those who were not of pure blood were called 'conversos'. John was born in 1542. His family also had 'converso' origins. John's family were poor. He found refuge in a school for orphans and when he was seventeen he worked at Nuestra Señora de la Concepciõn, a hospital established to serve those suffering from incurable diseases.

Teresa entered the convent of the Encarnačion in 1535 and John entered the Carmelite order in 1563. The Carmelites did not discriminate against those of 'Converso' blood. In 1567 John was ordained a priest and he met Teresa who persuaded him to join her reform.

Teresa recounts the drama of her religious life in her 'Life'. She describes a serious illness as a young woman which led her to the study and practice of prayer (Life, chs. 4-6). She searched for spiritual directors but could not find any (Life chapters 7-8, 23). She then describes her conversion to a deepening relationship with Christ, culminating in the point at which she says, "from here onward, it is a whole new life ... one that God lives in me". This period includes the famous Lenten meditation before a statue of Christ which showed his agony (Life, ch. 9). She began to experience the presence of Christ that helped her refocus her life. She tells us about her new life in Christ: "It

[2] see Teresa, Obras completas (Madrid: 1984), 306-308.

is a whole new book from here on forward – I mean a whole new life. The one up to here was mine. The one that I have lived since I began to speak of these prayer experiences is the one that God is living in me, or so it seems to be" (Life ch 23:1). This reveals for us what St. Paul said: "I have been crucified with Christ and I no longer live, but Christ lives in me. The life I now live in the body, I live by faith in the Son of God, who loved me and gave himself for me." (Gal 2:20).

One of the great gifts of John and Teresa is their ability to show us that this way of prayer is possible for us. The Inquisition banned many books precious to Teresa. Jesus became her teacher within. She tells us:

> "When they took away many books written in the vernacular so that they would not be read, I felt this keenly, because reading some of them gave me solace, and now I could not read them, since they were in Latin. But then God said to me, "Do not be sad; I will give you a living book." I could not understand why this was said to me … but then only a few days later, I understood it quite well…, for [since then] God has favored me with so much love as to teach me in so many ways that I have had little or even no need for books."

> (Life 26:5)

The collaboration between Teresa and John could be seen when Teresa became prioress at the Encarnaciõn. One of the sisters there said: "He had a gift for consoling those who came to him, by his words and in the cards he wrote… I received some myself – also some jottings about spiritual matters. I would deeply love to have them now" (Silvero de Santa Teresa, see Matthew, Infant of God, 19f). It was around this time Teresa's prayer life deepened and she wrote her "Interior Castle" in 1577.

However three days after Teresa completed her masterpiece, John was kidnapped by his conformed 'brothers'. He was imprisoned in Toledo where he was treated with much cruelty. He was starved, beaten and held prisoner in a dingy cell. Toledo was very cold in winter, asphyxiating in summer. The beatings gave him pain for many years. With this was psychological torture. His 'brother' would speak outside his cell hinting John's life was a waste, the reform had fallen apart. It was all happening together: physical and emotional abuse. His mind was crucified with anxiety. In his relationship with God, all was darkness. It is hard to believe such cruelty from a religious order. This has a sad parallel in modern times. Many have suffered abuse, especially children and vulnerable adults.

John suffered great inner darkness and it seemed "at times [the Lord] withdrew and left him in inner darkness along with the darkness of his cell" (Testimony of the nuns of Sabiote). In the first stanza of the Spiritual Canticle he wrote:

"Adónde te escondiste...?
Where have you hidden Beloved, and left me groaning?
You fled like a stag having wounded me;
I went out in search of you, and you were gone."

Yet it was here John wrote his most profound poems – 'The Dark Night of the Soul' and 'The Spiritual Canticle'. In the depth of darkness he found peace in God. John eventually escaped from Toledo and rejoined his community. All this time Teresa was livid. When she heard of the treatment John received she demanded it be reported to the Papal Nuncio. She hated injustice and cruelty. Her closeness to God made her more sensitive to injustice and cruelty.

We get a glimpse of what John suffered in the 'Living Flame of Love'. He says:

"...imparts the warmth of love, it does so with great torment and pain. And it is not delightful,... but it is consuming and contentious, making a person faint and suffer with self-knowledge... A person suffers from sharp trials in the intellect, severe dryness and distress in the will, and from the burdensome knowledge of their own miseries in the memory... In the substance of the soul they suffer abandonment, supreme poverty, dryness, cold… They find relief in nothing, nor does any thought console them, so oppressed are they by this flame…. it truly seems to the soul that God has become displeased with it and cruel."

(Living Flame, 1:19-20)

John was in communion with Jesus who felt the 'darkness' in his spirit (Mk 14:32-42). In spite of God's seeming absence his Spirit draws new life out of the darkness. John responded creatively to the deep darkness he felt. He responded with faith and acceptance. John said: "The humble are those who hide in their nothingness and know how to abandon themselves to God" (Sayings of Light and Love, no. 163). John was led through this darkness to an even deeper and more profound union with the one who loved him.

John speaks to people who feel unable to change. In our lives we sense a call to freedom, wholeness and authenticity. John said this was a call to reach out for God. Fear blocks us. We fear that we might find 'nothingness'. Ours is an age of anxiety. John and Teresa witness to the impact of God in their lives. John and Teresa knew the pain of loss, failure, stress and darkness. They are friends on our journey. John meets us at the threshold of our uncertainty. He assures us that what dwells beyond is not chaos and 'nothingness'. The darkness bears the Spirit of God, who broods over the waters of death (see Gen 1:1-2) and has power to bring forth a new-life, a resurrection. John and Teresa tell us it is Jesus the Christ we are seeking. By the power of the Spirit Jesus lives in us. He is the one who gives shape to the universe. John sees the world slung between Good Friday and Easter Sunday. In our darkness he finds Jesus' darkness and what John tells us is there is hope and new life. There is a resurrection. John died in 1591 and many people were attracted to him.

Take the case of the servant girl Juana: She found a John a life-long support. When she was an old woman, she still treasured a tiny locket containing his portrait. She suffered her own darkness and bewilderment. John wrote to console her: "But nothing is failing you… The person who desires nothing but God does not walk in darkness, however poor and dark she may be in her own sight" (Letter 19, to Juana de Pedraza, 1589).

The friars he lived with found him a kind person. He was joyful and easy to get on with. He was very gentle. These characteristics were forged out of love and pain. He loved to make people laugh and he lifted their spirits with music. In 1586 John founded a priory at Cordoba. Here the labourers were working on a stone wall which fell onto the section of the Monastery where John was. The friars and labourers frantically removed the rubble fearing that John may have been crushed to death. However when they found him he was crouched in a corner, laughing and joking with the worried man who found him. He said the Virgin Mary must have protected him with her cape.

John had fallen in love with Christ. His poetry after meeting Christ in his prison cell had the freshness of Easter morning. By the power of the Holy Spirit he experienced Christ's presence in his darkest hour. He wrote of this in his Canticle.

> "My beloved, the mountains,
> lonely wooded valleys,
> rare islands,
> thundering rivers,
> the whisper of love, carried by the breeze.
>
> The tranquil night
> at one with the rising dawn,
> the silence of music,
> the might sound of solitude
> the feast where love makes all new."

(Canticle A 14-14)

He experienced the love of God which surpasses all. In the letter to the Ephesians we read:

> "For this reason I kneel before the Father, from whom every
> family in heaven and on earth derives its name. I pray that

out of his glorious riches he may strengthen you with power through his Spirit in your inner being, so that Christ may dwell in your hearts through faith. And I pray that you, being rooted and established in love, may have power, together with all the Lord's holy people, to grasp how wide and long and high and deep is the love of Christ, and to know this love that surpasses knowledge—that you may be filled to the measure of all the fullness of God."

(Ephesians 3:14-19)

The love that Paul prays for here is the love John experienced in his heart. John doesn't tell us directly of how he had this experience, but in his writing we get glimpses of this visitation of love. "In the midst of obscurity" John speaks "of a kind of companionship and inner strength which walks with the soul and gives her strength" (2 Night 11:7). In his darkness there was disclosed to him Christ's love for him, a God who gives himself to the poor. This pattern is found in John's writing. Both John and Teresa knew it was for love we were created. We were created for union with God who is love. This is achieved by the Holy Spirit. We can never love God enough because He loves us infinitely. Our love must be always growing and must always be purified.

Teresa died in 1582, nine years before John died. The full maturity of her thought is found in the Interior Castle. In it she shows how the soul's relationship with God becomes more intimate and deep. Teresa was finally convinced to write her book after she received a vision from God. Diego, her confessor, wrote that God revealed to Teresa...

"...a most beautiful crystal globe, made in the shape of a castle, and containing seven mansions, in the seventh and innermost of which was the King of Glory, in the greatest splendour, illumining and beautifying them all. The nearer one got to the centre, the stronger was the light; outside the palace limits everything was foul, dark and infested with toads, vipers and other venomous creatures."

(Fray Diego, Confessor to Teresa)

The Interior Castle is divided into seven mansions (also called dwelling places), each level describing a step to getting closer to God. Teresa assured entrance into the first mansion was gained by prayer and meditation.

"The first three mansions are considered to be active prayer and asceticism. The first mansions begin with a soul's state of grace, but the souls are surrounded by sin and only starting to seek God's grace through humility in order to achieve perfection. The second mansions are also called the Mansions of the Practice of Prayer because the soul seeks to advance through the castle by daily thoughts of God, humble recognition of God's work in the soul and ultimately daily prayer. The third mansions are the Mansions of Exemplary Life characterized through divine grace a love for God that is so great that the soul has an aversion to both mortal and venial sin and a desire to do works of charitable service to man for the ultimate glory of God."

Andy Warhol shot an interesting set of films. He got different people to sit silently in front of the movie camera and remain silent. Many famous people agreed to these "screen-shots" as Warhol called them. People were often uncomfortable with just sitting there and felt the few minutes to be very long. In the short few minutes many found themselves getting in touch with their own inner reality. Teresa is teaching us here to be in touch with our own inner reality, but to realise we are held by love.

Teresa reminds us that heaven is not a geographical body but a relational reality – a qualitative way of being that God's indwelling presence activates in us. As we go deeper into our inner being (the Interior Castle) love enlarges our hearts.

In the fourth mansion Teresa uses Ps 119:32: "I have run the way of your commandments for you have broadened by heart (understanding)". We develop here the capacity to love. Teresa tells us to do what "best stirs us to love" (IC IV,1:7).

Teresa shows us that no matter what our circumstances are we can bring a loving heart to bear in any circumstances. We begin to see new possibilities. She tells us: "Perhaps we do not know what love is… it doesn't consist in great delight but in desiring with strong determination to please God in everything…" (IC IV, 1:7). Teresa goes on to tell us about her own struggles. We do not arrive at pure love all at once but we always have the capacity to cultivate a loving disposition. The signs of love are our desire to reach out in compassion. As long as we do that we are already praying.

She tells us it is difficult to 'erase' the mind when we sit in contemplative prayer: "Ordinarily the mind flies about quickly; only God can hold it fast in such a way as to make it seem that we are somehow loosed from the body" (IC IV, 1:8). She goes on: "I have been very afflicted at times in the midst of this turmoil of mind… It was an arduous thing for me that [my intellect] should be so restless at times" (IC IV, 1:8). She had to practice kindness to herself, not to beat herself up over those distractions. This was a gentleness she learned from John of the Cross. We have to tolerate our on inadequacies as we enter this state. She tells us:

> "Any disquiet and war can be suffered if we find peace where we live, as I have already said. But that we want to rest from the thousand trials there are in the world and that God wants to prepare us for rest and that within ourselves lies the disturbance cannot be anything but painful and even unbearable. These miseries will not afflict or assail everyone as much as they did me for many years because I was so wretched. But since it was something so painful for me, I think perhaps that it will be for you, too. And so I say that it is an unavoidable thing and should not be a disturbance or affliction for you. We must let the mill-clapper keep clacking on, and must continue grinding our flour, not stopping our work with the will and the understanding."
>
> (IC IV, 1:12-13)

We prepare a place of attentive silence where we can meet God who dwells in the centre of our being, the heart of the Castle. We come to experience unconditional love which transforms us:

> "What an expansion or dilation of the soul is may be clearly understood from the example of a fount whose water doesn't overflow into a stream because the fount itself is constructed of such material that the more water there is flowing into it the larger the trough becomes. So it seems is the case with this prayer and many other marvels that God grants to the soul, for He enables and prepares it so that it can keep everything within itself. Hence this interior sweetness and expansion can be verified in the fact that the soul is not as tied down as it was before in things pertaining to the service of God, but has much more freedom."
>
> (IC IV, 3:9)

Here we try to deal with the rambling of the intellect and enjoy this recollection: "almost everything lies in finding oneself unworthy of so great a gift and in being occupied with giving thanks" (IC IV, 3:8).

In the fifth dwelling place we begin to know God's love for us. Here the soul "comes to understand that God cherishes it particularly and has chosen it for union, in the same deliberate way that spouses choose and dedicate themselves to each other" (IC V, 1:2). We see we are precious in God's sight, we are honoured and he loves us (see Is 43:4). We are unique in God's eyes and we are, each in their own way, his beloved.

Henri Nouwen gives his reflection on being "chosen":

> "It is very hard for me to express well the depth of meaning the word "chosen" has for me, but I hope you are willing to listen to me from within. From all eternity, long before you were born and became a part of history, you existed in God's heart. Long before your parents admired you or your friends acknowledged your gifts or your teachers, colleagues, and employers encouraged you, you were already "chosen". The

eyes of love had seen you as precious, as of infinite beauty, as of eternal value. When love chooses, it chooses with a perfect sensitivity for the unique beauty of the chosen one, and it chooses without making anyone feel excluded."[3]

Teresa tells us we become absorbed "into the immediate presence of God". The soul is being transformed and empowered by the love it feels. The centre of the soul is where the exchanges of love between God and the soul take place. We become aware of God who lives in the heart of our being.

"Well see here, daughters, what we can do through the help of God: His Majesty Himself, as he does in this prayer of union, becomes the dwelling place we build for ourselves. It seems I'm saying that we can build up God and take Him away since I say that he is the dwelling place and we ourselves can build it so as to place ourselves in it. And, indeed, we can! Not that we can take God away or build Him up, but we can take away from ourselves and build up, as do these little silkworms. For we will not have finished doing all that we can in this work when, to the little we do, which is nothing, God will unite Himself, with His greatness, and give it such high value that the Lord Himself will become the reward of this work."

(IC V, 2:5)

The union in this dwelling place is "above all earthly joys, above all delights, above all consolations and still more than that". This union is felt "in the marrow of the bones" (IC V, 1:5). The relational identity into which the soul was invited in the fourth dwelling place is now being forged within the soul's own depths, bringing about a radical transformation of the soul. Temporarily suspended from all normal external and internal activity while it is in this state of union, the soul is absorbed into the immediate presence of God. The peace and love the soul experiences here leaves the soul in no doubt "that it was in God and God was in it (IC V, 1:8).

[3] Henri Nouwen, Life of The Beloved (New York: 1992), p. 53f.

Teresa uses two metaphors to describe this union and transformation. Firstly she uses the scriptural metaphor of the wine cellar of the Song of Songs, 2:4, which we cannot enter ourselves but God places us there (IC V, 1:11). Secondly this dwelling place is like the cocoon providing the safe space for the metamorphosis of the caterpillar. The cocoon is understood to be the "house of Christ" into which the soul comes to dwell. Teresa writes: "Once the silkworm is grown... it begins to spin the silk and build the house wherein it will die. I would like to point out that the house is Christ. Somewhere, it seems to be, I have read or heard that our life is hidden in Christ or in God (both are the same), or that our life is Christ". (IC 2:4 CF COL 3:3F). In Christ we become a new creation.

Teresa says in the Way of Perfection:

> "Turning to those who want to engage this journey and not stop until the end, which is to drink of this water of life, and how they must begin, I say that it is very important, in fact all-important – that they have a great and very determined determination not to stop until they arrive at the end, no matter who comes their way, whatever happens, whatever trials they must pass through, whoever murmurs against them, whoever arrives there, whoever dies on the road or does not have the heart for the trials that there are on it, even if the world drowns – as they so often say to us: "There are dangers there," "So-and-so lost her way here," "That one was deceived," "That one, even though she prayed a lot, got tripped up," "They lose their virtue," "It's not for women, since they can become delusional," "Better that they stick to their spinning," "Such complicated things are not necessary," or "Praying the Our Father and the Hail Mary is quite enough."
>
> (Way of Perfection, 21:2)

Teresa knows there are pitfalls on the way, but she has been there and that is why she is able to give courage to those who follow. She shows us this life of love is possible for us. 'The Century of the Self' was a

2002 British Television documentary by filmmaker Adam Curtis. He focuses on the work of psychoanalysts Sigmund Freud and Anne Freud and PR consultant Edward Bernays. One of the insights he had was that in the '60's people thought they could change the world. Many were disappointed as governments clamped down on protest movements, including using violence. In the '70's a new movement began focussing on the self: I can't change society but I can change myself. This is more true of the world I live in. In Latin America, for example, there are many who are engaged in trying to change the society in which they live. I believe a new ethic is needed that embraces both change of self, becoming who I am and from this a change in society. I found this in the writings of Georges Bernanos:

> "Whoever pretends to reform the Church with… the same means used to reform temporal society: not only will he fail in his undertaking, but he will infallibly end by finding himself outside the Church. I say that he finds himself outside the Church before anyone has gone to the trouble of excluding him from her. I say that it is he himself who excludes himself from her by a kind of tragic fatalism…. The only way of reforming the Church is to suffer for her. The only way of reforming the visible Church is to suffer for the invisible Church. The only way of reforming the vices of the Church is to lavish on her the example of one's own most heroic virtues. It's quite possible that Saint Francis of Assisi was not any less thrown into revolt than Luther by the debauchery and simony of prelates. We can even be sure that his suffering on this account was fiercer, because his nature was very different from that of the monk of Wittenberg. But Francis did not challenge iniquity; he was not tempted to confront it; instead, he threw himself into poverty, immersing himself in it as deeply as possible along with his followers. He found in poverty the very source and wellspring of all absolution and all purity. Instead of attempting to snatch from the Church all her ill-gotten goods, he overwhelmed her with invisible treasures, and under the hand of this beggar the heaps of gold and lust

began blossoming like an April hedge. Ah, yes: I'm well aware that in these matters comparisons aren't worth much, especially when seasoned with a little humor. Would you still allow me to say, however, in order to be better understood by some readers, that what the Church needs is not critics but artists?..., When poetry is in full crisis, the important thing is not to point the finger at bad poets but oneself to write beautiful poems, thus unstopping the sacred springs."

(Esprit, October 1951, p. 439f)

Saint Seraphim of Sarov said that when one soul attains peace thousands are saved. Teresa, John and Francis point out to us the way of attaining peace and love.

The sixth dwelling place (mansion) Teresa teaches is the space of final preparation for the fruition of union with God. She shows us how we grow. We are being loved into new life. We begin to know God who loves us infinitely. Reading the mystics such as Teresa and John we sense God loves the soul as if that person were the only person in the world. God is above our categories and love is His nature. We are His beloved. We are invited into relationship building with the world God has created. Our transformation draws others into God's sphere of influence, into His love. This is accomplished moment by moment, not all at once. Teresa tells us this requires a determination of the will. Many reach the door of this mansion but fear holds them back. George Herbert wrote:

"Love bade me welcome: yet my soul drew back,
Guiltie of dust and sinne,
But quick-ey'd Love, observing me grow slack
From my first entrance in,
Drew nearer to me, sweetly questioning,
If I lack'd any thing.

A guest, I answer'd, worthy to be here:
Love said, You shall be he.

I the unkind, ungrateful? Ah my deare,
I cannot look on thee.
Love took my hand, and smiling did reply,
Who made the eyes but I?

Truth Lord, but I have marred them: let my shame
Go where it doth deserve.
And know you not, says Love, who bore the blame?
My deare, then I will serve.
You must sit down, says Love, and taste my meat:
So I did sit and eat."

The idea of a banquet (a "party") is an image of where we met God in the Bible. In the Song of Songs we read: "He brought me to the banqueting house" says the Beloved, "and his banner over me was love" (Song of Songs 2:4). "Love bade me welcome" shows it is God's initiative to call us. We draw back "guiltie of dust and sinne" but Love's welcome gently leads us to share in God's love. This relational identity has been taught to us by love personified in Jesus and by the power of the Holy Spirit this presence is mediated to us.

This is a journey that we must make as individuals because each of us is unique and each must find his or her way. In this mansion "the soul is determined to take no other spouse" (IC VI, 1:1).

Teresa tells us we should have total trust in God. She tells the soul "who has with such willingness offered everything to God" to understand it itself no longer has any part to play. The soul here must be "determined now to do no more than… abandon itself into the hands of the one who is all powerful, for it sees the safest thing to do is to make a virtue of necessity" (IC VI, 5:2). Here, too, Teresa introduces the metaphor of a soul tossed about in a tempest.

> "Here this great God, who holds back the springs of water and doesn't allow the sea to go beyond its boundaries, lets loose the springs from which the water in this trough flows. With a powerful impulse, a huge wave rises up so forcefully that it lifts high this little bark that is our soul. A bark cannot

prevent the furious waves from leaving it where they will; nor does the pilot have the power, nor do those who take part in controlling the little ship. So much less can the interior part of the soul stay where it will, or make its senses or faculties do other than what they are commanded; here the soul doesn't care what happens in the exterior senses."

(VI, 5:3)

It takes courage to abandon ourselves to the living God. "It is a fearful thing to fall into the hands of the living God" (Heb 10:31). It is a new world for us, fearful at first but like George Herbert, Love makes us welcome. As Teresa says: "great courage is necessary" (VI, 5:4).

The soul is being pulled out of itself into the reality of God where it experiences bliss, meaning and full absorption. It also means that the soul, in contrasting movements, re-enters the depths of its own reality. We can be discouraged by what we see of ourselves. In this state, too, the soul takes into itself human weakness and suffering. Our prayer is for those who suffer. The life of union is meant to enlarge our hearts to others. We can pray and help those who suffer. In the sixth mansion the soul is not simply growing in its consciousness of God's presence. It is also manifesting and bringing God's presence to bear in our lives and the lives of others.

Teresa had 'intellectual' visions of her encounters with God. Teresa doesn't argue for the existence of God. By her prayer, love and life, she witnesses to her experience of God's love. As Jesus says: "by their fruits you shall know them" (see Mtt 7:16-20).

> "These are the jewels the Spouse begins to give the betrothed, and their value is such that the soul will not want to lose them. For these meetings remain so engraved in the memory that I believe it's impossible to forget them until one enjoys them forever, unless they are forgotten through one's own most serious fault. But the Spouse who gives them has the power to give the grace not to lose them."
>
> (IC VI, 5:11)

It is all new for us. "See, I make all things new" (Isa 43:18f, Rev 21:5, Isa 65:17). The newness removes us from our comfort zone and invites us to a new life in God. All the time, however, we remain sinners and weak. The process of transformation lasts a life-time.

At the beginning of chapter 7 Teresa tells us the soul's joy at the experience of freedom and deeper union only reinforces its understanding of the fragile state of humanity. For such a sensitive soul "sins are always... alive in the memory, and this is a heavy cross" (VI, 7:2). Bernard of Clairvaux once said "the soul loves itself for God's sake". God understands of what we are made and he looks for signs of love from us. Teresa tells us not to look at ourselves but to Christ and his embodied life. "To be always withdrawn from corporeal things and enkindled in love is the trait of angelic spirits, not of those who live in mortal bodies" (VI, 7:6). She goes on to say:

> "It's necessary that we speak to, think about, and become the companions of those who having had a mortal body accomplished such great feats for God. How much more is it necessary not to withdraw through one's own efforts from all our good and help which is the most sacred humanity of our Lord Jesus Christ."

We are human beings, not angels. We have to accept ourselves as we are and have the courage to accept acceptance, the acceptance and love of God for us.

As we persist in prayer in this mansion Teresa describes how the soul "will feel Jesus Christ, our Lord, beside it. Yet it doesn't see Him, neither with the eyes of the body nor those of the soul. This is called an intellectual vision, I don't know why" (VI, 8:2). She says "this vision imparts a special knowledge of God to the soul". She says she feared this once but she found reassurance.

> And although some persons put many fears in her, she was still frequently unable to doubt, especially when the Lord said to her: "Do not be afraid, it is I." These words had so

much power that from then on she could not doubt the vision, and she was left very much strengthened and happy over such good company. She saw clearly that the vision was a great help toward walking with a habitual remembrance of God and a deep concern about avoiding anything displeasing to Him, for it seemed to her that He was always looking at her.

(VI, 8:3)

And when we abandon ourselves into God's hands and allow him to work, Teresa tells us:

"This continual companionship gives rise to a most tender love for His Majesty, to some desires even greater than those mentioned to surrender oneself totally to His service, and to a great purity of conscience because the presence at its side makes the soul pay attention to everything. For even though we already know that God is present in all we do, our nature is such that we neglect to think of this. Here the truth cannot be forgotten, for the Lord awakens the soul to His presence beside it."

(VI, 8:4)

The Holy Spirit is the bond of love between the Father and the Son. He is working in this process and he unites us to the Father and the Son. Jesus told his disciples: ..."The Advocate, the Holy Spirit, whom the Father will send in my name, will teach you all things" (Jn 14:26). We learn by participating in the life of God. Teresa knew she was in the Spirit because of the peace, calm, improvement in the soul and love that came to grow in the soul (see VI, 5:10). She has come to know herself "in Christ".

Teresa understood human nature. We can be fearful and hold ourselves back. Alexander Lowen talks about our fear of change:

"Why do people keep repeating the same self-destructive behavior? To answer [this] question, I would compare the

141

character…to a shell. To step out of character is like being born or, more accurately, reborn. For a conscious individual this is a very frightening and seemingly dangerous move to make. The cracking of the shell is equivalent to a confrontation with death. Living in the shell seems to guarantee survival, even if it represents a severe limitation on one's life. To stay in the shell and suffer seems safer than to risk death for freedom and joy. This is not a consciously though out position."

(Alexander Lowen, The Voice of the Body
[Harrisburg:1958])

Teresa emphasises that we still are sinners. Carl Jung speaks of the 'shadow', that part of us that we do not like and repress. Both remind us we are not angels. We have to live with our imperfections (our 'shadow'). Jung warns us not to ignore the 'shadow':

"By not being aware of having a shadow, you declare a part of your personality to be non-existent. Then it enters the kingdom of the non-existent, which swells up and takes on enormous proportions… If you get rid of qualities you don't like by denying them, you become more and more unaware of what you are, you declare yourself more and more non-existent, and your devils will grow fatter and fatter."

(Carl Jung, Dream Analysis:
Notes of the Seminar Given in 1928-1930)

We have to recognise that we possess a 'shadow', the dark side of our personality, if only for the reason that we can be overwhelmed by it (Erich Neumann). In the prayer of union we become even more aware of the 'shadow', our sinfulness. Thérèse of Lisieux tells us that true sanctity consists in bearing patiently with our weaknesses and imperfections. We learn this patience and gentleness with ourselves in our union with Jesus. It is part of our growth as human beings. The seventh dwelling place speaks of the consummation of the union between God and the soul. This union consists of a participation in the Trinity. Christ has become a bridge for us to enter into the divine life.

This is achieved by the Holy Spirit. The soul shares in the divine energy that is there "whenever it takes notice" (VII, 1:9 and VII, 2:4). God sustains the soul here.

God is no longer experienced through the partial moments that characterize the sixth dwelling place. God is always present in the soul. Teresa refers to 1 Cor 6:17 where God and the soul become "one". St. Paul says: "But whoever is united with the Lord is one with him in Spirit". Teresa tells us of this union:

> "And each day this soul is more amazed, for these persons never seem to leave it, but it clearly beholds that they are within it. In the extreme interior, in some place very deep within itself, the nature of which it doesn't know how to explain, because of a lack of learning, it perceives this divine company."
>
> (VII, 1:7)

This experience of the presence of God does not keep the soul from daily activities. Rather it turns to them with new energies (VII, 1:8). Teresa was very active in her reform and the opening of new convents.

She describes the union of our spirit with Christ's and God using her favourite image of water:

> "Or it is like what we have when a little stream enters the sea, there is no means of separating the two.... Perhaps this is what Saint Paul means in saying The one who is joined or united to God becomes one spirit with God, and is referring to this sovereign marriage, presupposing that His Majesty has brought the soul to it through union.
>
> And [Paul] also says To me to live is Christ, and to die is to gain; and so it seems the soul here could say the same thing, because this is where the little butterfly that we spoke of before dies, and with great joy, because its life now is Christ. "
>
> (IC VII: 2:4-5)

This state produces peace, gentleness, love (the fruits of the Holy Spirit, see Gal 5:22-23) and this speaks for their authenticity. Even in this state we have to continue to grow and learn. We are still time bound sinners. This prayer will be perfected when we meet God in the next life. This prayer is a foretaste of Heaven. Teresa is a realist. We should always have humility – the virtue of truth. We are fallible human beings. She tells us:

> "Do you think that your very great humility and mortification, your service of others and great charity toward them, and your love of God is of small benefit? This fire of love in you enkindles the souls of others, and with every other virtue you will be always awakening them. Such service will not be small but very great and very pleasing to the Lord."
>
> (IC VII: 4:14)

John of the Cross felt that when we entered this state of prayer people would relate to us and come for solace and help. His order did not agree with him. Yet there is truth in what he felt. It is love that attracts people and heals. Contemplation is not a private enterprise. The soul loving God and God loving the soul produces fruit for others. In this mansion all is light and this radiates to others. This is a form of ministry. In her conclusion she says:

> "Once you get used to enjoying this castle, you will find rest in all things, even those involving much labour, for you will have the hope of returning to the castle, which no one can take from you."
>
> (IC Epilogue: 2)

East Coker:

> "Burnt Norton might have remained by itself if it hadn't been for the war, because I had become very much absorbed in the problems of writing for the stage and might have

gone straight from The Family Reunion to another play. The war destroyed that interest for a time: you remember how the conditions of our lives changes, how much we were thrown on to ourselves in the early days? East Coker was the result – and it was only in writing East Coker that I began to see the Quartets as a set of four."[4]

Eliot, for a time, in the 1930's moved from poetry to the theatre. 'Murder in the Cathedral' was his first play which gave him success. His next play, 'The Family Reunion', closed after only five weeks on the West End. Then the war closed the theatres. He returned to poetry in 'East Coker'. This was where the Eliot family originally came from. In 1937 Eliot visited St. Michael's church in East Coker. His ashes are interred there today. It is situated in a lush countryside in Somerset, west of London and not far from Stonehenge.

Eliot thought that the highest goal of a mature spirituality should be grounded in an ever-developing interplay between the Old and the New World, combining the profoundest skepticism with the deepest faith. The goal of the spiritual life is not "arriving" or "achieving" but exploring and still "moving into another intensity / for a further union, a deeper communion" (East Coker, V). We saw this in Teresa. Eliot speaks of humility: "Humility is endless" (EC, II). Eliot began to conceive the idea of the 'Four Quartets' built around the Heraclitean elements: air, earth, water and fire. 'East Coker' was first published in the New English Weekly in 1940. Here a brooding darkness replaced the "heart of light" from 'Burnt Norton'. 'East Coker' reflects the reality of England at war and he recalls his own ancestors. We are led in the poem through the opening meditative landscape of the first movement (The Open Field) to the temporary illumination of the second movement (Wisdom of Humility) from which we enter into the spiritual discipline of the third movement (Be Still), then the purgative lyric of the fourth movement (the Wounded Surgeon), finally arriving at the unitive vision of the fifth movement (Union and Communion).

---

[4] T. S. Eliot interviewed by John Lehmann, *New York Times Book Review* (November 29, 1953), p. 5.

In the first part of East Coker we are led from a peaceful daytime vision to a new midnight world:

> "In that open field
> If you do not come too close, if you do not come too close,
> On a summer midnight, you can hear the music
> Of the weak pipe and the little drum
> And see them dancing around the bonfire…"

He refers to the ghosts of the past. He was influenced by a work of Friedrich Gerstäcker called '*Germelshausen*'. This was a village placed under papal edict and was almost condemned to extinction, but once every hundred years it lives for the space of one day and then sinks under the earth. The 'lost village' is visited by a stranger from a completely different world.

Eliot was influenced, as we saw, by Dante. In the first section of East Coker he, like Dante in his Inferno, leads us to an implicit self-criticism, "a new and shocking valuation of all we have been". Eliot saw his work as being like music. As one listens to the music one is caught up in its beauty. It does not matter if you agree or not with the composer. It is the same with poetry. The listener does not have to believe like the poet. They can be caught up in the rhythms and rhymes as the poem is read.[5]

The poem begins:

> "In my beginning is my end. In succession
> Houses rise and fall, crumble, are extended,
> Are removed, destroyed, restored, or in their place
> Is an open field, or a factory, or a by-pass.
> Old stone to new building, old timber to new fires,
> Old fires to ashes, and ashes to the earth
> Which is already flesh, fur and faeces,
> Bone of man and beast, cornstalk and leaf.

---

[5] Eliot was influenced by Henri Bremond, Prayer and Poetry, translated by Algar Thorold (London: 1927).

Houses live and die: there is a time for building
And a time for living and for generation
And a time for the wind to break the loosened pane
And to shake the wainscot where the field-mouse trots
And to shake the tattered arras woven with a silent motto."

The first sentence is an inverse of Mary Stuart's motto, "En ma fin est mon commencement" (In my end is my beginning). The line carries the meaning that we are all called. We work towards a goal ("my end" – my telos). Hans Urs Von Balthasar speaks of Jesus coming to be the person he is called to be in his "mission" from God:

"Might not Jesus' consciousness of his mission have been that he had to abolish the world's estrangement from God in its entirety – that is, to its very end – or, in Pauline and Johannine terms, deal with the sin of the whole world? In that case, after his earthly mission, the decisive and (humanly speaking) immeasurable part was still to come...
.It cannot be denied that his earthly work, prayer and toil was the integral part of his entire task, that is, it cannot be said that the redeeming act was solely concentrated in the future, in the coming Cross....However, the awareness that his life is moving toward a "baptism", toward that "cup" he will have to drink (and which, when the hour comes, will prove humanly unbearable, stretching him beyond all limits, Mk 14:34, 36), means that his life cannot proceed along "wisdom" lines but must follow an "apocalyptic" rhythm. His life is running toward an akme that, as man, he will only be able to survive by surrendering control of his own actions and being determined totally by the Father's will (Lk 22:42 par)....If we can define the core of apocalyptic as the imminent expectation of God's final judgment of the old world, and therefore the change of aeon to a new world, we can say that this apocalyptic dimension – if Jesus lives within this horizon of expectation – is most definitely concentrated in him....[Yet] he cannot attain the goal and

end of his task by means of his human activity, but… must hand himself over to the Father for that purpose."

(Theodrama 3, p.110f)

His 'yes' to God's call is beyond all other calls.

In fact, what Von Balthasar develops is a notion of mission as constituting the person. He unfolds an analogy based on the maturation of an individual conscious subject who comes to know who she or he is precisely through interaction with others, and through the acceptance and fulfillment of commitments, goals, and acts of love. Ultimately, Von Balthasar argues, this constitution of the conscious subject as a fulfilled person, secure in her or his own identity, can only be accomplished by interaction with God.

> "It is when God addresses a conscious subject, tells him who he is and what he means to the eternal God of truth and shows him the purpose of his existence – that is, imparts a distinctive and divinely authorized mission – that we can say of a conscious subject that he is a "person". This is what happened, archetypically, in the case of Jesus Christ, when he was given his eternal "definition" – "You are my beloved Son." "

(Theodrama 3, p. 207)

We are called "in Jesus". We blossom as human beings by being known, loved and given a purpose. We see this in Jesus himself. His full humanity came to be actualised, personalised, by living out his mission in response to the Father's love by the power of the Holy Spirit. God's "idea" for each individual is…

> "unique and personal, embodying for each his appropriate sanctity…. The fulfillment of God's will does not mean carrying out an anonymous universal law which is the same for all; nor does it mean the slavish imitation of some fixed blueprint…. On the contrary it means freely realising God's loving plan, which presupposes freedom, and is, moreover,

the very source of freedom. No one is so much himself as the saint, who disposes himself to God's plan, for which he is prepared to surrender his whole being, body, should, and spirit."

(Thérèse of Lisieux, p. xii-xiii)

Jesus was fully human. Von Balthasar knew him as the 'Word' (Logos) made flesh and all creation was caught up in him:

> "...the relationship between the divine Person of the Logos and the totality of human nature; since he seems not to be an individual in our limited sense, he must somehow have adopted human nature as a whole. If this is so, it becomes credible that his work of atonement has affected the whole of human nature."

(Theodrama 3, p. 203)

Paul speaks of the mystical body in which each is given a gift ("charism") for the good of all:

> "Just as a body, though one, has many parts, but all its many parts form one body, so it is with Christ. For we were all baptized by one Spirit so as to form one body—whether Jews or Gentiles, slave or free—and we were all given the one Spirit to drink. Even so the body is not made up of one part but of many.
>
> Now if the foot should say, "Because I am not a hand, I do not belong to the body," it would not for that reason stop being part of the body. And if the ear should say, "Because I am not an eye, I do not belong to the body," it would not for that reason stop being part of the body. If the whole body were an eye, where would the sense of hearing be? If the whole body were an ear, where would the sense of smell be? But in fact God has placed the parts in the body, every one of them, just as he wanted them to be. If they were all one part, where would the body be? As it is, there are many parts, but one body."

(1 Cor 12:12-20)

We are all precious in the eyes of God. The Holy Spirit is active also in the hearts of those who do not know God. He is not confined.

Our existence can become prayer. Jesus' existence was an "existence as prayer". Francis of Assisi surrendered completely to God. Thomas of Celano (+1260) wrote this remark: Francis was "not so much praying as becoming totally prayer" (Francis of Assisi: Early Documents, p. 310).

We all have a unique dignity in God. This is not always recognised. We are given different messages from our culture, our environment. The world can be cruel and abusive. We still seek to find out where we belong. In the passage from East Coker above we have a reference to the Book of Ecclesiastes:

> "There is a time for everything,
> and a season for every activity under the heavens:
> a time to be born and a time to die,
> a time to plant and a time to uproot,
> a time to kill and a time to heal,
> a time to tear down and a time to build,
> a time to weep and a time to laugh,
> a time to mourn and a time to dance,
> a time to scatter stones and a time to gather them,
> a time to embrace and a time to refrain from embracing,
> a time to search and a time to give up,
> a time to keep and a time to throw away,
> a time to tear and a time to mend,
> a time to be silent and a time to speak,
> a time to love and a time to hate,
> a time for war and a time for peace."
> (Eccl 3: 1-8)

Qohelet's tragedy was he could not find his 'time'. Perhaps this was his 'mission', to give voice to those who thought life was useless ('hebel') and could not find their place. In the end he calls us to remember our creator in the midst of this:

"Remember your Creator
in the days of your youth,
before the days of trouble come
and the years approach when you will say,
"I find no pleasure in them"—
before the sun and the light
and the moon and the stars grow dark,
and the clouds return after the rain;
when the keepers of the house tremble,
and the strong men stoop,
when the grinders cease because they are few,
and those looking through the windows grow dim;
when the doors to the street are closed
and the sound of grinding fades;
when people rise up at the sound of birds,
but all their songs grow faint;
when people are afraid of heights
and of dangers in the streets;
when the almond tree blossoms
and the grasshopper drags itself along
and desire no longer is stirred.
Then people go to their eternal home
and mourners go about the streets."

(Ecclesiastes 12:1-5)

Eliot sought 'solitude' to find himself and in this poem leads others in their own ways. In quoting from Ecclesiastes Eliot sought a divine context for human experience and aligns his meditations with the Bible. He once said that Ecclesiastes is "as near to human literature or poetry as anything in the Bible."[6] Eliot could see the limitations of our human perspective and this formed part of his discipline of humility. The human and divine perspectives play against each other.

"In my beginning is my end. Now the light falls
Across the open field, leaving the deep lane

---

[6] He made this remark in an "Unpublished Address" to the Women's Alliance at Kings Chapel Boston, Dec 1, 1932. A copy of this manuscript exists at the Houghton Library of Harvard.

Shuttered with branches, dark in the afternoon,
Where you lean against a bank while a van passes,
And the deep lane insists on the direction
Into the village, in the electric heat
Hypnotised. In a warm haze the sultry light
Is absorbed, not refracted, by grey stone.
The dahlias sleep in the empty silence.
Wait for the early owl."

Here he speaks to us. He asks us to imagine standing on one side of a narrow road in the shadows of a fragrant afternoon, along with breathing in a silence that takes no note of itself. The imagery of "the deep lane", the dark afternoon, the "empty silence" and "the early owl" suggest a transition from light to the absence of light. As the "empty alley" of Burnt Norton here on a summer midnight in an open field the poet comes upon a marriage dance.

"In that open field
If you do not come too close, if you do not come too close,
On a summer midnight, you can hear the music
Of the weak pipe and the little drum
And see them dancing around the bonfire
The association of man and woman
In daunsinge, signifying matrimonie —
A dignified and commodiois sacrament.
Two and two, necessarye coniunction,
Holding eche other by the hand or the arm
Whiche betokeneth concorde. Round and round the fire
Leaping through the flames, or joined in circles,
Rustically solemn or in rustic laughter
Lifting heavy feet in clumsy shoes,
Earth feet, loam feet, lifted in country mirth
Mirth of those long since under earth
Nourishing the corn. Keeping time,
Keeping the rhythm in their dancing
As in their living in the living seasons"

The archaic language used by Eliot helps connect us with the ages past, his own ancestors. His ancestor Sir Thomas Elyot strongly associated marriage with dance. The dance at the still point becomes a grace manifesting sign of God's presence. The sacramental dance that Eliot imagines will be transfigured later in the poem. In the traditions Eliot shows us here the sacramental life is lived by a person who wholly, naturally gives of herself or himself to the service of the moment. Sacramental means God is present in that moment. He is present when the relationship between persons and ritual form is openly, honestly chosen by each partner who surrenders to it. It involves mutual self-giving. Each moment forms part of our 'mission' in becoming who we are.

The previous idyllic version of the summer wedding dance, the symbol of harmony, gives way to images of confusion disrupting the order of the seasons. The second movement of East Coker begins with short, sharp statements:

> "What is the late November doing
> With the disturbance of the spring
> And creatures of the summer heat,
> And snowdrops writhing under feet
> And hollyhocks that aim too high
> Red into grey and tumble down
> Late roses filled with early snow?
> Thunder rolled by the rolling stars
> Simulates triumphal cars
> Deployed in constellated wars
> Scorpion fights against the Sun
> Until the Sun and Moon go down
> Comets weep and Leonids fly
> Hunt the heavens and the plains
> Whirled in a vortex that shall bring
> The world to that destructive fire
> Which burns before the ice-cap reigns."

Apocalyptic images of disharmony swirl around: "Until the Sun and Moon go down" and "Comets weep and Leonids fly". The serene vision has been eclipsed by "that destructive fire / Which burns before the ice-cap reigns". Eliot goes on to speak of his dissatisfaction with his own poetry:

> "That was a way of putting it—not very satisfactory:
> A periphrastic study in a worn-out poetical fashion,
> Leaving one still with the intolerable wrestle
> With words and meanings. The poetry does not matter.
> It was not (to start again) what one had expected."

The poet reflects "the intolerable wrestle / With words and meanings", words that both strive and fail to adequately articulate the power of the singular Word. The divine mystery cannot be caught by our words. Behind the words lies the tremendous mystery of God. No matter how breathtaking a statement may be it cannot come close to the reality of God's relational presence.

East Coker unfolds in the shadow of darkness: the darkness of the sky over the field; the darkness of late November; the darkness his ancestors had peered into; and the spiritual darkness into which the poet enters. The Leonids mentioned are showers of meteors occurring in November. The poet wonders:

> "What was to be the value of the long looked forward to,
> Long hoped for calm, the autumnal serenity
> And the wisdom of age?

Eliot wonders were his forebears wrong to assert that through diligent practice and patience comes wisdom.

> "Had they deceived us
> Or deceived themselves"

We must seek wisdom in our own time. So much of what we called wisdom is not wisdom.

"For the pattern is new in every moment
And every moment is a new and shocking
Valuation of all we have been. We are only undeceived
Of that which, deceiving, could no longer harm.
In the middle, not only in the middle of the way
But all the way, in a dark wood, in a bramble,
On the edge of a grimpen, where is no secure foothold,
And menaced by monsters, fancy lights,
Risking enchantment."

The poet has been shaken loose from old habits of mind by the uniqueness of the moment he finds himself in. He tells us "the pattern is new in every moment". He reflects on his situation. He is like Dante who begins his quest...

"In the middle of the journey of our life
I come to myself in a dark wood
Where the straight [or right] way was lost."
                              (Dante, Inferno, canto 1)

Here Dante, at the midpoint of his life, having strayed, finds himself in a dark wood, lost and also confronted by terrifying animals. 'Grimpen' was not a word in its own right. It was the place-name of a village and parish in Arthur Conan Doyle's book 'The Hound of the Baskervilles'.

Eliot sees the darkness that lies in the human heart. True wisdom is seen as humility. The way to true wisdom is through humility. A dictionary definition of humility accentuates humility as a low self-regard and sense of unworthiness. In a religious context humility means a recognition of self in relation to God. It means not having pride or haughtiness nor indulging in self-deprecation. The term 'humility' is derived from the Latin word 'humus' meaning ground. Humility means being grounded in truth. Eliot tells us:

"Do not let me hear
Of the wisdom of old men, but rather of their folly,
Their fear of fear and frenzy, their fear of possession,

> Of belonging to another, or to others, or to God.
> The only wisdom we can hope to acquire
> Is the wisdom of humility: humility is endless.
>
> The houses are all gone under the sea.
>
> The dancers are all gone under the hill."

Eliot felt, with good reason, that the law of progress had proved illusory at the start of the Second World War. Eliot directed us to 'humility', not boasting about human wisdom. True humility means for Eliot choosing to surrender oneself into ever-deepening relationships with the unique particulars of one's current situation. We have to be true to ourselves and in truth open ourselves to the Divine. We need strength in dark times – not from ourselves or of other generations but from God. The pattern of life is in constant flux and every moment comes a new and shocking revelation. The only wisdom is "humility". Practising humility in this context of powerlessness opens a person to the liberating possibilities of grace.

The third movement is prepared for by the closing lines of the second movement – "The houses are all gone under the sea / The dancers are all gone under the hill." These lines introduce the threatening spectre of mortality. Here he echoes Milton's 'Samson Agonistes'. In the Old Testament Samson the warrior is blinded and in Milton's work he complains about the darkness in which he now lives.

> "O dark, dark, dark, amid the blaze of noon....
> The sun to me is dark
> And silent as the moon,
> When she deserts the night,
> Hid in her vacant interlunar cave."

Of course in this Eliot verse, the 'dark' is not blindness but death. The vacant interstellar spaces are a compelling reminder of Pascal's 'le silence éternel de ces espaces infini m'effraie' – the eternal silence of those infinite spaces frightens me (Pensée, 91).

Eliot begins movement three as follows:

> "O dark dark dark. They all go into the dark,
> The vacant interstellar spaces, the vacant into the vacant,
> The captains, merchant bankers, eminent men of letters,
> The generous patrons of art, the statesmen and the rulers,
> Distinguished civil servants, chairmen of many committees,
> Industrial lords and petty contractors, all go into the dark,
> And dark the Sun and Moon, and the Almanach de Gotha
> And the Stock Exchange Gazette, the Directory of Directors,
> And cold the sense and lost the motive of action.
> And we all go with them, into the silent funeral,
> Nobody's funeral, for there is no one to bury."

All of us, the poet and all the people mentioned are included in the silent funeral's inevitable presence. In the 1930's Eliot had become suspicious of fame especially in the face of death's inevitability and he includes himself among the "eminent men of letters" in the catalogue of those who are mortal. The Almanach de Gotha is the register of European royalty and nobility. All will die. The temporal world is darkness. Eliot is also referring to John of the Cross's 'Dark Night of the Soul'. In the darkness of apparent abandonment the Spirit is working to bring forth new life. Eliot says:

> "I said to my soul, be still, and let the dark come upon you
> Which shall be the darkness of God. As, in a theatre,
> The lights are extinguished, for the scene to be changed
> With a hollow rumble of wings, with a movement of darkness on darkness,
> And we know that the hills and the trees, the distant panorama
> And the bold imposing facade are all being rolled away—
> Or as, when an underground train, in the tube, stops too long between stations
> And the conversation rises and slowly fades into silence
> And you see behind every face the mental emptiness deepen

Leaving only the growing terror of nothing to think about;
Or when, under ether, the mind is conscious but conscious
of nothing—
I said to my soul, be still, and wait without hope
For hope would be hope for the wrong thing; wait without
love,
For love would be love of the wrong thing; there is yet faith
But the faith and the love and the hope are all in the waiting.
Wait without thought, for you are not ready for thought:
So the darkness shall be the light, and the stillness the
dancing.
Whisper of running streams, and winter lightning.
The wild thyme unseen and the wild strawberry,
The laughter in the garden, echoed ecstasy
Not lost, but requiring, pointing to the agony
Of death and birth."

Eliot said in a letter he wrote to his friend Paul Elmer More: "I know a little what is the feeling of being alone – I will not say with God but alone in the presence and under the observation of God – with the feeling of being stripped, as of frippery, of the qualifications that ordinarily most identify one: one's heredity, one's abilities, and one's name." (Jan 11, 1937, in Princeton University Library). The Darkness here is like the movement of darkness upon darkness when theatre lights are extinguished; it is the mental darkness that lies behind the emptiness of those in the Tube when conversation stops. It is like when one is under an anesthetic when the "mind is conscious of nothing". It is the 'Night' of John of the Cross. In 'The Ascent of Mount Carmel' (I, ii, 1) we read:

> "We can offer three reasons for calling this journey toward union with God a night. The first has to do with the point of departure, because the individual must deprive himself of his appetite for worldly possessions. This denial and privation is like a night for all the senses.
> The second reason refers to the means or the road along which a person travels to this union. Now this road is faith, and for the intellect faith is also like a dark night.

The third reason pertains to the point of arrival, namely God. And God is also a dark night to man in this life. These three nights pass through the soul, or better, the soul passes through them in order to reach divine union with God."

John's life at one stage, as we saw, was undermined suddenly. Life seemed hopeless. Circumstances conspired to break up the whole. Eliot and his generation found themselves in this darkness. It was in the darkness that John met God.

"En una noche oscura
So dark the night! At rest and hushed my house,
I went with no one knowing upon a lover's quest
– Ah the sheer grace! – so blest,
my eager heart with love aflame and glowing.

In darkness, hid from sight
I went by secret ladder safe and sure
– Ah grace of sheer delight! –
so softly veiled by night,
hushed now my house,
in darkness and secure.

Hidden in that glad night,
regarding nothing as I stole away,
no one to see my flight,
no other guide or light
save one that in my heart
burned bright as day.

Surer than noonday sun,
guiding me from the start this radiant light
led me to that dear One
waiting for me, well-known..."

Even in the darkness there is a blessedness. God is there even if for a time he seems to be silent. In John's darkness he felt a "hidden, peaceful, loving inflow of God". He says: "If it is given room, it will inflame the spirit with love" (1 Night 10:6). In the Night his love is felt as pain but the dawn does come. The Night, the Darkness, takes us to the heart of the world's suffering. It declares the world's wounds to be spaces through which God may enter. John offers a spirituality which embraces those who cannot go on. The disempowered, the inarticulate, the broken are a focus of God's action on the world. John shows us the Gospel Jesus welcoming the broken and desolated. Eliot echoes these themes when he tells us: "Be still". He tells us to travel 'without hope'. He did not mean 'no hope' but all is now abandoned into God's hands. What He wills is our hope.The darkness of the present moment is still an opportunity for God to illumine the soul. It is through stillness, not holding on to old ideas of love, that light comes in. Eliot concludes this movement:

> "You say I am repeating
> Something I have said before. I shall say it again.
> Shall I say it again? In order to arrive there,
> To arrive where you are, to get from where you are not,
>   You must go by a way wherein there is no ecstasy.
> In order to arrive at what you do not know
>   You must go by a way which is the way of ignorance.
> In order to possess what you do not possess
>   You must go by the way of dispossession.
> In order to arrive at what you are not
>   You must go through the way in which you are not.
> And what you do not know is the only thing you know
> And what you own is what you do not own
> And where you are is where you are not."

Here Eliot echoes John of the Cross:

> "With such vigilance you will gain a great deal in a short time.
> Many blessings flow when the four natural passions (joy, hope, fear and sorrow) are in harmony and at peace. The following maxims contain a complete method for

mortifying and pacifying them. If put into practice these maxims will give rise to abundant merit and great virtues. Endeavour to be inclined always:

not to the easiest, but to the most difficult;

not to the most delightful, but to the most distasteful;

not to the most gratifying, but to the less pleasant;

not to what means rest for you, but to hard work;

not to the consoling, but to the unconsoling;

not to the most, but to the least;

not to the highest and most precious, but to the lowest and most despised;

not to wanting something, but to wanting nothing.

Do not go about looking for the best of temporal things, but for the worst, and, for Christ, desire to enter into complete nakedness, emptiness, and poverty in everything in the world."

(Ascent of Mount Carmel, Book 1, 13:5-6)

This is the discipline we need in the Darkness in which we find ourselves.

In the fourth movement Eliot introduces the 'wounded surgeon':

"The wounded surgeon plies the steel
That questions the distempered part;
Beneath the bleeding hands we feel
The sharp compassion of the healer's art
Resolving the enigma of the fever chart."

The idea of the wounded healer is found in Jung. He said we had to be in touch with our own brokenness and 'shadow' in dealing with others. Accepting ourselves helps us accept others. Our brokenness teaches us. Henri Nouwen told a story to illustrate the idea of Wounded Healer:

A Rabbi who came across the prophet Elijah said to him:
"Tell me – when will the Messiah come?"
Elijah replied, "Go and ask him yourself."

161

"Where is he?" said the Rabbi.

"He's sitting at the gates of the city," said Elijah.

"But how will I know which one he is?"

"He is sitting among the poor, covered with wounds. The others unbind all their wounds at the same time and bind them up again, but he unbinds only one at a time and binds them up again, saying to himself, "Perhaps I shall be needed; if so, I must always be ready so as not to delay for a moment."

Nouwen adds, "What I find impressive in this story are these two things: first, the faithful tending of one's own woundedness and second, the willingness to move to the aid of other people and to make the fruits of our own woundedness available to others."

What this story also might illustrate is the idea that to become 'The wounded healer' there is a level of sacrifice that may need to take place. In order to fully embrace becoming a healer you must give over a part of yourself to the people that need your help.

Nietzsche recognised the transformative potential of negative experiences, and while you may not go as far as he did, to wish suffering upon those closest to you, it can be a consoling thought that hurtful experiences could be the very things that lead us to a more enlightened view of the world and a stronger version of ourselves.

(Henri Nouwen, The Wounded Healer [London:2014])

In Greek mythology, the centaur Chiron was a wounded healer after being poisoned by one of Hercules' arrows. We are all wounded. For Jung "a good half of every treatment that probes at all deeply consists in the doctor's examining himself... it is his own hurt that gives a measure of his power to heal. This, and nothing else, is the meaning of the Greek myth of the wounded physician."[7]

---

[7] quoted in Anthony Stevens, Jung (Oxford: 1994), p. 110.

Akira Kurosawa's film "Drunken Angel" centers upon the efforts of Doctor Sanada, himself an alcoholic, to sustain a young gangster against tuberculosis counseling him to abandon his self-destructive lifestyle. The character Dr. House, in the television series House, has physical and emotional scars. They are both a burden and a driving force in his need to fix the problems of others.

Jesus is the ultimate wounded healer. He suffered loneliness, death and rejection. He is the one Eliot refers to. He knows us and our wounds. In the Mass and other sacraments we can meet this Jesus and allow him heal us: "the wounded surgeon plies the steel / That questions the distempered part." The celebration of the Eucharist displays the full mystery of Jesus – his life, teaching, suffering, death and resurrection. Eucharist embodies the incarnate Logos. It is here the poet comes for sustenance. He says:

> "The dripping blood our only drink,
> The bloody flesh our only food:
> In spite of which we like to think
> That we are sound, substantial flesh and blood—
> Again, in spite of that, we call this Friday good."

The Eucharist makes present the healing benefits of Jesus' life, death and resurrection. That is why "we call this Friday good."

It is not just individuals who need healing:

> "The whole earth is our hospital
> Endowed by the ruined millionaire,
> Wherein, if we do well, we shall
> Die of the absolute paternal care
> That will not leave us, but prevents us everywhere."

What starts with the individual must spread to the whole 'hospital', that is the world we live in.

The fifth movement brings all the different parts together. The multiple connections between "beginning" and "ending" deepen his discovery that the spiritual goal is not to be achieved by "arriving" but by ever renewed striving. We are always growing. The final movement of East Coker begins by recalling the poet's earlier paraphrase of Dante:

> "So here I am, in the middle way, having had twenty years —
> Twenty years largely wasted, the years of l'entre deux guerres
> Trying to use words, and every attempt
> Is a wholly new start, and a different kind of failure
> Because one has only learnt to get the better of words
> For the thing one no longer has to say, or the way in which
> One is no longer disposed to say it. And so each venture
> Is a new beginning, a raid on the inarticulate
> With shabby equipment always deteriorating
> In the general mess of imprecision of feeling,
> Undisciplined squads of emotion. And what there is to conquer
> By strength and submission, has already been discovered"

The poet underscores the darkness of the poem with the depression felt as the poet recalls wasted years. The middle way refers to his struggle with language. He had spent twenty years trying to overcome the "intolerable wrestle / with words and meanings". There is another possibility. In the Bhagavad Gita, the great war in which Krishna reveals himself to Arjuna as god takes place on two battlefields simultaneously: Kurukshetra, the literal place of the battle and dharma-kshetra, the field of dharma (the spiritual battleground). The two wars could refer to the outer war (World War II) and to the always-raging inner battle between acting and acting-without-acting (the Gita's teaching).[8] Many interpreters see Eliot as speaking of the two World Wars. Perhaps he meant both. Eliot saw his words as "a raid on the inarticulate / With

[8] Kenneth Paul Krame, Redeeming Time: T.S. Eliot's Four Quartets (Cambridge: 2007), p. 95ff.

shabby equipment". Eliot is aware that as soon as he speaks his words are altered in and by time passing.

Therefore he goes on:

> "There is only the fight to recover what has been lost
> And found and lost again and again: and now, under conditions
> That seem unpropitious. But perhaps neither gain nor loss.
> For us, there is only the trying. The rest is not our business."

He strives to remember encounters with the Logos. He remembers, then forgets. In this way he hopes to introduce grace into every moment. He hopes to become detached and humble. He comes to a growing realisation that...

> "Not the intense moment
> Isolated, with no before and after,
> But a lifetime burning in every moment..."

Love is more truly human when it is not dependent on how he may feel in this moment or at this place. Being loved and living in love do not depend on the here and now. Rather he knows he is loved and called by God and this love transforms every moment into one moment of eternity. The Eucharist is important in realizing this love.

The poem concludes:

> "Love is most nearly itself
> When here and now cease to matter.
> Old men ought to be explorers
> Here or there does not matter
> We must be still and still moving
> Into another intensity
> For a further union, a deeper communion
> Through the dark cold and the empty desolation,
> The wave cry, the wind cry, the vast waters
> Of the petrel and the porpoise. In my end is my beginning."

We are called to a 'deeper communion' – time becomes redeemable when it is immersed in the sacred. We must always explore and grow. There is no time when we achieve perfection – we remain as humans who struggle with our sinfulness, our 'shadow'. Every new day brings a new event, new questions. In stillness we meet God and that overflows into our living: "We must be still and still moving". We can gain inner strength in desolate times when "The wave cry, the wind cry, the vast waters / Of the petrel [Peter] and the porpoise [Christ]. The "vast waters" (which becomes in 'The Dry Salvages' the sea all around us) contain the 'petrel' and the 'porpoise'. The petrel is a small bird that flies so close to the water that it appears to be walking on water. Hence the name, 'Petrel', the little Peter. This directs the readers attention to the Christ.

The porpoise, according to sailors, often appears in the waters just before a storm at sea and is thus associated with Christ as the one who calms the storm.

Chapter 5

The Dry Salvages:

(The Dry Salvages—presumably les trois sauvages—is a small group of
rocks, with a beacon, off the N.E. coast of Cape Ann, Massachusetts.
Salvages is pronounced to rhyme with assuages.
Groaner: a whistling buoy.)

This explanation was placed by Eliot at the beginning of The Dry Salvages.
Eliot spent most of his summers in Massachusetts. He considered this his
spiritual home. Here Eliot looks back at his American roots for his poetry:
He loved to sail off the coast of Cape Ann where the Dry Salvages' rock
ledge was a seamark. Not only was the young Eliot steeped in the lore of
Cape Ann he became familiar with the encompassing ocean. The Dry
Salvages is re-discovery of youthful adventure and educational awakenings
in the New World. The last lines of East Coker – "The wave cry, the wind
cry, the vast waters / Of the petrel and the porpoise" – tie the two poems
together, making the two quartets a single continuous work.[1] The Dry
Salvages might be called Eliot's New World Quartet because he returns to
his American roots and he finds new meaning in them, a meaning which
goes back to the religious origins of New England. He now sees that the
world is new in every moment.[2] Eliot addressed the ongoing power of his
childhood experiences in a 1932 essay on "Wordsworth and Coleridge".

> "There might be the experience of a child of ten, a small boy
> and peering through sea-water in a rock-pool, and finding a
> sea-anemone for the first time: the simple experience (not so
> simple, for an exceptional child, as it looks) might be dormant
> in his mind for twenty years, and to re-appear transformed in
> some verse-context charged with great imaginative pleasure."[3]

---

[1] A. David Moody, Thomas Sterns Eliot: Poet (Cambridge: 1994), p. 222-34.

[2] op. cit., p. 14.

[3] T. S. Eliot, "Wordsworth and Coleridge" in The Use of Poets and the Use of Criticism
(London: 1933), p. 78f.

In his youth he remembered the great Mississippi river. Eliot once told an audience: "you will notice... that this poem begins where I began, with the Mississippi; and that it ends where I and my [second] wife expect to end, at the parish church of a tiny village in Somerset."[4] Vivienne died in 1947 and Eliot married again later in life. Eliot would not re-marry while Vivienne was still alive.

For Eliot the way up and the way down penetrate the Quartets. The 'way up' is his experience of the Divine, but in the next three Quartets the way down is among human beings, the lifeless faces he sees on the underground. Eliot's life among others is like the river. He bears the wounds of his past and yet seeks to live the life of faith among those he meets. He learned disinterestedness from the Indian scriptures, not to be concerned with the fruits of action: he forces forward as a flawed man; that is his reason for humility. The only hope is not to hope. What matters is that he surrender to the Divine and allow God to work through him and his flaws. The Blitz in London and the Second World War form the backdrop the last Quartets. He emphasises strength from within in the Quartets. He wrote the Quartets while he was a fire-warden during the Blitz. His aim was "to get beyond time and at the same time deeper into time". We must get in touch with the beyond in our mindset. Eliot thought of how Beethoven's last Quartet goes right through to the spirit of the listener. In this sense Eliot thought that Beethoven communicated beyond music. He tries to communicate here "beyond poetry".

The river, the Mississippi, that appears in the first part functions symbolically. The river flows with an accumulation of human experiences moving through time in an endless flux of successive moments replacing one another. The river also appears in Mark Twain's 'Huckleberry Finn'. It embodies both a powerful natural force and an innocent dignity.

The river observes human life from its place in nature. Those who live beside the river in the flux of time (builders of bridges, dwellers in cities, and worshippers of the machine) are reflected in the river's "waiting, watching and waiting". For Eliot it flows through "the nursery bedroom", through youth, adulthood and death, making the seasonal changes of "the April dooryard" and "the autumn table" and "the winter gaslight". Eliot speaks of his boyhood memories thus:

[4] T. S. Eliot, "The Influence of Landscape on the Poet", Daedalus, 89 no. 2 (Spring 1960), p. 422.

"I do not know much about gods; but I think that the river
Is a strong brown god—sullen, untamed and intractable,
Patient to some degree, at first recognised as a frontier;
Useful, untrustworthy, as a conveyor of commerce;
Then only a problem confronting the builder of bridges."

The impulse that dominates the first movement is that of two temporal images. The first is that of the ocean (prehistoric time) and that of the river (personal time) which runs to the ocean.

A balance exists between sea and river. There is an intersection between the two: the lifeblood of nature's cycles bound up in time and the boundless expanse of the sea's timelessness:

"The river is within us, the sea is all about us;
The sea is the land's edge also, the granite
Into which it reaches, the beaches where it tosses
Its hints of earlier and other creation:
The starfish, the horseshoe crab, the whale's backbone;
The pools where it offers to our curiosity
The more delicate algae and the sea anemone.
It tosses up our losses, the torn seine,
The shattered lobsterpot, the broken oar
And the gear of foreign dead men. The sea has many voices,
Many gods and many voices."

The line "The river is within us, the sea is all about us" is central to the Quartet. The river's flow "sullen, untamed and intractable" courses through it. This passage shifts the poem's focus to the primordial, all embracing sea. This is one of the most musical passages of the Quartets.

The sea resembles a nautical museum of death. The sea tosses up debris onto the beach for inspection, ints of earlier creation. The sea, on the other hand, reminds us of "ceaseless flux, an endless motion to no end, not the human time of chronometers, but the time of the ground swell or undulating movement caused by distant storms or earthquakes."[5]

[5] Nancy K. Gish, Time in the Poetry of T. S. Eliot: A Study in Structure and Theme (Totowa, NJ: 1981), p. 108.

As the ebb and flow of waves along "the land's edge" continues, the assonance (resemblance of sounds) and the dissonance (lack of harmony) of the sea's many voices move inland: "The salt is on the briar rose / The fog is in the fir trees". There is a rhythmic undertow in the verse not unlike the undertow in the ocean. The sea's primordial, unfathomable abyss interrupts the dwellers in chronological time. The different voices of the sea – the "sea howl" and the "sea yelp", the "whine in the rigging" and "the wailing warning from the approaching headland" – powerfully evolve the threatening menace of this vast body of water:

> "And under the oppression of the silent fog
> The tolling bell
> Measures time not our time, rung by the unhurried
> Ground swell, a time
> Older than the time of chronometers, older
> Than time counted by anxious worried women
> Lying awake, calculating the future,
> Trying to unweave, unwind, unravel
> And piece together the past and the future,
> Between midnight and dawn, when the past is all deception,
> The future futureless, before the morning watch
> When time stops and time is never ending;
> And the ground swell, that is and was from the beginning,
> Clangs
> The bell."

Human time emerges from primordial time. Anxious women lie awake at night worrying about their men out at sea. They struggle to make sense of past events in light of future possibilities. There is a difference between their anxious preoccupation of "counting" time and the unhurried bell's "measuring time". The bell's "clang" also produces momentary silence. Recalling the clanging bell of the fourth movement of Burnt Norton, the "tolling bell" later in the fourth movement will become the Angelus bell calling to mind the angel Gabriel's annunciation and the birth of Christ, through whom new life emerges from death.

In the opening sestina of the second movement the poet ponders three types of annunciation, which are associated with three senses of death. The human or physical death marks the first annunciation. The apparently meaningless pattern of death seems to end any real possibility for redemption. We are given the image of...

> "The silent withering of autumn flowers
> Dropping their petals and remaining motionless"

Here there is no possibility for prayer.

The second or "last annunciation" corresponds to the failing vital powers of psychological death. This is akin to drifting in a boat "with a slow leakage" that moves towards no fixed destination. This annunciation is accentuated by the driving ennui of mindless habits and failing pride. Those who suffer this are like fishermen lulled by the incessant rhythms of the sea – "failing", "sailing", "bailing". They descend into unknowing.

The poet then turns to the third annunciation that he calls the "one annunciation". This is the annunciation of spiritual death and rebirth. Here calamity and annunciation are set in juxtaposition:

> "There is no end of it, the voiceless wailing,
> No end to the withering of withered flowers,
> To the movement of pain that is painless and motionless,
> To the drift of the sea and the drifting wreckage,
> The bone's prayer to Death its God. Only the hardly, barely
>   prayable
> Prayer of the one Annunciation."

The "one annunciation" announces the coming of divine incarnation. Like the "one end" and the "still point" in the previous Quartets the "one Annunciation" points towards a uniquely redemptive event, offering hope through intercessory words addressed to the Virgin Mary. In the midst of "the drifting wreckage" of life the presence and the possibility of prayer distinguishes the one Annunciation (of the glorious death-rebirth in the spirit) from the others.

In the second section the poem's tone shifts. In longer, more discursive lines, the poet ponders the complex pattern to human history in a new light compared to what he said in the past.

"It seems, as one becomes older,

That the past has another pattern, and ceases to be a mere
    sequence —

Or even development: the latter a partial fallacy

Encouraged by superficial notions of evolution,

Which becomes, in the popular mind, a means of disowning
    the past.

The moments of happiness — not the sense of well-being,

Fruition, fulfilment, security or affection,

Or even a very good dinner, but the sudden illumination —

We had the experience but missed the meaning,

And approach to the meaning restores the experience

In a different form, beyond any meaning

We can assign to happiness."

The mystical moment was recorded in 'Burnt Norton'. It is now retrieved "in a different form", one that includes and transmits the present and the past as well. On the one hand the "sudden illumination" embodies an emotional recollection of a past event, which is recalled in memory and restored in the present moment. It also signifies giving new meaning to events that occur in the present.

He says "We had the experience but missed the meaning". Eliot used Heraclitus' idea of the logos and he combined this with Martin Buber's idea that the logos does not occur in us, but between us as "speech with meaning". Logos is translated as *word*. In Greek philosophy it means the soul of the world. In Christianity it means the Word of God and Jesus is the Word made flesh (John 1:14). Von Balthasar has a strong sense of God's Logos invisibly infusing all creation. He suggsts that...

> "...however secular this human world may seem as culture, art, philosophy, pedagogy and technology, it can yet be a response to God's call, and so a bringing back of man and the world to God. Thus is responding to God's Word man will be able to 'redeem' the word lying deeply hidden in the nature of things, to say what each thing says."[6]

---

[6] Hans Urs Von Balthasar, The Word, Scripture and Tradition, Explorations in Theology (San Francisco: 1989), 1:28.

Words only come to expression in our relationship, I-Thou. The logos joins us to the Cosmos from which, as Buber wrote, "from which we came and which comes from us", and from which we obtain "the shaped order of what is experienced by us and what is known as experienceable, a shape that grows and changes."[7]

In this shaping and reshaping of the cosmos, the poet not only engages his past but also the past generations and cultures that enrich and deepen his realisation. Eliot has in mind the written words of past generations. They become "living words" when we hear the voice of the one who wrote them. He came to see that "moments of happiness" and "moments of agony" flow together in all "currents of action".

While personal moments of happiness and agony inform the uniqueness of each individual,

> "the meaning
> Is not the experience of one life only
> But of many generations"

Big city dwellers who live beside the great river have forgotten who strong the river is:

> "The backward look behind the assurance
> Of recorded history, the backward half-look
> Over the shoulder, towards the primitive terror."

This makes us aware of the sea's wreckage. This brings to mind the agony of physical and psychological death that are part of life. When we get in touch with our own agony we see more clearly another's agonizing moments. If a new possibility for redeeming time is to open up, that redemption must address and overcome whatever triggers distress and anguish. We might have mystical moments but we cannot remain there. It must lead us to caring for the pain of others for it to be complete.

Having recalled that past agonies still reside in the past, the second movement goes on to say:

[7] Martin Buber, The Knowledge of Man: A Philosophy of the Inter-human (New York: 1965), p. 105ff.

> "The bitter apple, and the bite in the apple.
> And the ragged rock in the restless waters,
> Waves wash over it, fogs conceal it;
> On a halcyon day it is merely a monument,
> In navigable weather it is always a seamark
> To lay a course by: but in the sombre season
> Or the sudden fury, is what it always was."

Here we remember what he said in an earlier line – "the river is within us, the sea is all about us". Time, like the sea, both destroys and preserves. On the one hand, an abiding monument to the passage of time, the "ragged rock" in the restless waters off the coast of Cape Ann is "seamark / To lay a course by" to passing ships in good weather. On the other hand, it is around the figure of "ragged rock" that the unfolding spirit of The Dry Salvages gathers.

The "ragged rock" echoes imagery from Eliot's 1934 "*Choruses from The Rock*," in which the Rock, who speaks as a character in the play, combines St. Peter ("You are Peter, and on this rock I will build my church" [Matt 16:18]) with 2 Samuel 22:2, "the Lord is my rock, my fortress, and my deliverer." We are invited to "make perfect" our will by the grace of the incarnate Son of God, Jesus.

In the third movement we see Eliot's reaction to the Bhagavad Gita. Buber stated that a text can become person-like for the reader. The otherness of the text can reflect back the reader's own historical and cultural presuppositions. We are invited to reflect on values and meanings of the text. The reader then shares with the wider community what they have read.[8] For Buber a genuine meeting (in which redeeming reciprocity occurs) between a person and what comes to meet that person (nature, another person or spirit becoming forms) is said to involve choosing and being chosen and, simultaneously, acting and surrendering into a reciprocal relationship. Similar criteria hold for a genuine encounter with the spirit of a text as it becomes language.

Here Eliot recalls his intellectual and spiritual encounter with the Bhagavad Gita. The Gita's opening lines – "In the field of dharma (righteousness, law,

[8] Martin Buber, I and Thou (New York: 1958), p. 128.

virtue), in the field of Kuru (physical land belonging to the clan of Kuru)" – offers us a perspective to the themes of time explored in The Four Quartets. Alongside the field of logos (timeless moments of reaction with the world, or with the Word common to all) dwells the field of time.

The third movement begins:

> "I sometimes wonder if that is what Krishna meant—
> Among other things—or one way of putting the same thing:
> That the future is a faded song, a Royal Rose or a lavender
>   spray
> Of wistful regret for those who are not yet here to regret,
> Pressed between yellow leaves of a book that has never been
>   opened.
> And the way up is the way down, the way forward is the way
>   back."

Eliot was using the technique of using other poetic voices to widen his insight. It is through dialogue that differing religions can influence each other. Rabbi Heschel said that when dialogue is true one tradition can enrich others.[9]

Here Eliot uses Krishna's "fare forward". This suggests a movement towards awakening to fuller consciousness. Arjuna reveals to Krishna that his being is overcome with the question of how he should lead his life: "My mind is confused as to my duty" (11:7) and it "runs / After the wondering senses, / Then it carries away one's understanding" (11:67). The spirit of wondering is at the heart of the Gita. Krishna meets Arjuna and tells him to "fare forward" in battle and points out to him the futility of worrying about the future. Like a modern-day Arjuna the reader of The Dry Salvages is urged to "fare forward" into life's battles not by "escaping from the past / Into different lives, or into any future" since "you are not the same people who left that station / Or who will arrive at any terminus." The poet warns that struggling to escape from the past in the future is futile:

> "You cannot face it steadily, but this thing is sure,
> That time is no healer: the patient is no longer here."

[9] Abraham Joshua Heschel, No Religion is an Island, Union Seminary Quarterly Review 21, No. 2 (January 1966), p. 117-131.

The "fare forward" seems to contradict what the poet said earlier about stillness. The "still point" does not move but it can determine our movements. Our spiritual life can have a still centre but it influences our lives as we "fare forward". Eliot brought together elements from other religions. This dialogue was ahead of its time.

He writes:

> "At nightfall, in the rigging and the aerial,
> Is a voice descanting (though not to the ear,
> The murmuring shell of time, and not in any language)
> Fare forward, you who think that you are voyaging;
> You are not those who saw the harbour
> Receding, or those who will disembark.
> Here between the hither and the farther shore
> While time is withdrawn, consider the future
> And the past with an equal mind."

One learns to treat future and past with "an equal mind". If you are to "fare forward" then you move without attachment to the ego into a new equanimity, a deeper communion with self and with life. From the Gita Eliot integrated 'Karma yoga', the renunciation of the fruits of action and 'Bhakti yoga', the spiritual path focused on loving devotion towards any personal deity. The words "fare forward" include Burnt Norton's "descend lower" and East Coker's "be still". He lives now without attachment to outcomes. He surrenders his will and as we will see later abandons himself to the will of God, whatever that might contain. Arjuna abandons himself to the will of Krishna without being attached to the outcome. Humans cannot be totally free from desires but, as Krishna teaches, one can be free from attachments to desires. Desire produces more desires which are never satisfied even if they are attained. Attainment only produces more desires. I often have the discussion with a friend of mine about when can we say we have enough. In the end we always find there is always a desire for something more. We are never really satisfied. In Eliot's poem whether one suffers shipwreck or arrives safely at port, realising life's destination demands "faring forward" with an "equal mind" that is with "actionless action" made possible by one's intention, surrender and divine grace. Jean-Pierre de Caussade said that God reveals himself through the daily events, restrictions, cares and sufferings of ordinary life and that we grow spiritually by fully recognising and accepting his merciful will in every situation.[10] St. Paul says: "we know that in all things God works for the good of those who love him" (Rom 8:28). Eliot continues:

"At the moment which is not of action or inaction
You can receive this: "on whatever sphere of being
The mind of a man may be intent
At the time of death"—that is the one action
(And the time of death is every moment)
Which shall fructify in the lives of others:
And do not think of the fruit of action.
Fare forward."

In Krishna's teaching one's last words can liberate one from rebirth if they are wholly concentrated upon and surrendered to Krishna. Here Eliot gives us a reminder of Krishna's word to Arjuna about dying "the good death":

"On whatever sphere of being
The mind of man may be intent
At the time of death
There will he go in the next life. (XIII:5-6)

The moment of death is every moment. One should therefore be detached as if this moment were the last. Eliot appropriates Krishna's insights. In the beginning of East Coker he said: "In my end is my beginning". Our personal actions bear fruit in the lives of others when our behaviour consists in ending old habits and beginning without attachments. Eliot suggests that spiritual death arises when we encounter the divine presence. The redeeming of time is brought about by moments of self-sacrifice. We behold "the other" and care for their needs.

We become open to the divine and wait to hear his voice:

"O voyagers, O seamen,
You who came to port, and you whose bodies
Will suffer the trial and judgement of the sea,
Or whatever event, this is your real destination.'

[10] Jean-Pierre de Caussade, Abandonment to Divine Providence (Indiana: 2010)

177

> So Krishna, as when he admonished Arjuna
> On the field of battle.
> > Not fare well,
> But fare forward, voyagers."

If we are fortunate enough to meet the Divine we can discover that our "destination" is not a place toward which we travel but a transformation of awareness occurring in the traveling itself.

Martin Buber had an experience that teaches us we can have "mystical" experiences but we are called to live in the moment and be present to the person who comes to us. One day in July 1914, Buber was deep in prayer and caught up in a mystical ecstasy when he received a visit from a young man named Mehe. Buber was friendly towards him, but so inwardly absorbed by the mystical experience he had just emerged from that he was not present in spirit. Buber was no indifferent or abstracted in the usual sense. He conversed attentively and openly with Mehe and answered the questions he asked; but he failed to guess the question that the young man did not put into words. Two months later, one of Mehe's friends came to see Buber and told him of Mehe's death at the front during World War 1 and what his meeting with Buber had meant to him. He had come to Buber, not casually, for a chat, but to ask a question which in the end he could not voice.

Buber later wrote to Maurice Friedman that Mehe died out of that kind of despair that may be defined partially as 'no longer opposing one's own death'. Buber felt that in his conversation with Mehe, he had withheld himself, had not responded as a whole person to the demands of the situation. This meeting brought about a conversion in Buber. Mehe had wondered about putting his trust in existence, but had died without this hope.

After his experience with Mehe, Buber no longer divided his life into the 'everyday' and a 'beyond', where illumination and rapture hold sway. He reached for the present with all who came to him, wishing to enter into dialogue. He said:

> "Since then I have given up the 'religious' which is nothing but the exception, extraction, exaltation, ecstasy; or it has given me up. I possess nothing but the everyday, out of which I am never taken. The mystery is no longer disclosed, it has

escaped or it has made its dwelling here where everything happens as it happens. I know no fullness but each mortal hour's fullness of claim and responsibility. Though far from being equal to it, yet I know that in the claim I am claimed and may respond in responsibility, and know who speaks and demands a response."[11]

In the fourth movement Eliot speaks of the Virgin Mary. From his earliest childhood he was familiar with Our Lady of Good Voyage in Gloucester, Massachusetts. The fourth movement opens with this image:

"Lady, whose shrine stands on the promontory,
Pray for all those who are in ships"

This is the lady who prayed the "Prayer of the one Annunciation" of the second movement. She is petitioned to protect all travelers.

Coleridge, too, spoke of Mary's role in protecting travelers – the healing of the Mariner in the poem "The Rime of the Ancient Mariner". Healing begins with sleep. The Mariner says:

"Oh sleep! it is a gentle thing,
Beloved from pole to pole!
To Mary Queen the praise be given!
She sent the gentle sleep from Heaven,
That slid into my soul."

Mary had already been invoked earlier in the poem, in the brief prayer: "Heaven's mother send us grace" (line 178) when the spectre-ship first appeared and now the prayer is answered in the grace of sleep and a prescient dream of further grace. Mary, here, counterbalances the demonic feminine, the "Night-mare Life in Death" and frees the Mariner from her curse.

Eliot, too, addressed her as "Queen of Heaven". Eliot was devoted to Mary and he prayed the rosary, often meditating on the mystery of the Agony in the Garden. He says:

[11] Maurice Friedman, Martin Buber's Life and Work: The Early Years (Detroit: 1988), p. 188-190.

"Repeat a prayer also on behalf of
Women who have seen their sons or husbands
Setting forth, and not returning:
Figlia del tuo figlio,
Queen of Heaven."

Eliot refers here to Saint Bernard's mystical prayer in the final canto of Dante's 'Paradiso'. "Figlia del too figlio" means daughter of your son. He encapsulates here the mystery of the Incarnation, the Logos become flesh (John 1:14). These names show Mary's cooperation with Jesus in his mission of healing the world.

In 'Ash Wednesday' Eliot wrote:

"Blessèd sister, holy mother, spirit of the fountain, spirit of the
    garden
Suffer us not to mock ourselves with falsehood
Teach us to care and not to care
Teach us to sit still
Even among these rocks,
Our peace is His will
And even among these rocks
Sister, mother
And spirit of the river, spirit of the sea,
Suffer me not to be separated

And let my cry come unto Thee."

Mary is the Jewish Virgin, the Greek 'Theotokos' (mother of God) and the animating spirit of the garden. When Eliot remains in silence, surrendering to God's will, his peace grows. These prayers are addressed to the "Lady of Silences" who is also "Calm and distressed / Torn and most whole".

Eliot finishes with a prayer on behalf of those unable to hear the bell that tolled in the opening movement of this quartet.

"Also pray for those who were in ships, and
Ended their voyage on the sand, in the sea's lips
Or in the dark throat which will not reject them

Or wherever cannot reach them the sound of the sea bell's
Perpetual angelus."

The first movement of The Dry Salvages closed with a ringing bell that announced the death of the first annunciation ("Time and the bell have buried the day"), here the sound of the bell ashore suggests the perpetual rebirth of the one Annunciation. In his death and resurrection Jesus is alive. The Angelus is a prayer that recalls the Incarnation, the Logos taking on flesh. Mary is asked to intercede for those who are vulnerable in a double sense. There are those who are in danger of being shipwrecked spiritually. Loneliness and despair can destroy us. Eliot asks her to intercede for those who have the possibility of dying without apprehending the message of the Incarnate Word. In this way Eliot places all of suffering humanity into the prayer of Mary. Mary loved God and surrendered all her being to God. She lives in God forever interceding for all her children. Eliot uses the Bhagavad Gita where Arjuna surrendered to the will of Krishna. This, in Eliot's world, helped throw light on Mary's giving herself to God's will. Mary accepts God's will in whatever it may lead to. She bears the One who gives light to others and she is devoted to her Son. She embodies self-emptying surrender of dying to self in every moment.

Henri Nouwen suffered many internal battles. He was insecure about relationships. He had an abiding feeling of unworthiness. He feared that in some way if people knew who he really was they would neither love nor respect him. This afflicted him all his life. He, too, found solace in contemplating the figure of Mary, the mother of Jesus. One of his favourite icons was Our Lady of Vladimir,[12] Our Lady of tenderness. As he contemplated the icon he was led out of himself and away from the compulsive and divisive milieu of the world and entered the liberating and uniting milieu of God. He felt he was led by Our Lady into the inner life of God. He began by seeking eye contact with the eyes of the Virgin. He wanted her to look at him, to notice him as a unique individual and to become friends. He found her eyes looked inward and outward at once. The look inward to the heart of God and outward to the world. There is a mystic union between the creator and creation. She sees the eternal in the temporal, the divine in the human. Her eyes gaze upon the infinite spaces of the heart where joy and sorrow are transcended in spiritual unity. Mary is completely

---

[12] Henri Nouwen, Behold the Beauty of the Lord (Indiana: 1987), p. 46-64.

open to the Holy Spirit, giving her whole being to the creative power of God. Yet, Nouwen points out, she sees us with the same eyes she sees Jesus. In beholding the child she sees all of humanity as his sisters and brothers. With her hands she guides us to her Son. In coming to know him we are invited to let go of our old ways and accept the good news that we are beloved of God. The whole image expresses Mary's song: "My soul proclaims the greatness of the Lord and my spirit exults in God my saviour" (Lk 1:46). Her hands lead us to approach Jesus without fear. Just as the body of the risen Lord still carries the wounds of his suffering, so too the glorified Mother of God is the woman whose heart has been pierced by sorrow.

In contemplating the child Jesus in the icon Nouwen notices how the child gives himself in love to the Virgin. His arm holds her in an affectionate embrace. His eyes are fixed on her with complete attentiveness. The image reverberates with the prayer of Jesus for his disciples:

> "When the paraclete comes,
> whom I shall send to you from the Father,
> the Spirit of truth, who issues from the Father,
> he will be my witness."

(Jn 15:26)

The Holy Spirit is the Comforter (the Paraclete) who makes the love of God revealed in Jesus present to us today. The icon speaks to the heart. The Russian mystics describe prayer as descending with the mind into the heart and standing there in the presence of God. Prayer takes place when and where the heart speaks to heart, that is where the heart of God is united with the heart that prays. This knowing God becomes loving God, just as being known by God is being loved by God (Beauty of the Lord, p. 34f).

The fifth movements of Burnt Norton and East Coker opened with an attempt to make sense of the ever-present, ever changing gap between words and meaning. Here in The Dry Salvages Eliot returns to the theme of time. At the outset of the fifth movement Eliot calls attention to the misleading ways in which people try to control the temporal process. The poet begins by mocking pseudo-mystical approaches that "communicate with Mars, converse with spirits", or "report the behaviour of the sea monster". He, in an earlier time, referred to Madame Sosostris, "famous clairvoyante", in The Waste Land:

"Madame Sosostris, famous clairvoyante,
Had a bad cold, nevertheless
Is known to be the wisest woman in Europe,
With a wicked pack of cards. Here, said she,
Is your card, the drowned Phoenician Sailor,
(Those are pearls that were his eyes. Look!)
Here is Belladonna, the Lady of the Rocks"

Madame Sosostris is a figure of spurious guidance. She foresees approximately the future of the Waste Land, the drowned sailor, the Lady of the Rocks and the one-eyed merchant. Her inscrutability is strategic and financially advantageous. Eliot says with a deft touch: "One must be so careful these days."

In contrast to the pseudo-mystical Madame Sosostoris the poet now realises more accurately that:

"to apprehend
The point of intersection of the timeless
With time, is an occupation for the saint—
No occupation either, but something given
And taken"

To Eliot the redemption worked by Jesus is something the saints really appreciate. The present suffering can appear to the rest as being the only reality. It is hard to see God in the present moment. Eliot was writing during the Blitz. He goes on to say that to escape the horror of the present suffering one needs to be transfigured by "a lifetime's death in love / Ardour and selflessness and self-surrender." In the 'Dark Night' John of the Cross met God and this gave him strength. All can learn from him to allow God to work in our darkness.

In Jesus, the Word made flesh, we see "the point of intersection of the timeless / With time". Finding God in the darkness is what the saints achieve, but "For most of us, there is only the unattended / Moment, the moment in and out of time". Yet the Incarnation is before us. By prayer we can find we are not alone in the darkness.

"The distraction fit, lost in a shaft of sunlight,
The wild thyme unseen, or the winter lightning
Or the waterfall, or music heard so deeply
That it is not heard at all, but you are the music
While the music lasts. These are only hints and guesses,
Hints followed by guesses; and the rest
Is prayer, observance, discipline, thought and action.
The hint half guessed, the gift half understood, is Incarnation."

Eliot's experience in the Rose garden is an initiation into the ways of God. That "timeless moment" inspires practical, day-to-day spiritual disciplines: "prayer, observance, discipline, thought and action". He sees moments of light. In Burnt Norton he referred to the voices of children: "There rises the hidden laughter / Of children in the foliage". The children symbolise the possibility of a new reality.

The moments of "timelessness" must be retained in memory and then restored through a disciplined imagination. The entire poem moves towards an experience of grace. In *"Choruses from The Rock"* Eliot wrote:

"Then came, at a predetermined moment, a moment in time
    and of time,
A moment not out of time, but in time, in what we call history:
    transecting, bisecting the world of time, a moment in time
    but not like a moment of time,
A moment in time but time was made through that moment:
    for without the meaning there is no time, and that moment
    of time gave the meaning. "

These are the infinite moments of reconciliation when the infinite comes to the finite moment. They are moments of grace. These experiences tell us we are not alone, that we are accepted and loved. They are moments of peace that we must keep before us as we face the moments of life and the moments of darkness we meet. By sharing his experience Eliot helps us understand our own experiences and gives us hope in the darkness.

The "intersection point" between timeless realisation and time bound spiritual practice overcomes the moment "driven by daemonic, chthonic / Powers" and through grace one is freed from "past and future alike". One can live in the "now" in the presence of God.

"Here the impossible union
Of spheres of existence is actual,
Here the past and future
Are conquered, and reconciled,
Where action were otherwise movement
Of that which is only moved
And has in it no source of movement—
Driven by daemonic, chthonic
Powers. And right action is freedom
From past and future also."

Union, here, meets the genuine giving and sharing between the Divine and us. In earlier drafts Eliot had used the word "meeting". Now in his union and meeting with the Presence he faces the reality of the here and now moment.

Eliot concludes The Dry Salvages with the following:

"For most of us, this is the aim
Never here to be realised;
Who are only undefeated
Because we have gone on trying;
We, content at the last
If our temporal reversion nourish
(Not too far from the yew-tree)
The life of significant soil."

Eliot contrasts those who experience truth directly (he calls saints) and the rest of us (who at best receive hints and make guesses). Evelyn Underhill (whose writings Eliot used) says: "the imperfect and broken life of sense is mended and transformed into the perfect life of spirit".[13] These moments of the Divine encounter encourage us to engage in the world as we find it and gain courage to confront reality. Our strength and healing have to come from within. That is why Eliot recommends spiritual practice daily. He went to Mass daily. He recited the rosary. These are some of the practices he engaged in. This is how he brought "timelessness" to bear on time.

---

[13] Evelyn Underhill, Mysticism: A Study in the Nature and Development of Man's Spiritual Consciousness (New York: 1911), p. 120.

Chapter 6

Little Gidding

The word for Spirit in Hebrew, *ruach*, can mean wind. It means energy. Ruach can mean in God an emanation of His life-force, the breath of God. Ruach implies a power that is within the breath and wind. The Holy Spirit is the power coming from Yahweh, the name for God. It is Yahweh's power that puts all things into motion. It is Yahweh's power through the Spirit that breathes life into creation and makes all things live.

The Greek word for Spirit is *pneuma* which means to breathe, blow and also wind. The Spirit, like the wind, is invisible, immaterial and powerful. In the Gospel of John we read: "the wind blows where it pleases. You hear its sound but you cannot tell where it comes from or where it is going. So it is with everyone born of the Spirit." (Jn 3:8). John plays on the double meaning of pneuma here. The Holy Spirit is a power, an emanation, a power that goes out from the Father and is poured upon his people (Isaiah 32:15, 44:3; Acts 2:17). In the Gospel of John we hear Jesus say: "But the helper, the Holy Spirit whom my Father will send in my name will teach you all things and bring to your remembrance all the things that I said to you" (Jn 14:26). By living "in the Spirit" we experience God's presence and come to know him in love. The Holy Spirit is the Spirit of love. He is the "lord and giver of life".

We come to understand Jesus through the Holy Spirit. In Genesis 1:2 we read: "The spirit (ruach) of God was hovering over the surface of the earth". In Isaiah we see God rest his spirit on his servant: "Behold, my servant whom I uphold... I have put my Spirit (ruach) upon him" (Isa 42:1). Then in the Gospel of Luke we see Jesus in the local synagogue when he says:

> "And the scroll of the prophet Isaiah was handed to him,
> and he opened the scroll and found the place where it was
> written:
> The Ruach of YHVH is upon me, because he has anointed me."
> (Luke 4:17-18a; Isa 61:1)

Psalm 33 shows the relation between word and Spirit:

> "By the Word of the Lord the heavens were made,
> And by the Ruach of his mouth all their host."

(Ps 33:6)

By the power of the Spirit Jesus is born and throughout his ministry the Spirit rests on him. Jesus tells us: "My words are Spirit and life" (John 6:63). The Spirit is active in Jesus' words and as we come to know these words and the Word, we grow and have life. We are called to be "in Jesus" by the power of the Holy Spirit. Living a "spiritual life" is breathing with the life and breath of God who is within us and among us. Henri Nouwen understood the spiritual life as a journey inward and a journey outward in community and mission. He says:

> "The journey inward is the journey to find the Christ dwelling within us. The journey outward is the journey to find the Christ dwelling among us and in the world. The journey inward in communion requires the disciplines of solitude, silence, prayer, meditation, contemplation, and attentiveness to the movements of our heart. The journey outward in community and mission requires the disciplines of care, compassion, witness, outreach, healing, accountability, and attentiveness to the movement of other people's hearts. These two journeys belong together to strengthen each other, and should never by separated."[1]

Here we remember Eliot's paradox of the way up and the way down being the same. Here we grow inwardly and this affects our life in the world and our relationship with others.

In "The Living Flame of Love" the poetry and commentary are very close. St. John of the Cross wrote it for Doña Ana de Peñalosa. She was recently bereaved. She lost both her husband and her only child. John consoled her and she supported the Carmelites who came to Granada. John wrote 'Living Flame' for her and at her request he wrote the commentary. This helps us see the life of prayer is meant for all.

---

[1] Henri Nouwen, "Generation Without Fathers", Commonweal 92 (June 1970), p. 287-294.

"...once obscure and blind,
now give forth, so rarely, so exquisitely,
both warmth and light to their Beloved.
How gently and lovingly
you wake in my heart,
where in secret you dwell alone;
and in your sweet breathing,
filled with good and glory,
how tenderly you swell my heart with love."

John last met Teresa in 1581. He then moved to Baeza before he was transferred to Granada. He was extremely busy in Granada during his time as superior of Teresa's convents and monasteries in southern Spain. It was during this busy time that he wrote 'Living Flame'. Ana took the sisters to her own home before the convent was built. Ana found in John a compassionate listener who helped her in her grief after the deaths of her husband and daughter. During the last year of his life John continued to write to Ana. He suffered persecution again from his own friars. John dedicated 'The Living Flame' to her.

Medieval mystics spoke of the inner self as "the spirit", "the centre", "the depth". John wants to say "yes, but more so". He speaks of "in the middle of the heart of the spirit", the "intricate substance of the depth of the soul", even the "infinite centre" (see L F 2:10; 3:68; 2:8).

He, too, finds that words are difficult to come by to speak of his experience. He says:

> "No words have been invented for the works of God in such souls. The only language to cope with them is acceptance for oneself, experience, joy and silence."
>
> (Living Flame 2:21)

John's universe is 'drenched' in the outpouring of the love of God. The Holy Spirit is the personalised love of God. John's images of the work of the Spirit are flame, fire, blazing, burning. John says where God is concerned "love is never idle; it is in continuous movement" (Living Flame 1:8).

The Spirit that John knows is an "infinite fire of love", able to set the heart "blazing more intensely than all the fire in the world" (Living Flame 2:2). His presence is like a fiesta in the soul, "like a song that is new, always new, wrapped round with joy and love" (Living Flame 1:9; 2:36). Love grows in the soul. It spirals upwards with increasing velocity (Living Flame 3:79).

An awareness of the self-communicating God by the power of the Spirit penetrates the whole poem. The Spirit is a person, "the Spirit of your bridegroom", the breath of Christ. God gives himself freely to others. Nothing else would satisfy the "liberality of his generous grace". He gives himself totally (Living Flame 2:6; 1:3, 6).

The Spirit hovers over us to enter, pass in and once in, bus through until he finds the deepest core of the human person. John tells us it seems that God has no other concern but for that individual alone. John says: "... but that he is all for her alone" (Living Flame 2:36). God finds his union with the soul "a glad celebration" (Living Flame 1:8). John puts the following words on the lips of God:

> "I am yours, and for you, and I am pleased to be as I am that I may be yours and give myself to you."
>
> (Living Flame 3:6)

This favour is by the grace of God:

> "When a person loves another and does her good, he does her good and loves her with his own personality and character. So with your Bridegroom, who is in you: it is as he who he is that he shows you favour."
>
> (Living flame 3:6)

As the seal, so the impress and as the flame, so the burn: the measure of God's desire to give and his guarantee is himself. The Living Flame here discloses the greatness of the human person. John speaks of "the deep caverns of the soul" and "only the infinite can find them". When these caverns "are empty and pure, the thirst and hunger and sense of spiritual longing is more than can be borne... The capacity of these caverns is deep, because that which they can hold is deep and infinite; and that is God" (Living Flame 3:18, 22). For John, Paul's phrase comes to life: "I live, but

189

not I, but Christ lives in me" (Gal 2:20 quoted in Living Flame, 2:34). The person is "utterly bathed now in glory and love, in her innermost core pouring out nothing less than rivers of glory" (Living Flame 1:1). John shares his experience of faith. He takes us back to Easter morning and lets us glimpse the Father's love for his Son:

> "Love! Love on fire, lavish, active: you are glorifying me as much as my soul can bear it and hold it."
>
> (Living Flame 1:17)

The Living Flame John talks about purifies us. He uses the image of the log in the fire. He says the flame of love is the Spirit of the Bridegroom, the Holy Spirit.

> "The soul feels him within itself not only as a fire that has consumed and transformed it but as a fire that burns and flares within it, as I mentioned. And that flame, every time it flares up, bathes the soul in glory and refreshes it with the quality of divine life."
>
> (Living Flame 1:3)

As the Holy Spirit purifies us we only see the act of purification but John tells us we will be filled with love by the Holy Spirit:

> "We can compare the soul in its ordinary condition in this state of transformation of love to the log of wood that is ever immersed in fire, and the acts of this soul to the flame that blazes up from the fire of love. The more intense the fire of union, the more vehemently does this fire burst into flames. The acts of the will are united to this flame and ascend, carried away and absorbed in the flame of the Holy Spirit, just as the angel mounted to God in the flame of Manoah's sacrifice [Jgs. 13:20].
>
> Thus in this state the soul cannot make acts because the Holy Spirit makes them all and moves it toward them. As a result all the acts of the soul are divine, since both the movement to these acts and their execution stem from God."
>
> (Living Flame 1:4)

The grace of union with God is a foretaste of eternity. John tells us:

> "Yet it does not enjoy eternal life perfectly since the conditions of this life do not allow it. But the delight that the flaring of the Holy Spirit generates in the soul is so sublime that it makes it know that which savours of eternal life. Thus it refers to this flame as living, not because the flame is not always living but because of this effect; it makes the soul live in God spiritually and experience the life of God in the manner David mentions: My heart and my flesh rejoiced in the living God [Ps. 84:2]."
>
> (Living Flame 1:6)

John's aim is that we be open and experience this love. He did in his deepest darkness. His life was a witness to the truth of the words he wrote. John speaks of the importance of love:

> "It is noteworthy, then, that love is the inclination, strength, and power for the soul in making its way to God, for love unites it with God. The more degrees of love it has, the more deeply it enters into God and centres itself in him. We can say that there are as many centres in God possible to the soul, each one deeper than the other, as there are degrees of love of God possible to it. A stronger love is a more unitive love, and we can understand in this manner the many mansions the Son of God declared were in his Father's house [Jn. 14:2]."
>
> (Living Flame 1:13)

The process of growing in love continues. The wound of love is only cured by love. God's love reaches the very centre of a person and he transforms it in love. He uses the image of a crystal for the soul. Teresa's mansion was made of crystal.

> "When light shines in a clear and pure crystal, we find the more intense the degree of light, the more light the crystal has concentrated within it and the brighter it becomes; it can become so brilliant from the abundance of light received that it seems to be all light."
>
> (Living Flame 1:13)

John speaks of the "wound of love" in the second stanza. He speaks of a purely internal cauterisation of the soul effected by the Holy Spirit and then he speaks of "another and most sublime way" of burning in which the soul is wounded internally in such a manner the flame of divine love fills it so entirely that "it seems to the soul that the whole universe is a sea of love in which it is swallowed" (Living Flame 2:10). In this case God may allow the effect of this interior love to pass outward in the senses "as was the case when the Seraph wounded St. Francis; when the soul is wounded by love with fire wounds, the effects extend to the body and the wounds are marked on the body and it is wounded just as the soul is" (Living Flame 2:13). For John priority is given to the interior wound.

Thérèse of Lisieux was a Carmelite nun and saint (+1897). Her family were very loving but her mother Zélie died when Thérèse was young. Pauline, her sister, took the place of her mother but she left to join the Carmelites. This was traumatic for the young Thérèse who was very ill afterwards. Her family feared she was lost. Thérèse describes her cure in the following words:

> "Finding no help on earth, poor little Thérèse also turned towards her heavenly Mother and prayed with all her heart for her to have pity on her at last. All of a sudden the blessed Virgin appeared to me beautiful, more beautiful than anything I had ever seen before. Her face expressed an ineffable goodness and tenderness, but what went right to the depths of my soul was THE BLESSED VIRGIN'S RAVISHING SMILE. Then all my pain vanished, two large tears welled up on my eyelashes and silently rolled down my cheeks, but they were tears of pure joy. Ah! I thought, the blessed Virgin has smiled at me, how happy I am – but I will never tell anyone, for then MY HAPPINESS WOULD DISAPPEAR."
>
> (MsA, 30r°-v°)

At age 14 she felt the call to join the Carmelites, but she was too young. She went on pilgrimage to Rome and met the Pope, Leo XIII, and she asked him for permission to join early. He told her when God willed it, it would happen. Thérèse did join the convent at age 15.

Before this she had what she called her complete conversion. On Christmas Eve of 1886 after midnight Mass she heard her father make an unkind comment. She was extremely sensitive and a remark like this could hurt her deeply. She went to her room.

> "In an instant Jesus, content with my good will, accomplished the work I had not been able to do in ten years." After nine sad years she had "recovered the strength of soul she had lost" when her mother died and, she said, "she was to retain it forever". She discovered the joy in self-forgetfulness and added, "I felt, in a word, charity enter my heart, the need to forget myself to make others happy – Since this blessed night I was not defeated in any battle, but instead I went from victory to victory and began, so to speak, "to run a giant's course"."
>
> (MsA, 45°)

In Lisieux she developed what she called her "little way". She did not feel she could accomplish great things, but she could abandon herself into the hands of God in absolute trust.

> "I will seek out a means of getting to Heaven by a little way – very short and very straight little way that is wholly new. We live in an age of inventions; nowadays the rich need not trouble to climb the stairs, they have lifts instead. Well, I mean to try and find a lift by which I may be raised unto God, for I am too tiny to climb the steep stairway to perfection. [...] Thine Arms, then, O Jesus, are the lift which must raise me up even unto Heaven. To get there I need not grow. On the contrary, I must remain little, I must become still less."
>
> (MsB 3r°-4v°)

She said her vocation was love and this embraced all vocations. She read St. Paul's letter to the Corinthians where Paul enumerates the differing charisms; but in the end he says "the greatest of these is love" (1 Cor 13:13). In the last eighteen months of her life she suffered terribly. Her love and faith were tested, but she won through. It is not easy for our generation to appreciate this. We run from pain. Thérèse became one with those who felt they had lost God.

In his apostolic letter 'Salvifici Doloris' (1984) Pope St. John Paul deals with suffering and redemption. He writes:

> "The Redeemer suffered in place of man and for man. Every man has his own share in the Redemption. Each one is also called to share in that suffering through which the Redemption was accomplished. He is called to share in that suffering through which all human suffering has also been redeemed.
>
> In bringing about the Redemption through suffering, Christ has also raised human suffering to the level of the Redemption. Thus each man, in his suffering, can also become a sharer in the redemptive suffering of Christ."

The New Testament basis for these sufferings is found in the Letter to the Colossians 1:24: "Now I rejoice in my sufferings for your sake, and in my flesh complete what is lacking in Christ's affliction for the sake of his body, that is, the Church". Thérèse joined her sufferings with Christ. The rich soul for Thérèse is a chosen one whose sufferings are mysteriously joined with the redemptive suffering of Christ and is used for the redemption of others. When the account of her life 'The Story of a Soul' was published many were deeply touched by her. During the First World War the French soldiers who felt abandoned found great solace in her writings. There were many accounts of healings at Thérèse's intercession. As St. Paul said "… death is at work in us, but life in you" (2 Cor 4:12).[2] Thérèse did not read widely but she was devoted to John of the Cross. His spirit touched her.

She often felt dryness in prayer. During the retreat preceding her clothing with the habit she wrote: "In my relation with Jesus, nothing: dryness, sleep (Letter to Mother Agnes) and i a letter to Sister Marie she wrote: "Your little lamb can say nothing to Jesus; and more important, Jesus says nothing to her."

In faith she believed the darkness was luminous but still it was darkness. From 1892 she is left in complete aridity. Yet she believes in faith that the Holy Spirit is instructing her and working in her soul: "My Beloved is instructing my soul: He speaks to it in the silence, in the darkness." (letter to Céline).

---

[2] see my Thérèse and the Little Way of Love and Healing (Athlone: 2013) for a discussion of Thérèse and her spirituality.

The flame of Divine Love did show itself once. She tells us:

> "A few days after the oblation of myself to God's Merciful Love, I was in the choir, beginning the Way of the Cross, when I felt myself suddenly wounded by a dart of fire so ardent that I thought I should die. I do not know how to explain this transport; there is no comparison to describe the intensity of that flame. It seemed as though an invisible force plunged me wholly into fire.... But oh! what fire! what sweetness!"
>
> (Novissima Verba, p. 32)

When Mother Prioress asked her if this rapture was the first she had experienced, she answered simply: "Dear Mother, I have had several transports of love, and one in particular during my Novitiate, when I remained for a whole week far removed from this world. It seemed as though a veil were thrown over all earthly things. But, I was not then consumed by a real fire. I was able to bear those transports of love without expecting to see the ties that bound me to earth give way; whilst, on the day of which I now speak, one minute – one second – more and my soul must have been set free. Alas! I found myself again on earth, and dryness at once returned to my heart." True, the Divine Hand had withdrawn the fiery dart – but the wound was unto death!

But soon, she returned to her normal dryness. God worked in the darkness: "Do not think I am always bathed in consolation; oh! no, my consolation is in not having any on earth. Without showing himself, without making his voice heard, Jesus instructs me in secret. That is not through books, for I do not understand what I read" (MsB, 1r°).

The following is a letter she wrote in 1890 to her sister, Mother Agnes. It indicates the characteristics of her journey:

> "But the little solitary must tell you of the itinerary of her journey. Here it is: Before they started, it seemed that her Spouse asked her in what country she wished to travel, what road she wished to follow .... the little bride answered she had only one desire, to come to the summit of the mountain of Love....

Then Jesus took me by the hand and brought me into a subterranean way, where it is neither hot nor cold, where the sun does not shine, and rain and wind do not come; a tunnel where I see nothing but a brightness half-veiled, the glow from the downcast eyes in the Face of my Spouse....

I do not see that we are advancing towards the mountain that is our goal, because our journey is under the earth; yet I have a feeling that we are approaching it, without knowing why."

(Letter to Agnes)

On reading these lines we see how John of the Cross nourished her spiritual life: "I have obtained many spiritual lights through the work of Saint John of the Cross. When I was seventeen and eighteen they were my only food" (MsB, 83v°).

She reached a state where she no longer asked for anything except the accomplishment of God's will in her soul "without any creature being able to set obstacles in the way". She said she could speak these words of the Spiritual Canticle of John:

"In the inner wine cellar
I drank of my Beloved, and, when I went abroad
through all this valley
I no longer knew anything,
and lost the herd that I was following.

Now I occupy my soul
and all my energy in his service;
I no longer tend the herd,
nor have I any other work
now that my every act is LOVE.

(Spiritual Canticle, st 26 and 28)

Or rather:
After I have known it
LOVE works so in me
that whether things
go well or badly

love turns them to one sweetness
transforming the soul
in ITSELF.

(Canticle, st 27)

In st 3 of the Canticle we read "without support yet with support." We see paradoxes like this in Eliot. Thérèse says we might fail on the way but "knowing how to draw profit from everything love quickly consumes everything that can be displeasing to Jesus". Love leaves nothing but a humble and profound peace in the depths of the heart. (MsB, 83r°).

Thérèse found in John reassurance. She found in his writings the description of that darkness and peaceful emptiness she felt. She saw God's action behind the darkness and the emptiness she was experiencing. She lived out in faith John of the Cross's teachings and embodied his teaching in her life. John said that there were many different roads to sanctity.

Teresa spoke about the need for living out what one experienced in prayer in the real experience of life. "What the Lord desires is works" she says, "one must never hesitate to leave one's devotions to give help to a sick person" (V IC, 31:11). Thérèse wished her love to be pure and self-giving. She read the message of John of the Cross who spoke about an act of pure love:

> "The smallest movement of pure love is more useful to the church than all other works put together.... Thus, it is of greatest importance that our souls be exercised much in Love so that being consumed quickly we do not linger here on earth..."
>
> (Spiritual Canticle, 29:3)

Thérèse wrote: "It is, then, of the greatest importance that the soul exercises herself much in love in order that consuming herself rapidly, she hardly stops here below and arrives promptly in seeing God Face to Face (General Correspondence II, p. 1129).Here she paraphrases John's Living Flame (1:6).

In the last year of her life Thérèse was really ill and suffered much. In the infirmary when she was coughing up blood and suffering mental, spiritual and physical torment she kept the 'Spiritual Canticle' and 'The Living Flame of Love' (bound in s single volume) beside her. She suffered out of love for others. People who discovered Thérèse found in her a loving presence with them in their sufferings. She suffered a deep darkness and temptation against faith. Those who discovered Thérèse found solace in reading her. In the twentieth century, after her death, many people who asked her intercession found healing. She became known as the great healer of the twentieth century.

John was her strength in her deep loneliness:

> "Ah, it is incredible how all my hopes have been fulfilled. When I used to read St. John of the Cross, I begged God to work out in me what he wrote, that is, the same thing as though I were to live to be very old; to consume me rapidly in Love, and I have been answered."
>
> (Carnet Jaune, 8. 31. 9)

For Thérèse John was the Saint of Love par excellence. She felt that John had expanded her whole being: "with love not only did I advance, I actually flew" (MsA, 80v°). The love of John and Thérèse was 'agape', manifested by Jesus Christ and bestowed through him on his disciples by the gift of the Holy Spirit. 'Agape' is the Greek work for love in the sense of pure gift. God is "agape" (1 Jn 4:8,16). Thérèse saw love as the unique way to attain divine union. Thérèse spoke of being enflamed by the Spirit of Love in her poetry:

> "The Spirit of Love sets me aflame with his fire
> Flame of Love, consume me unceasingly
> Deign to set me aflame with your fire. (PN 17:2)
>
> At her voice, my delighted soul
> Is set aflame with the fire of Love. (PN 22:12)
>
> Remember the ever gentle Flame
> Which you wanted to enkindle in hearts.
> You put this Fire of Heaven in my soul.
> I also want to spread its intense heat.
> One weak spark, O mystery of life,
> Is enough to light a huge fire.

That I want, o my God,
To carry your Fire far and wide.
Remember. (PN 24:17)
And the fire of love which consumes my soul
Shall never go out!... (PN 26:9)

Once the blessed Trinity,
Gazing upon your soul,
Marked you with his Flame
And revealed his beauty to you.

Your heart was all inflamed
At this blessed word.
You gave life for life
To Jesus your beloved.

Now, happy victim
Who sacrifice yourself to Love,
Taste the joy, the intimate peace,
Of sacrificing yourself each day.

Your soul longs for Love.
That is your shining star.
Love will be your martyrdom,
Love will open the Heavens for you. (PN 29)

> Your voice echoes in my soul.
> I want to resemble you, Lord.
> I crave suffering.
> Your fiery word
>   Consumes my heart!...

I thirst for Love, fulfill my hope.
Lord make your Divine Fire grow within me.
I thirst for Love, so great is my suffering.
Ah! I would like to fly away to you, my God!...

> Your Love is my only martyrdom.
> The more I feel it burning within me,
> The more my soul desires you...
> Jesus, make me die
>   Of Love for You!!!... (PN 31)

Thérèse wrote in another poem:

> "Mon Bien-Aimé, mon Frère,
> J'ai soif d'Amour…"

> My Beloved, my brother,
> I thirst for love.

Thérèse put the words "I am thirsty… I thirst for love". Jesus thirsts for love and Thérèse responded by loving Jesus and loving him in all her brothers and sisters.

Being transformed in the living flame of love, Sr. Thérèse wanted to communicate this fire to everybody around her and to the whole world. "This is my prayer. I ask Jesus to draw me into the flames of His love, to unite me so closely to Him that He live and act in me. I feel that the more the fire of love burns within my heart, the more I shall say: 'Draw me,' the more also the souls who will approach me (poor little piece of iron, useless if I withdraw from the divine furnace), the more these souls will run swiftly in the odor of the ointments of their Beloved" (Ms C, p. 257 [36r°]).

She lived out what John had said. Her life was a life of love for all and her death was the 'death of love'. Her new life is in doing good to those she loves. We remember what John said:

> "This flame of love is the spirit of its Bridegroom, who is the
> Holy Spirit. The soul feels him within itself not only as a fire
> that has consumed and transformed it but as a fire that burns
> and flares within it, as I mentioned. (…) Such is the activity of
> the Holy Spirit in the soul transformed in love: the interior acts
> he produces shoot up flames for they are acts of enflamed
> love, in which the will of the soul united with that flame, made
> one with it, loves most sublimely."

> (Living Flame, 1:7)

Time and Solitude:

Stavrogin: ... in the Apocalypse the angel swears that there'll be no more time.

Kirillov: I know. It'a quite true, it's said very clearly and exactly. When the whole of man has achieved happiness, there won't be any time, because it won't be needed. It's perfectly true.

Stavrogin: Where will they put it then?

Kirillov: They won't put it anywhere. Time isn't a thing, it's an idea. It'll die out in the mind.

(F. Dostoevsky, The Possessed)[3]

Like Eliot, Dostoevsky meditated on time. For Tarkovsky, time is necessary to human beings so that, made flesh, they may be able to realise themselves as personalities. Time and memory merge into one another. They are like the two sides of a medal. In his films he shows moments of blissful beauty and harsh realities. He saw film as being something like music. It reaches straight through to the heart. Film can do the same. There is an intangible quality to being human, a potential for deep emotional experiences which cannot be grasped through logic or reason, which cannot be fully described in words, but in music, cinema, this part can be touched. We can add poetry to the mix. Tarkovsky (and Eliot) did not use their art to indoctrinate. They shared their vision and allowed their audience find their own meaning. Art, says Tarkovsky, allows us see the world with its beauty and ugliness, its compassion and cruelty, its infinity and its limitations. Art is close to a religious experience and its creation, an act of faith. His work is a type of prayer.

In his film 'Rublev' the film is broken up into different chapters. One of the last chapters is called 'Silence'. Here Rublev experiences a crisis of faith – not his faith in God but in human beings. He saw the cruelty, greed and lack of compassion that make up the human condition. When he begins to live out his calling as an icon painter he begins to see that Jesus became human to heal the human condition and by his love raise up fallen human beings.

---

[3] quoted by Andrei Tarkovsky, Sculpting in Time: The Great Russian Filmmaker Discusses his Art (Austin, Texas: 1998), p. 57.

He came that we might have life and have it to the full (Jn 10:10). The icon guides us into another world of love. It addresses us in our fallenness and misery. If we were perfect then there would be no need for art of any kind – there would be no need for Rublev or Tarkovsky and, for us, T. S. Eliot. Tarkovsky said we have to use our time on earth to improve each other spiritually. Art must serve this purpose. His films explored our world in search for understanding.

In the film 'Rublev' he comes to a more compassionate view of broken humanity. He sees that reconciliation between God and human beings is at the core of Jesus' mission. Tarkovsky says:

> "A true artistic image gives the beholder a simultaneous experience of the most complex, contradictory, sometimes even mutually exclusive feelings ... We cannot comprehend the totality of the universe, but the poetic image is able to express that totality."

> (Sculpting in Time, p 108)

No artist can work in an ideal situation. Some pressure from reality must exist. We must live with ambiguity. For Tarkovsky we must live our own experience of reality. In an interview Tarkovsky gave called "A Poet of the Cinema" he was asked what advice would he give to young people. He said seek solitude and live alone. He was aware how people run from solitude and silence, but he counseled young people not to be afraid. They would discover themselves in solitude and come to be the people they are meant to be.

Henri Nouwen is a good guide for exploring the lonely landscape of much of life. He reflects on how our loneliness can become 'solitude'. He looks at figures like John the Baptist, St. Anthony of the desert, Charles de Foucauld. "For them solitude is not a private therapeutic place. Rather it is a place where the old self dies and the new self is born, the place where the emergence of the new man and the new woman occurs."[4] Solitude involves a journey where we descend into ourselves, an inner search. There in the desert of the individual heart, a conversion slowly takes place. Because we fear loneliness, we are afraid of the process. Nouwen himself understood

[4] Henri Nouwen, The Way of the Heart (San Francisco: 1981), p. 26f.

this deeply. He suffered a deep breakdown in the mid 1980's. He had to put into practice in his loneliness what he had written for others. With the support of the community we was in he began to heal.[5] His writing and life give us courage to stay with our loneliness and by the grace of the Holy Spirit allow our place of loneliness become a place of solitude where we meet God.

Little Gidding:

Following the completion of 'The Dry Salvages' Eliot's health declined. It was during this time he started writing 'Little Gidding'. He was not happy with his first attempt but he reworked it again and the poem was finished by September 1942 and was published in "The New English Weekly'.

Little Gidding is a small village in Cambridgeshire, England. It was the home of a small Anglican religious community established in 1626 by Nicholas Ferrar, two of his siblings and their extended families. It was founded around adherence to Christian worship in accordance with the Book of Common Prayer. The community was made up of married people who aimed at being a Christian community. The community was broken up by Cromwell and his forces and the community was dispersed. The community wanted to explore could they live the faith and devote their lives as families to prayer, work and charity. Eliot was a Board member of the Society of Friends of Little Gidding.

Eliot believed that wisdom cannot be pursued in isolation, but requires a community of support. Lacking a common logos the world can be at odds with itself. We do not support each other.

In our day there are people who want to come together to pray, worship and live their faith in love in the community. I see in them shoots of renewal. There is a huge treasury of spiritual wisdom in the churches. We need to recover this spirituality and express it anew in the world we live in.

Dom Laurence Freeman, O.S.B., was quoted in The Tablet, an English Catholic weekly, saying:

[5] Henri Nouwen, The Inner Voice of Love (New York: 1996).

"It is puzzling and frustrating to try and understand how the mainline Churches, despite all their determination and resources, still seem unable to connect with the profound spiritual needs of our time." Many young people, he says, are ready for idealistic and sacrificial commitment and hungry for inspiration. And yet, instead of discovering in the Church an inclusive vision, and a comprehensive philosophy of life and spirituality, they "dismiss what they find as narrowness of mind, intolerant dogmatism, internal feuding, inter-denominational sectarianism, medieval sexism" and, their most damning criticism, "the lack of spiritual depth."[6]

It is by learning together who we are in God and living from that place we can bring light to the worlds. Donald Nicholl speaks of:

"…the agony of being human which consists in the fact that from the very beginning there is implanted in us a longing for unconditional love, for agape, which we ourselves are not only powerless to supply but whose nature is infinitely beyond anything human beings can even imagine. So every plan, however radical, to change the human condition – whether by moving mountains or by genetic engineering or by giving away all one's possessions, even one's body – all of that will prove to be nothing unless we receive the Holy Spirit who alone has the power to change human hearts."[7]

Communities like Little Gidding explored the reality of being human, the restless searchings of the heart. This is what influenced Eliot. He saw the need for such a spirit in the modern world. I have met many people searching for something to believe in and who have the desire to explore faith, prayer and community. They need a place and a community where they can be accepted and where they can explore their questions. With many people taking their lives we need to provide places of welcome where people can discuss their emotional issues and find acceptance.

[6] see James Roose-Evans, The Tablet, December 17-24, 2004.

[7] Donald Nicholl, Holiness: A Call to Radical Loving, Grail: an Ecumenical Journal (1989), p. 77f.

Over the entrance to Little Gidding church, a stone memorial bears Nicholas Ferrar's words: "This is None other But the House of God and the Gate of Heaven". Here in the final Quartet we get Eliot's view of Little Gidding. We encounter here the fire that is the Holy Spirit, the Lord and giver of life. The Spirit "stirs the dumb spirit" and quickens the soul. Eliot wished to juxtapose the fires of Inferno with the fire of the Holy Spirit. He states:

> "Winter scene. May.
> Lyric. air earth water end &
> demonic fire. The Inferno.
>   They vanish, the individuals, and
> our feeling for them sinks into the
> flame which refines. They emerge
> in another pattern & recreated & reconciled
> redeemed, having their meaning to-
> gather not apart, in a union
> which is of beams from the central
> fire. And the others with them
> contemporaneous.
>
> Invocation to the Holy Spirit.

He sees the Holy Spirit coming to the Inferno of the person who feels alone. The person is healed and transformed and the transformed person gives to others in turn. Initially in the poem we find ourselves in mid-winter – he calls it the mid-winter spring calling to mind what he said in East Coker: "What is the late November doing / With the disturbance of the spring...?" This is a far cry from "April is the cruelest month..." of the Waste Land. The winter season "between melting and freezing" is trans-seasonal. Light is reflected from ice, fire is not consumed. The sky is clear. The poet is in harmony with nature; "the soul's sap quivers". Death and rebirth coexist.

The dualities between winter and spring dissipate in the season of "Midwinter spring", a season that is "not in the scheme of generation." The midwinter "zero summer" blazes with the Pentecostal fire of the Holy Spirit into the natural sphere like the sun reflecting off the frozen pond. We recall Burnt Norton. Now Eliot's soul can thrive, ripen and bring forth fruit. The earlier Quartets spoke of places that could entrap us between past and future, where we could live in fear. Here in Little Gidding, where the power of the incarnate logos had shaped a believing community, Eliot discovered that what held that community together was prayer. Eliot saw that "the praying mind" was central to the community. Here private prayer and community prayer fuse together.

Eliot brings us to the "dull facade" of the church. We are invited to enter:

> "...what you thought you came for
> Is only a shell, a husk of meaning
> From which the purpose breaks only when it is fulfilled
> If at all. Either you had no purpose
> Or the purpose is beyond the end you figured
> And is altered in fulfilment."

In spite of all appearances the church for Eliot embodies the whole of spiritual substance. There are brass tablets with the Lord's Prayer, the Ten Commandments and the Apostles' Creed. Above these tablets there is an arch stained glass window depicting Christ on the cross, flanked by his mother, Mary, and the beloved discipled.

Eliot recalls those who worshipped here (like Ferrar and the poet George Herbert). The poet continues...

> "If you came this way,
> Taking any route, starting from anywhere,
> At any time or at any season,
> It would always be the same: you would have to put off
> Sense and notion. You are not here to verify,
> Instruct yourself, or inform curiosity
> Or carry report. You are here to kneel
> Where prayer has been valid. And prayer is more
> Than an order of words, the conscious occupation
> Of the praying mind, or the sound of the voice praying.
> And what the dead had no speech for, when living,
> They can tell you, being dead: the communication
> Of the dead is tongued with fire beyond the language of the
> living."

Now we are placed where the Spirit is embodied. It is hard to speak of the Holy Spirit, but in holy people we see him embodied. We see the effects of the Holy Spirit in a holy life. The Eucharist was celebrated and, for Eliot, the prayer of the community was real.

Eliot had written an earlier poem called "Usk", This was a landscape poem where he warned against putting faith in the "old enchantments" of fertility rituals or the grail legend. Instead he sought the Spirit:

> "Where the gray light meets the green air
> The hermit's chapel, the pilgrim's prayer."

In this place of Little Gidding ("where prayer has been valid") and at this moment he recognises that what he used to think (that prayer is "the conscious occupation / Of the praying mind") is not fully the truth. He finds himself in union with those who prayed here in the past and the great saints who taught him. Commenting on the lines "You are here to kneel / Where prayer has been valid", Eliot once said:

> "What I mean is that for some of us, a sense of place is compelling. If it is a religious place, a place made special by the sacrifice of martyrdom, then it retains an aurora. We know that once before a man gave of himself here and was accepted here, and it was so important that the occasion continues to invest the place with its holiness."[8]

As we enter this place in company with the poet we are called to leave the reasoning mind and kneel humbly in prayer. We enter into communion with God in the Holy Spirit and surrender to him. Eliot was asked what he experienced when he prayed. He "described the attempt to concentrate, to forget self, to attain union with God."[9] He sits in peace and speaks with the One he knows loves him (St. Teresa).

---

[8] Quoted by William Levy and Victor Scherle, Affectionately, T. S. Eliot (London: 1968), p. 41f.

[9] Stephen Spender, "Remembering Eliot" in T. S. Eliot: The Man and his Work (London: 1967), p. 59.

In Poets' Corner in Westminster Abbey on January 4th, 1967, a stone was set to commemorate Eliot's life and death. It contains lines from Little Gidding:

Thomas
Stearns
Eliot
O.M.
Born 26 September 1888
Died 4 January 1965
"the communication
of the dead is tongued
with fire beyond
the language of the living."

The dead can refer to those who influenced him. It also refers to those who have died to themselves and surrendered to God in love. Eliot had already pointed to this. In East Coker he spoke of the necessary "...agony / Of death and rebirth" (East Coker III). In The Dry Salvages he said "the time of death is every moment" (Dry Salvages III), and he pointed to the suggestion that the "intersection of the timeless / With time" occurs "in a lifetime"'s death in love" (Dry Salvages V).

A kind of unity exists between the dead and the living. We share with them in abandoning ourselves into the hands of God. I think of Thérèse of Lisieux here. We allow ourselves to be lifted by the grace of the Holy Spirit. We come, as we are, to be transformed in love. Prayer's communication is "tongued with fire". This expression of tongues and flames comes from the Acts of the Apostles where the Holy Spirit comes upon the Apostles and Mary.

"When the day of Pentecost came, they were all together in one place. Suddenly a sound like the blowing of a violent wind came from heaven and filled the whole house where they were sitting. They saw what seemed to be tongues of fire that separated and came to rest on each of them. All of them were filled with the Holy Spirit and began to speak in other tongues as the Spirit enabled them."

(Acts 2:1-4)

This Spirit gives birth to a new community and it is the same Holy Spirit who gives new life to the one who prays. In his healing we become detached from addictions. Ferrar described how the group would pray and they would continue their prayer in their work. Eliot learned from him and he also remembered those who had influenced him like the Church of England bishop Lancelot Andrewes (+1626) and the poet John Donne (+1631). In prayer he learned to give himself to God in a prayer beyond words.

> "Here, the intersection of the timeless moment
> Is England and nowhere. Never and always."

Prayer might take place in one place but its effect is timeless and is not confined to one place. We are part of a great community past and present who seek to find God and themselves in God. Genuine prayer is only possible because of the intersection between "here and now" and "never and always". God is always present and in prayer we become present to Him. This is Eliot's experience of Little Gidding. It is the prayer of Teresa of Avila and John of the Cross. Through all these witnesses we are called to find our place.

Movement Two begins as follows:

> "Ash on an old man's sleeve
> Is all the ash the burnt roses leave.
> Dust in the air suspended
> Marks the place where a story ended.
> Dust inbreathed was a house—
> The walls, the wainscot and the mouse,
> The death of hope and despair,
>   This is the death of air."

The impact of the war becomes obvious in this part. The death of air is "the death of hope and despair", the death of the earth "laughs without mirth". The experience of being a fire warden comes through. The ghost who appears later in the poem is a purgatorial figure compounded out of such figures as Dante. The "death of hope and despair" catches the emotions of that time. Eliot referred to broken people in the Waste Land: "A crowd flowed over London Bridge, so many / I had not thought death had undone so many." Now even the water and sand are "parched" and "eviscerated", devoid of all life.

> "Dead water and dead sand
> Contending for the upper hand."

This recalls East Coker where he said: "Bone of man and beast, cornstalk and leaf" both "live and die". This is the "death of earth".

Eliot goes on to spiritual death and rebirth. If we can die to our old ways of being and become transformed anew then we have the courage to face physical death and the threat of physical death. We get strength from inside:

> "Water and fire succeed
> The town, the pasture and the weed.
> Water and fire deride
> The sacrifice that we denied.
> Water and fire shall rot
> The marred foundations we forgot,
> Of sanctuary and choir.
>   This is the death of water and fire."

Water and the Spirit have overtones of Baptism and the fire of the Holy Spirit. The Spirit comes upon us and renews our heart. In an earlier draft Eliot included these lines which illustrate the theme of death and rebirth.

> "Fire without and fire within
> Shall purge the unidentified sin.
> This is the place where we begin."

The dove symbolises the Holy Spirit. This is a contrast to "the dark dove" the bombers that rained down death and destruction:

> "In the uncertain hour before the morning
>   Near the ending of interminable night
>   At the recurrent end of the unending
> After the dark dove with the flickering tongue
>   Had passed below the horizon of his homing
>   While the dead leaves still rattled on like tin
> Over the asphalt where no other sound was..."

This dove brings destruction, death and despair. We need strength from another – "water and fire".

Eliot then describes his meeting with a ghost-like figure. Eliot scholars argue as to the identity of this ghost-like figure. It is probably an amalgam of poets from the past. He has aspects of Dante and Eliot tries to imitate Dante's style (the so-called terza-rima). This encounter brings Eliot to an intimate self-encounter:

> "So I assumed a double part, and cried
> And heard another's voice cry: 'What! are you here?'
> Although we were not. I was still the same,
> Knowing myself yet being someone other—
> And he a face still forming; yet the words sufficed
> To compel the recognition they preceded.
> > And so, compliant to the common wind,
> > Too strange to each other for misunderstanding,
> In concord at this intersection time
> > Of meeting nowhere, no before and after,
> > We trod the pavement in a dead patrol."

This echoes Dante's meeting with Brunetto Latini whom Dante met in Hell (Inferno, 15, 18-87). It asks who is present before him? What needs do "you" bring to the text. In Burnt Norton Eliot said: "My words echo / Thus, in your mind". Eliot is questioning himself and his work.

In and earlier draft he had included the lines...

> "Although we were not. I was always dead
> > Always revived, and always something other,
> > And he a face changing."

The confrontation between the poet and his envisioned double produces deliberate renunciation of "last season's" creative efforts: "For last year's words belong to last year's language / And next year's words await another voice."

He now answers the voice by disclosing what death has helped him to realise:

"Since our concern was speech, and speech impelled us
　　To purify the dialect of the tribe
　　And urge the mind to aftersight and foresight,
Let me disclose the gifts reserved for age
　　To set a crown upon your lifetime's effort.
　　First, the cold friction of expiring sense
Without enchantment, offering no promise
　　But bitter tastelessness of shadow fruit
　　As body and soul begin to fall asunder.
Second, the conscious impotence of rage
　　At human folly, and the laceration
　　Of laughter at what ceases to amuse.
And last, the rending pain of re-enactment
　　Of all that you have done, and been; the shame
　　Of motives late revealed, and the awareness
Of things ill done and done to others' harm
　　Which once you took for exercise of virtue.
　　Then fools' approval stings, and honour stains..."

Eliot uses the phrase "to purify the dialect of the tribe...". Purifying language shows itself in a communal speaking and listening in the service of meaning. His challenge is to refine language and revitalise speech. This was the poet's purpose. the mysteries he speaks of are eternal but the language used to explore these mysteries changes from generation to generation.

The poet's mind is urged "to after sight and foresight". He looks at past events in his life with honesty and sincerity. His self-centered, capricious and virtueless acts evoke a "rending pain" that stings the soul. Yet as he comes to accept himself and his past a new creativity is born. The ghost tells him:

"...From wrong to wrong the exasperated spirit
　　Proceeds, unless restored by that refining fire
　　Where you must move in measure, like a dancer."

The remedy comes via a "refining fire" of deformation?? and endless humility in which one moves "like a dancer" in harmony with the divine. The necessary renewal of spirit occurs at the intersection of his life and his art, where the one enriches the other... As we saw earlier, in Tarkovsky, if all were perfect then there would be no need for art. It is out of humanity's failures, weaknesses and infinite longing that creativity is born. The words spoken to Eliot by the ghost were "tongued with fire". They were words that expressed the Holy Spirit moving in the human heart.

On his purgatorial walk around the barbed streets Eliot finds himself in harmony with another mystic who lived in troubled times, Julian of Norwich. She said:

> "And all shall be well
> and all manner of things shall be well."

Julian of Norwich (+1416) was an English anchorite of the Middle Ages. An anchorite was one who lived in a room attached to the church. During her lifetime the Black Death and Peasants Revolt took place. Then, as in Eliot's time, it did not seem that all would be well. In 1373 when she was seriously ill she received visions of the Crucified Christ. She called them "Revelations of Divine Love" (she also called them "Showings") and it is from this the above quotation comes. After death comes resurrection. Julian witnesses to the hope found in the Book of Revelation: "He will wipe away every tear from their eyes. There will be no more death or mourning or crying or pain, for the old order of things has passed away." (Rev 21:4). Later in the poem Eliot will quote Julian. In the midst of darkness Eliot had found hope.

He looked on those of the past who strove to purify their lives...

> "We were born with the dead;
> See they return and bring us with them."

In Eliot's early years a gap yawned between The Waste Land and the white towers of Wren's churches. In the Quartets the opposition of time and eternity is resolved as Eliot found points of intersection, in art, in the life of Church and in the Church, the community of faith. In his youth he had hoped for heavenly bliss in the here and now:

> "Your heart would have responded
> gaily... beating obedient
> To controlling hands."

Now, in his maturity, he contents himself with reconciliation and relief. He knows now he is imperfect and has hurt those he loved. He now sees as an artist who "knows he is but a vessel of an emotion, where others, not he, must drink". His struggle with language parallels the effort at the perfect life. Eliot points towards the place of fulfillment by pointing towards it. The greatness of his work is because of the authenticity of the search. All, whether or not they share his beliefs, can admire the work. He superimposes upon the bomber ("the dark dove") the dove of the Holy Spirit.

In the third movement of Little Gidding he talks again about 'detachment'. Proper detachment involves not grasping at things to fill the infinite needs of the Spirit. We are both finite and infinite beings. Viktor Frankl spoke of our need for meaning. Once in a concentration camp two fellow inmates came to him. The wanted to give up. He asked them 'what does life expect of you?' They thought about that and thought of their family and community, the people who needed them. They continued to live and hope. His work of therapy is called Logotherapy. The term Logotherapy is based on the word 'Logos'. Here Logos means meaning.

Perfect detachment is attachment to ultimate meaning…

> "The use of memory.to.detach oneself
>   ones own
> From the past.–they vanish & return
> in a different action.a new
> relationship. If it is here, then, why
> regret it?…
> Detachment & attachment
> only a hair's width apart."

His memory of a "timeless moment" (Burnt Norton) points the ways towards redeeming time. He says:

> "… This is the use of memory:
> For liberation—not less of love but expanding
> Of love beyond desire, and so liberation
> From the future as well as the past. Thus, love of a country
> Begins as attachment to our own field of action

And comes to find that action of little importance
Though never indifferent. History may be servitude,
History may be freedom. See, now they vanish,
The faces and places, with the self which, as it could, loved
them,
To become renewed, transfigured, in another pattern."

Eliot saw the need of the healing of memories. He felt reconciliation with God and himself. Then he remembers the moments of grace. The Holy Spirit expands human love. In contemplation love becomes renewed "transfigured, in another pattern". The memory of grace frees him. He is led from past oriented compulsions to a condition "not less of love but expanding / Of love beyond desire'.

Here he recalls Dame Julian of Norwich (+1416). She was a contemporary of Geoffrey Chaucer. She, as we saw, was a solitary person living in a cell (an anchoress) who devoted her life to prayer and meditation. Here Eliot integrates these lines from her "Revelation of Divine Love":

"Sin is Behovely, but
All shall be well, and
All manner of thing shall be well."

For Julian to say 'Sin is Behovely' she means a necessary and unavoidable aspect of human behaviour shall be transformed into joy and glory. For Eliot the effects of sin can be overcome by entering into the presence of God by devotion, prayer and sacrifice.

Eliot finds this peace: "If I think again of this place" and the people associated with it...

"All touched by a common genius,
United in the strife which divided them"

They sought peace in the middle of a civil war. Charles I stayed there after his defeat by Cromwell. Both sides prayed at Little Gidding, but in the end Cromwell broke up the community. Charles I was a martyr figure for Eliot.

As his mind slips back and forth among memories of all these earlier people he turns again to Julian and adds these lines to her "Sayings"...

> "And all shall be well and
> All manner of thing shall be well
> By the purification of the motive
> In the ground of our beseeching."

The term "beseeching" tells us about the notion of journeying, of not possessing, of enduring until the end. Julian writes:

> "Beseeching is a true and gracious enduring will of the soul, united and joined to our Lord's will by the sweet, secret operation of the Holy Spirit."
>
> (Showings XIV, ch 41)

In Julian's words,

> "Our Lord brought all this suddenly to my mind, and revealed these words and said: I am the ground of your beseeching."
>
> (43 ibid)

Beseeching is closely related, for Julian, with real prayer. She writes that one needs to pray wholeheartedly, even though one may feel nothing; for in dryness and in barrenness, in sickness and in weakness, then is your prayer most pleasing to God, though you think it almost tasteless to you. In other words, "all shall be well," insofar as our motives are inspired by faith and rooted in prayer that invites divine grace into the foundation of our action.

For Eliot "the time of death is every moment". We have to live in the moment and allow the Spirit work in us.

All Eliot has spoken about in the other Quartets is affirmed and celebrated by the cleansing fire that is the Holy Spirit. In the fourth movement of Little Gidding we read:

> "The dove descending breaks the air
> With flame of incandescent terror
> Of which the tongues declare

The one discharge from sin and error.
The only hope, or else despair
    Lies in the choice of pyre or pyre —
    To be redeemed from fire by fire."

Dante spoke about having to pass through fire, which did not burn him. It is a fire of purification. Here we come close to Eliot. Prayer is the first movement, the "incandescent terror" that leads one to decide between the flame of senseless death and destruction and the eternal flame of redemptive love. In the fire of Dante's Purgatorio he speaks of the refining, redeeming fire: "You would not lose one hair" (Purgatorio, canto 27, 27).

Eliot suggests also a choice between worlds of opposing wills – the will to power on earth (leading to the Inferno) or the will of God (perfected in the fire of Purgatorio). In the Bhagavad Gita there are two fires: the fire of desire, passion and anger (III: 37, 39) and the fire of wisdom that transforms works of desire to ashes (IV: 37).

Eliot recalls here the scene at Pentecost when "without warning a powerful wind filled the entire house". Divided tongues as of fire appeared among them and a tongue rested on all of them. "All of them were filled with the Holy Spirit and began to speak in other languages, as the Spirit gave them the ability" (Acts 2:3-4). The experience of spiritual death / rebirth brings with it the realisation of renewed life. We become open to the new world of resurrected life.

"Who then devised the torment? Love.
Love is the unfamiliar Name
Behind the hands that wove
The intolerable shirt of flame
Which human power cannot remove.
    We only live, only suspire
    Consumed by either fire or fire."

Eliot speaks of suffering and how we can use it for purification. Love's fire is with us in our suffering (John of the Cross) and in the end liberates us. This is the message of John's 'Living Flame of Love'. Eliot says: "We only live, only suspire / Consumed by either fire or fire."

East Coker spoke of the "wounded surgeon". Frankl's teaching about finding meaning shows us that we are more than a collection of chemicals we are victims of conflicting impulses and desires. We have a spirit. By being in touch with our brokenness we can with the power of the Holy Spirit become compassionate and loving to others. All people are precious. We should not just see people for their utility. The fire of the Spirit burns at the still point of compassionate love.

The last movement starts:

> "What we call the beginning is often the end
> And to make an end is to make a beginning.
> The end is where we start from. And every phrase
> And sentence that is right (where every word is at home,
> Taking its place to support the others,
> The word neither diffident nor ostentatious,
> An easy commerce of the old and the new,
> The common word exact without vulgarity,
> The formal word precise but not pedantic,
> The complete consort dancing together)
> Every phrase and every sentence is an end and a beginning,
> Every poem an epitaph. And any action
> Is a step to the block, to the fire, down the sea's throat
> Or to an illegible stone: and that is where we start."

Eliot sees his life as a continuous movement. He does not stay situated in one moment. Life is meant to be lived in each moment.

> "We die with the dying:
> See, they depart, and we go with them.
> We are born with the dead:
> See, they return, and bring us with them."

"We die with the dying" to the extent we share in and empathise with their sufferings. At the same time "we are born with the dead" in that we are continually renewed by the genius and compassion of previous generations. The interplay between death and rebirth recalls the "new and shocking / Valuation of all we have been (East Coker). For Eliot once said of the mystics "They live in us even as we die in them."[10]

---

[10] T. S. Eliot, Preface in "The Testament of Immortality", ed. N. Gangalee (London: 1940), p. 136.

Approaching the hour of winter dusk Eliot tells us:

> "The moment of the rose and the moment of the yew-tree
> Are of equal duration. A people without history
> Is not redeemed from time, for history is a pattern
> Of timeless moments. So, while the light fails
> On a winter's afternoon, in a secluded chapel
> History is now and England."

The movement of retrieval and renewal of past timeless moments brings us to a new fullness of life and gives a new meaning to the present moment. The Divine is both eternal and present. The rose and the yew underscore the insight by evoking temporal and eternal life simultaneously.

In the transition to the concluding passage of Little Gidding Eliot calls on the anonymous English author of "The Cloud of Unknowing". The author tells us that redemption and healing is an act of mutual love: "With the drawing of this Love and the voice of this / Calling". The author of the Cloud tells us that we are awakened by the power of God's unending love for humankind. The "Cloud" reveals a loving God who desires to enter into union with those who turn wholeheartedly towards the divine.

The "calling" is the impulse of love which impels us to perform what we are called to do and to be. Eliot speaks of this love: "Love is itself unmoving / only the cause and end of movement / Timeless, and undesiring / Except in the aspect of time" (Burnt Norton V), "Love is most nearly itself / When here and now cease to matter" (East Coker V), "a lifetime's death in love / Ardour and selflessness and self surrender (Dry Salvages V) and "With the drawing of this Love and the voice of this Calling" (Little Gidding V). These show the stream of love and compassion that underlines the Quartets. He places before us the transforming power and the redeeming power of love. We come to see that human life is redeemable when unconditional love, implicitly present from the beginning, renews the face of the world by in-dwelling the poet's relationship to the world.[11]

---

[11] Kenneth Paul Kramer, Redeeming Time: T. S. Eliot's Four Quartets (Plymouth: 2007), p. 172.

In the last lines of the Quartets he tells us:

> "We shall not cease from exploration
> And the end of all our exploring
> Will be to arrive where we started
> And know the place for the first time."

At the end (being present here and now) of our exploration "we" (poet and reader) are brought back to our "beginning" (always right here, right now). We continue to seek, to understand. These words give substance to these lines:

> "What we call the beginning is often the end
> And to make an end is to make a beginning.
> The end is where we start from."

We are called to reenter the world but with different eyes. We approach our lives and the lives of others with the eyes of love. We see God's love for all and we see people in His eyes. We experience each day as if it were a new day. We surrender to God's will in what meets us at each moment.

Eliot recalls the "moments":

> "Through the unknown, remembered gate
> When the last of earth left to discover
> Is that which was the beginning;
> At the source of the longest river
> The voice of the hidden waterfall
> And the children in the apple-tree
> Not known, because not looked for
> But heard, half-heard, in the stillness
> Between two waves of the sea.
> Quick now, here, now, always—
> A condition of complete simplicity
> (Costing not less than everything)"

The "music of poetry" shows Eliot's willingness to go back into the world of living. His experience of grace, his relationship with the Divine, reconstitutes his meetings with the world. He no longer sees the world as

"The Waste Land". The imagery of the dance ("Quick now, here, now, always") and the quiet of the still point fold into one:

> "And all shall be well and
> All manner of thing shall be well
> When the tongues of flame are in-folded
> Into the crowned knot of fire
> And the fire and the rose are one."

The "Fire" ("the Living Flame of Love") and "rose" are united. the "rose" can refer to Mary, who embodied the Spirit. Eliot sees the co-inherence of diversity and unity, of timelessness and time, of self and letting go of self, of contemplation and action. By moments of love we experience we begin to find our places in the world, in time, only to remember "where we started / And know the place for the first time."

Chapter 7

Wounds into Honour

"But Jesus, who in this vision informed me of everything needful to me, answered with these words and said, 'Sin is befitting, – but all shall be well, and all shall be well, – and all manner of things shall be well.'"

This comes from Julian of Norwich's 'Revelations of Divine Love' (Chapter 27). Many of us have wrestled with this. We saw Eliot use it at the end of his Four Quartets. Eliot wrote during the Blitz and many more horrors were revealed as the War wore on. How could he say (following Julian) that all things will be well? Julian herself wrestled with this revelation. She could see so much in her own lifetime and yet she said this.

Julian lived from 1343 – ca. 1416. She was an anchorite of the Middle Ages. An Anchorite is someone who withdrew from society. They often lived in cells attached to churches. The ceremony in which they became an anchorite was similar to a funeral because they were now dead to the world. Julian became an anchoress in her cell, attached to St. Julian's Church, Norwich. Margery Kempe, a celebrated mystic, writes an account of her meeting with Julian. Nothing is known about Julian's family name or her history. In 1373, aged thirty, Julian became seriously ill and those around her thought she would die. During her agony she received a series of visions or "showings" of the passion of Jesus the Christ. She recovered from her illness and wrote two versions of her experience. The first one, the shorter form, was written soon after. The longer version appeared twenty years later and is the result of her mature reflection on her experiences. She wrote in the Vernacular, the first major work by a woman in English. She was a contemporary of Geoffrey Chaucer (+1400) who wrote 'The Canterbury Tales'. Their works, Julian and Chaucer, were the first masterpieces in the English language.

Julian's World:

"All will be well" must have sounded strange in Julian's word, as it sounded strange in Eliot's world and as it sounds strange in ours. She lived through the aftermath of one of the most extraordinary moments in human history – the Black Death, 1348-9. The effect on the population was devastating. In Norwich it is estimated that 7000 of the 12000 inhabitants died. Julian would have been a young girl at the time. In the Plague people died horribly and suddenly and in great numbers. There were mass graves everywhere. The situation was compounded by diseases in cattle and crop failures. The country was in a state of famine. Julian did not speak of the plague directly but in her book she shows compassion for the sick and dying.

A form of the plague returned in 1361 and this time the plague was a form that was particularly virulent among children. It continued to hit the forlorn city four times between 1369 and 1387. Julian would have seen all these plagues during her life. The plague was possibly the cause of her life-threatening illness. In the 'Revelations' she describes a body lying on the earth:

> "At this time I saw a body lying on the earth, a body which looked dismal and ugly, without shape and form, as it were a swollen, heaving mass of stinking mire."
>
> (Chapter 64)

This description comes from what she saw herself in the victims of the plague.

The physical suffering brought about through plague, famine and failed harvests erupted into political turmoil in the Peasants' Revolt of 1381. The attempts by royal officials to collect poll taxes in Essex turned into violence, and rallied by the sermons of John Ball, angry representatives of society headed for London. They were led by Wat Tyler and demanded the removal of unfair taxes, an end to serfdom and the removal of corrupt government officials. In the rioting that ensued, prisons were opened, law books were burned. The Chancellor, Simon

Sudbury, was beheaded on Tower Hill. The revolt was quelled by the personal intervention of young King Richard II.

In Norwich the same issues that led the men of Kent and Essex to march on London had provoked riots and chaos. Geoffrey Litster led a band of rebels to Norwich castle which they pillaged. It took the intervention of Bishop Henry Despenser to suppress the violence. He travelled to Norwich with an armed force and defeated the rebels in the Battle of North Walsham. Despenser led the assault himself, gaining him the title of "The Fighting Bishop". He crushed the defeated rebels and ruled with an iron fist. This would be the same bishop who took Julian's vows.

In her time England and France were at war – The Hundred Years War. This drained manpower from the land. Knights, peasants and bondsmen went off to battle. Initially enthusiasm ran high. At the same time Scotland invaded England but was repelled.

After the successes at Crécy and the taking of the port of Calais English fortunes declined. Taxes and manpower were being poured into a bottomless pit which offered few returns. By the time of Edward III's death in 1375 most of the initial gain had been taken from him and the morale of the country was low.

The Bishop of Norwich aroused much resentment. He had been ruthless in the way he quelled the peasants' riots. There would not have been any riots if the peasantry had not been pushed over the brink of despair, first by the calamities of plague and famine, and then by harsh taxation tactlessly imposed. The people saw how the Bishop lived in luxury through it all.

He became more unpopular again by this warlike actions. There was a schism in the papacy. Urban VI, the Roman claimant to the papacy, encouraged a general crusade against the supporters of his rival Clement. This was then led by the Bishop of Norwich, Henry Despenser. Urban VI promised full remission of sins to those who gave military or financial support to his cause. At first enthusiasm was high but the crusade was a disaster. The Bishop himself straggled home in disgrace. The selling of indulgences embittered a lot of people. Also the actions of those who fought (in the name of God) alienated many people by their looting and pillage.

Added to the mix was John Wycliffe (+1384). He was a priest who attacked the privileged status of the clergy, condemning the way many lived in luxury. He also advocated translation of the Bible from the Latin Vulgate into Middle English. This is the form of English that existed at that time and is the language Julian originally used. This version became known as Wycliffe's Bible. Wycliffe's follower were known as Lollards. This was the derogatory nickname given to those without an academic background educated (if at all) only in English. They attacked the veneration of the saints, the sacraments, requiem masses, transubstantiation, monasticism and the existence of the Papacy. While Wycliffe opposed the Peasants' Revolt, one of the peasants' leaders, John Ball, preached Lollardy. The royalty and nobility then saw the Lollards as a threat not only to the church but to English society in general. Persecution against the Lollards broke out and Bishop Despenser burned many of them at the stake. He had actually called for the death penalty for the Lollards and Henry IV, the King, acquiesced. Julian wrote in English and there were those who looked on her as possibly being a Lollard. She, too, had used the vernacular.

Johannes Gutenberg invented the printing press around 1440 which revolutionised printing. However, in Julian's time there were more primitive methods of printing which made the dissemination of books more than in former times. This is why John Wycliffe's Bible was so important. Julian's writing would reach a larger audience in her time.

In this world Julian became ill. Her mother stayed by her bed thinking she was going to die. A priest placed a crucifix before Julian's eyes. Then suddenly all the pain left and her visions began. In her revelations she describes Christ's sufferings. At the same time her revelations were also spiritual. She saw how great is God's love for us, "enfolding us like our clothing". God embraces us with a love "so tender that he may never desert us". Her visions were concerned with God, Christ and the Trinity, but also with Mary, with Christ's death and our death. For Julian the soul's home is in God.

"Greatly should we rejoice that God dwells in our soul – and rejoice yet more because our soul dwells in God. Our soul is created to be God's home, and the soul is at home in the uncreated God."

(Chapter 54)

Julian recovered and wrote of her experiences in 'Revelations of Divine Love'. Her words were comforting to a generation in turmoil and pain.

Julian emphasised the importance of love. She experienced this love in contemplating her visions. She said:

"And he who loves in this way is saved, and so I wish to love, and so I do love, and so I am saved."

(Short Text, Chapter 6)

To convince people of unconditional love was a difficult one. People lived in a world of betrayal and violence. For Julian love emanates from and is unconditionally supplied by God. Her visions focused on the Cross, Christ's passion and suffering. Her mantra throughout is "love was his meaning". She even opens the book with the phrase: "this is a revelation of love". For Julian God is everywhere and in everything. Her God is the very ground of her being. She says of God's love spreading out:

"...there is a spreading outwards of length, and breadth, and of height and of depth without end, and all is one love."

(Chapter 59)

Julian lived out this message. This was why she was so attractive and many people went to her "cell" to talk to her. She carried the pain of her generation to God. In her silent contemplation she gathers all who suffer and brings it to the love of God. She brings the wounds and pain of humanity to the source of our being and our re-creation. She brings this pain to God so that he can bring new life, hope and possibility and joy to those who experience this pain. In a darkened world Julian was a beacon of hope and love. Julian would say we are "onyd" (one) with

God. When we pray on behalf of another we are creating a space for God to enter that life. We allow God to look after the needs of the one prayed for.

Julian had a profound respect for the individual human beings. Her love for broken humanity is rooted in God. We are his creation:

> "For I saw in the same revelation that if the blessed Trinity could have created man's soul any better, any fairer, any nobler than it was created, the Trinity would not have been fully pleased with the creation of man's soul. But because it made man's soul as beautiful, as good, as precious a creature as it could make, therefore the blessed Trinity is fully pleased without end in the creation of man's soul."
>
> (Chapter 68)

Her favourite conception of us is grounded in her experience of the love of God manifested in the passion of Christ. The love he has shown for us in his suffering and death shows that in God's esteem of us we are worth the very life of God. Our self-esteem is grounded in the boundless esteem God has for us. Depression and despair blind us to our worth. We have a fundamental goodness in that we are made in the image and likeness of God (Gen 1:26-28). We often fall from that image. Julian describes our fall and God reaching out to us in one of her visions:

> "And in this time I saw a body lying on the earth, which appeared oppressive and fearsome and without shape and form, as it were a devouring pit of stinking mud; and suddenly out of this body there sprang a most beautiful creature, a little child, fully shaped and formed, swift and lively and whiter than the lily, which quickly glided up to heaven."
>
> (Chapter 64)

Julian identifies the pit with the wretchedness we experience here on earth and the beautiful child with the cleanness and purity of our souls. Julian starts with the premise that the self is created and loved by God and is of great beauty and worth in his sight. We are in a pit and blind to our inner reality. God reaches down to us to heal and lead us to life in him.

Julian spoke of the soul as the citadel of God, his chosen dwelling place. Julian says:

> "I saw the soul as wide as if it were an endless citadel, and also as if it were a blessed kingdom, and from the state in which I saw it, I understood that it is a fine city. In the midst of that city sits our Lord Jesus, true God and true man, a handsome person and tall, highest bishop, most austere king, most honourable lord. And I saw him splendidly clad in honours."
>
> (Chapter 68)

This theme is of central importance to Teresa of Avila. As we saw, she likens the soul to a beautiful castle made of very clear crystal. In this castle are many rooms or mansions (see John 14:2). In the centre of this castle God himself dwells. Teresa says:

> "As he himself says, he created us in his image and likeness. Now if this is so – and it is – there is no point in our fatiguing ourselves by attempting to comprehend the beauty of this castle; for; though it is his creature, and there is therefore as much difference between it and God as between creature and Creator, the very fact that His Majesty says it is made in his image means that we can hardly form any conception of the soul's great dignity and beauty."
>
> (Interior Castle 1:1)

God rules Heaven and Earth but he dwells at the heart of our being. He lives in us. He has made his abode in us. Jesus says: "Abide in me, as I abide in you" (John 15:4). The word for abide in Greek is "*menein*". This word has the same word "*mone*" which was translated as mansion or rooms in John 14:2. Julian and after her Teresa's words act as a commentary on these texts. Their lives were living witnesses to this reality. We dwell in God and God in us.

Wounds into Honours:

Bob Dylan's song "I Contain Multitudes" contains the words "I'm a man of contradictions / I'm a man of many moods". Each of us are complex. Our inner worlds contain so much confusion and chaos. In our hearts there lies a brokenness and loneliness we fear and run away from. Julian helps us face our fears, our loneliness and our failures. All of us "contain multitudes".

The task of spirituality is to become a whole person, integrating our sensuality with our substance in union with God. Julian's teaching and life was rooted at every point in the passion of Jesus the Christ. The Cross, considered in terms of human behaviour showed wickedness, a manifestation of malice, deceit, cruelty, religious and political hypocrisy. Yet, in Julian's eyes, Jesus went to the cross because of his solidarity with and compassion for suffering and sinful humankind. Jesus died because he refused to compromise his claims of God's love and compassion for suffering human beings. Those who truly see and experience God's love in Jesus are those who become more sensitive to human hurt and can respond, mediating God's own compassion. Julian speaks of Christ's pains which she saw in vision form.

> "And yet in all this time that Christ was present to me, I felt
> no pain except for Christ's pains."
>
> (Short Text, page 74)

Julian contemplated the tension between the experience of love and compassion of God, on the one hand, and the suffering of the world, both physical and spiritual. This is what Jesus shared on the cross.

As Julian contemplated Christ the more horrendous evil and suffering appeared to her:

> "So I saw how Christ has compassion on us because of sin;
> and just as I was previously filled with suffering and
> compassion at Christ's Passion, so now I was filled in part
> with compassion for all my fellow Christians. And then I

saw that each instance of kind compassion that a man feels
for his fellow Christians out of love – it is Christ in him."

(Short Text, p. 20)

And in that compassion which she felt for her suffering fellow
Christians, she finds it hard to believe that in all the suffering and harm
that all will be well, as Jesus had promised her:

> "But I stayed contemplating this generally, sorrowfully, and
> mournfully, addressing our Lord in this way in my thoughts
> in very great awe, 'Ah, good Lord, how could all be well,
> in view of the great harm which has come upon your
> creatures through sin?' And in this I wished, as much as I
> dared, to receive some clearer explanation to set my mind
> at ease about this."

(Chapter 29, p. 76)

She sees all around her that all things are not well. Sin is the cause of
our brokenness. It is the woundedness at the heart of our personality. We
hurt each other. Julian was shown that "Adam's sin was the greatest
harm ever done or ever to be done until the end of the world" (p. 76).
We hear in Julian's words an echo of Saint Paul: "For as in Adam all die,
so in Christ all will be made alive" (1 Cor 15:22). Often we suffer at the
hand of others we perpetuate with our heads. We feel locked into a
heartless, cruel world, bereft of humanity and compassion. To look
sincerely at our alienation, brokenness and sinfulness means we have to
look into its causes and effects. This involves self scrutiny at the most
painful level.

> "Sin is the sharpest scourge that any chosen soul can be
> struck with, a scourge which lashes men and women and
> utterly shatters them, and damages them in their own eyes
> to such an extent that they think themselves unworthy of
> anything except, as it were, to sink into hell."

(Short Text, p. 20)

We are all broken and lonely in so many ways. This is the door through which we allow Christ enter our lives. Julian does not understand fully the purpose of all the world's sufferings but she is assured that this will not be the end. It's a mystery hidden in the heart of God. In the Book of Revelation we read:

"Then the angel showed me the river of the water of life, as clear as crystal, flowing from the throne of God and of the Lamb down the middle of the great street of the city. On each side of the river stood the tree of life, bearing twelve crops of fruit, yielding its fruit every month. And the leaves of the tree are for the healing of the nations. No longer will there be any curse. The throne of God and of the Lamb will be in the city, and his servants will serve him. They will see his face, and his name will be on their foreheads. There will be no more night. They will not need the light of a lamp or the light of the sun, for the Lord God will give them light. And they will reign for ever and ever."

(Rev 22:1-5)

In Isaiah we read what God says: "On this mountain... the Lord God will wipe away all tears from their faces" (Isa 24:7f). Now God accomplishes this in the new Heaven and the new Earth. God gives his people the "water of life" (Rev 21:6f). This lives out the promise of Isaiah: "All you who are thirsty come to the water, You who have so many cares, come receive grain and eat" (Isa 55:1). The new city is radiant with God's glory (Isa 60:1-2, Ezek 43:3-5, Zech 2:5). Here in the new city God and the Lamb reside. The verses quoted above show a Paradise restored. There is the tree of life here. Julian's visions are in line with these scriptural quotations. We read of the New Heaven and Earth:

"Then I saw "a new heaven and a new earth," for the first heaven and the first earth had passed away, and there was no longer any sea. I saw the Holy City, the new Jerusalem, coming down out of heaven from God, prepared as a bride beautifully dressed for her husband. And I heard a loud voice from the throne saying, "Look! God's dwelling place is now among the people, and he will dwell with them. They will be his people, and God himself will be with them and be their God. 'He will wipe every tear from their eyes. There will be no more death' or mourning or crying or pain, for the old order of things has passed away."

(Rev 21:1-4)

God is forming "the new Earth and the Heavens" from our world, our sufferings. Our lives in union with Christ lay the foundations for this new world. God makes us his partners in this. God's dream is for an end to suffering and he calls us to work with him in this. Julian trusted in God because she knew the overwhelming love of God revealed in Jesus.

Julian did not trivialise misery by pretending to have an explanation that trivialises our pain. We are helped to face the suffering of Jesus who fully shares in our pain. Saint Paul says: "I have gained... an uprightness from God, based on faith, that I may come to know him and the power of his resurrection, and partake of his sufferings by being moulded into the pattern of his death, striving towards the goal of resurrection from the dead" (Phil 3:9-11). By the power of the Holy Spirit we come to share in the power of the resurrection. Julian hopes for the peace that passes all understanding. She has a vision of the restored Eden. She says:

"And in this I saw that he does not want us to be afraid to know the things that he reveals; he reveals them because he wants us to know them, and through this knowledge he wants us to love him and take delight and endlessly rejoice in him. And because of the great love which he has for us, he reveals to us everything which at the time is to his glory and our benefit. And the things which he wants to keep secret for now, he still, out of his great goodness, reveals them without full disclosure, and in this revelation he wants us to believe and understand that we shall see them indeed in his eternal bliss. Then we ought to rejoice in him for all that he conceals; and if we do this willingly and humbly we shall find great comfort in it, and we shall have endless thanks from him for it."

(Chapter 31, p. 84f)

God works through our tears and sufferings in mysterious ways. We abandon ourselves in trust. Julian had come to know "the love of Christ which is beyond knowledge" and "was filled with the utter fullness of God" (Eph 3:19). Her revelations echo Paul's prayer in Ephesians: "... so that with God's holy people you will have the strength to grasp the breadth and the length, the height and the depth" of God's love (Eph 3:18). This work is accomplished by the Holy Spirit. He is "endless delight". Julian tells: "The Father is pleased, the Son is glorified and the Holy Spirit takes delight" (Chapter 23, p. 78). The Holy Spirit turns bitterness into the hope of God's mercy: "And then the wounds begin to heal and the soul to revive." (Chapter 39, p. 88). The Holy Spirit is endless life dwelling in our souls who "protects us most seemly and effects a peace in the soul" (Chapter 48, p.102).

Sin according to Julian is the marring and twisting of the image of God that is in us. She says sin has "no substance". She points to a day of complete wholeness and fulfillment when all sin and its consequences of pain and sorrow will be taken away. She speaks about the Lord's assurance that sin, alienation, loneliness and its afflictions are temporary and will come to an end:

"You shall suddenly be taken from all your suffering, from all your distress and from all your unhappiness. And you shall come up above, and you shall have me for your reward, and you shall be filled full of joy and bliss. And you shall never have any kind of suffering, any kind of sickness, anything displeasing, nor any disappointed desires, but always joy and bliss without end. Why then should it bother you to suffer for a while, since it is my will and my glory?"

(Short Text, p. 28)

She tells us when we are in pain "we should pass over it, and place ourselves in the endless delight that is God" (Chapter 15, p. 51). "The love which made Jesus suffer surpasses all his sufferings, as much as heaven is above the earth." In just the same way as his love surpasses all his sufferings, so will our eternal bliss and reward surpass our own.

> "...and grace transforms our sorrowful dying into holy, blessed life; for I saw most certainly that just as our contrariness brings us pain, shame, and sorrow here on earth, so, on the contrary, grace brings us solace, honour, and bliss in heaven – and to such an extent that when we come up and receive the sweet rewards which grace has created for us, then we shall thank and bless our Lord, rejoicing without end that we ever suffered sorrow."
>
> (Chapter 48, p. 103)

Too often we can think of examples where suffering brings about bitter, twisted personalities, broken in themselves and inflicting further harm and brokenness on others. Julian held out hope to even these that one day they would find peace.

Julian shares another of her visions. It is that of the Lord and Servant. The Lord sits in state, while the servant tries to do his best. The servant, however, comes to grief. He...

> "...falls into a 'slade' (a valley or hollow). Although seriously injured, the servant's greatest misery is that, having fallen, he cannot now see his lord – even though the lord is very near – and 'like someone who was weak and foolish for the moment, he was intent on his own feelings'"
>
> (Chapter 51, p. 106f)

Julian saw that the Lord had love and compassion for the one who fell.

> "For our courteous Lord does not want his servants to despair because they fall often and grievously; for our falling does not prevent him from loving us. Peace and love

are always in us, being and working, but we are not always in peace and love. But he wants us to pay attention to this: that he is the foundation of our whole life in love..."

(Chapter 39, p. 89)

The reward for the servant is that the wounds he received would be "turned into high, surpassing honour and endless bliss". One result of the servant falling into the ditch was that his understanding was injured because he could no longer look upon the Lord. He felt completely alienated. He knows neither himself nor his Lord. This blindness is all too real. It prevents us from recognising that at bottom we seek the good and wish to know the love of God.

> "His expression was merciful, the colour of his face was a beautiful brown, with most handsome features; his eyes were black, most beautiful and becoming, his looks all full of loving pity; and within him there was a lofty sanctuary, long and broad, all full of endless heavens. And the loving regards with which he looked continually at his servant, and especially when he fell – it seemed to me that it could melt our hearts for love and break them in two for joy."

(Chapter 51, p. 109)

Our wounds are transformed into honours by God (Chapter 39, p. 89). The Lord reached down to the servant, washed him and healed his wounds.

> "In the same way we know that when man fell so deeply and so wretchedly through sin, no other help was forthcoming to restore man except through him who made man. And he who made man for love, by the same love would restore man to the same blessedness and surpassingly more. And just as we were made like the Trinity in our first creation, our creator wished that we should be like Jesus Christ our Saviour, in heaven without end, by virtue of our remaking."

(Chapter 10, p. 54)

Laughter is never far from the surface in Julian. In the fifth revelation she saw all the power of evil personified in the devil and saw how the passion of Christ made his power impotent. She tells us:

> "I also saw our Lord scorn his malice and discount him as nothing, and he wants us to do the same. At the sight of this I laughed heartily, and that made those who were around me to laugh, and their laughter was a pleasure to me. In my thoughts I wished that my fellow Christians had seen what I saw."
>
> (Short Text, p. 12)

Even though we still suffer from blindness and weakness, Julian says we should have joy because our Lord protects us and leads us into increasing light and wholeness.

> "But our good Lord, the Holy Spirit, who is endless life dwelling in our soul, protects us most securely, and effects a peace in the soul, and gives it comfort by grace, and accords it to God, and makes it compliant. And this is his mercy and the path on which our Lord continually leads us, as long as we are here in this changeable life."
>
> (Chapter 48, p. 102)

The idea of Heaven as "a banquet" is an image that runs through scripture. Ps 107:9 tells us: "For he has satisfied the thirsty soul and the hungry soul he has filled with what is good". In Isa 55:1-2 we read:

> "Ho! Every one who thirsts, come to the waters;
> And you who have no money come, buy and eat.
> Come, buy wine and milk
> Without money and without cost.
> "Why do you spend money for what is not bread,
> And your wages for what does not satisfy?
> Listen carefully to Me, and eat what is good,
> And delight yourself in abundance."

In Matthew 22:2 Jesus says: "The kingdom of Heaven may be compared to a king who gave a wedding feast for his son". For Julian Heaven is not a solemn affair, but a party, a banquet, full of gladness and joy. Even now we can experience some of that joy in the Holy Spirit. She says:

> "Then I saw the Lord take no seat in his own house, but I saw him reign royally in his house, and he filled it full of joy and delight, himself eternally gladdening and comforting his beloved friends most friendlily and most courteously, with marvelous melody of endless love in his own fair, blessed face, which glorious face of the Godhead fills heavens full of joy and bliss."

(Chapter 48)

Jesus suffered but Julian tells us he had joy in his heart when a soul came to him. "I tell you in the same way that there will be more rejoicing in heaven over one sinner who repents than over ninety-nine righteous persons who do not need to repent" (Luke 15:7). We are all invited to come to the party.

Julian spent her life meditating on the mystery of the Cross. There are two realities for Julian: sin and God's love. Nothing mediates between these two realities except sin's defeat of love, the Cross. When she is tempted to look beyond the Cross to heaven, she resists, because she wants to see only the Cross as God's love for us (Chapter 3). For Julian the conflict between sin and love is the final conflict, and the Cross is the final outcome of that conflict. Sin is of its nature violent and wages war on love. Love is absolute vulnerability. Love has no strategy of violence. The Cross is the victory of love over sin. Love is stronger than death or sin. Sin has failed to engage love in its own violent battleground. In this way its power is exhausted. The Resurrection, then, is the meaning of the Cross. The vulnerability of love, its refusal of violence is stronger than sin's power to kill (Chapter 3).

In the Gospel of John we read: "and when I am lifted up from the earth, I will draw all people to myself." (John 12:32). Julian prayed to experience living compassion for Jesus in his sufferings. In her vision of the Cross which healed her she said:

"But in this I never asked for any bodily vision or any kind of revelation from God, but for compassion, such as it seems to be a naturally sympathetic soul might feel for our Lord Jesus, who for love was willing to become a mortal man. And I longed to suffer with him, while living in my mortal body, as God would give me grace."

(Chapter 3, p. 43).

She became one with Jesus in her suffering. In the communion of love she prayed for the world's pain. This is why troubled people in a troubled age made their way to her.

St. Paul reminds us:

"But if Christ is in you, then even though your body is subject to death because of sin, the Spirit gives life because of righteousness. And if the Spirit who raised Jesus from the dead is living in you, he who raised Christ from the dead will also give life to your mortal bodies because of his Spirit who lives in you."

(Romas 8:10-12).

"...This Spirit helps us in our weakness. We do not know how to pray as we ought, but the Spirit himself intercedes for us through wordless groanings. And he who searches our hearts knows the mind of the Spirit, because the Spirit intercedes for God's people in accordance with the will of God."

(Romans 8:26f)

Julian, in one of her earlier visions, saw creation:

"And in this he showed me something small, no bigger than a hazel-nut, lying in the palm of my hand, and I perceived that it was round as any ball. I looked at it and thought: What can this be? And I was given this general answer: It is everything which is made. I was amazed that it could last, for I thought that it was so little that it could suddenly fall into nothing. And I was answered in my understanding: It lasts and always will, because God loves it; and thus everything has being through the love of God."

(Chapter 5, p. 45)

As Julian contemplates the tiny ball, so delicate and tender, she sees the whole universe. God is its Creator, protector and lover (Chapter 5). We are called to make our home with God:

"This little thing which is created seemed to me as if it could have fallen into nothing because of its littleness. We need to have knowledge of this, so that we may delight in despising as nothing everything created, so as to love and have uncreated God. For this is the reason why our hearts and souls are not in perfect ease, because here we seek rest in this thing which is so little, in which there is no rest, and we do not know our God who is almighty, all wise and all good, for he is true rest."

(Chapter 5, p. 45)

St. Augustine said: "You have made us for yourself, and our heart is restless until it rests in you" (Confessions 1,1). God, as creator, brings the Cosmos out of chaos, and Easter out of Good Friday. Our hope is in him that he would bring from the confusion of our lives and world a new life and new world. "Behold, I am making all things new" (Rev 21:5). God created everything for love, "and by the same love it is preserved" and "the goodness everything has is of God" (Chapter 8, p. 50). "God is in man and in God is all" (Chapter 9, p. 52).

The poet William Blake had this insight:

"To see a World in a Grain of Sand
And a Heaven in a Wild Flower
Hold Infinity in the palm of your hand
And Eternity in an hour"

(Auguries of Innocence)

Saint Benedict, too, saw all creation in the mote of a sunbeam.

For Julian all things are as nothing without God. In our prayers we recognise that what we ultimately seek is God and our life in him.

In her "Revelations of Divine Love" Julian refers to Jesus as "mother" and the one he called 'Father' as 'Mother'. God is greater than our categories and he (she) is greater than our ideas of Fatherhood and Motherhood. Julian says:

> "So Jesus Christ who sets good against evil is our real Mother. We owe our being to him – and this is the essence of motherhood! – and all the delightful, loving protection which ever follows. God is as really our Mother as he is our Father."
>
> (Chapter 59)

> "So Jesus is our true Mother by nature at our first creation, and he is our true Mother in grace by taking on our created nature."
>
> (Chapter 59)

> "A mother can give her child milk to suck, but our dear mother Jesus can feed us with himself, and he does so most courteously and most tenderly with the holy sacrament, which is the precious food of life itself... The mother can lay the child tenderly to her breast, but our tender mother Jesus, he can familiarly lead us to his blessed breast through his sweet open side..."
>
> (Chapter 60)

Here she taps into the Biblical revelation of who God is. In Ps 131 we read:

> "O Lord, my heart is not lifted up;
> my eyes are not raised too high;
> I do not occupy myself with things

too great and too marvelous for me.
But I have calmed and quieted my soul,
like a weaned child with its mother;
my soul is like the weaned child that is with me.

O Israel, hope in the Lord
from this time on and forevermore.

(Ps 131:1-3)

There is a deep serenity in the words of the Psalmist. A proud heart and haughty eyes are the signs of great ambition; a trait that is absent in the humble individual. A weaned child is one whose hunger has been satisfied and who now rests contently at its mother's breast. The psalm represents God as a mother who has given of her very self for the child. We are summoned to trust as the little child.

In the Book of Isaiah, the part called Deutero-Isaiah, we see the prophet use the image of God as mother. The prophet promises the people deliverance from exile. To counter the exiles' disbelief, the prophet says:

"Can a mother forget the baby at her breast
and have no compassion on the child she has borne?
Though she may forget,
I will not forget you!
See, I have engraved you on the palms of my hands;
your walls are ever before me."

(Isa 49:15f)

The image underscores the unbreakable bond God has with Israel. God's commitment to Israel remains secure – "see, I have carved you on the palms of my hands." In Isa 66:13 we read

"As a mother comforts her child,
so will I comfort you;
and you will be comforted over Jerusalem."

(Isa 66:13)

Julian describes Jesus as mother. Here again she is very biblical… In Chapter 23 of Matthew's Gospel Jesus denounced the leaders in Jerusalem. Then the tone shifts as Jesus shows his sadness for the city which destroys God's messages and later Jerusalem would be ruined. Jesus is sad at the fate of Jerusalem. He says:

> "Jerusalem, Jerusalem, you who kill the prophets and stone those sent to you, how often I have longed to gather your children together, as a hen gathers her chicks under her wings, and you were not willing."
>
> (Matthew 23:37)

Jesus' care is like that of a mother. Julian's revelations lead us back to this insight. All will be well.

Conclusion

"The Darkness Shall be the Light" is a spiritual journey with T. S. Eliot. His poem 'The Waste Land' (1922) shows a world that is barren and hopeless. In writing 'The Waste Land' Eliot found he no longer lived there. He recovered his faith. This is seen in his poem 'Ash Wednesday' (1930). This led him to the 'Four Quartets'. The last three of the Quartets were written during World War II. In East Coker the world has become dark, the darkness of the war and world. He helps us enter into ourselves and face our own darkness and find strength there, a strength born of God.

"But the faith and the love and the hope are all in the waiting,
Wait without thought, for you are not ready for the thought:
So the darkness shall be the light, and the stillness the dancing."

(East Coker)

Printed in Great Britain
by Amazon